# FISHING WITH
# NATURAL
# BAITS

FISHING

# VLAD EVANOFF

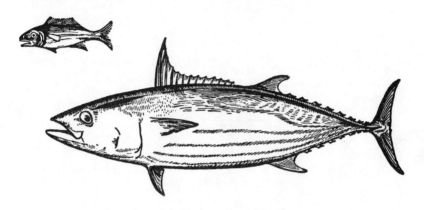

# WITH
# NATURAL
# BAITS

*Illustrated by the Author*

PRENTICE-HALL, INC., Englewood Cliffs, N.J.

*Design by Linda Huber*

*Fishing with Natural Baits* by Vlad Evanoff
Copyright © 1975, 1959, by Vlad Evanoff
All rights reserved. No part of this book may be
reproduced in any form or by any means, except
for the inclusion of brief quotations in a review,
without permission in writing from the publisher.
Printed in the United States of America
Prentice-Hall International, Inc., London
Prentice-Hall of Australia, Pty. Ltd., Sydney
Prentice-Hall of Canada, Ltd., Toronto
Prentice-Hall of India Private Ltd., New Delhi
Prentice-Hall of Japan, Inc., Tokyo
10 9 8 7 6 5 4 3 2 1

Library of Congress Cataloging in Publication Data
Evanoff, Vlad.
Fishing with natural baits.
Edition of 1959 published under title:
Natural baits for fishermen.
1. Bait. I. Title.
SH448.E82 1975    799.1'2    75-15658
ISBN 0-13-319699-2
ISBN 0-13-319681-X pbk.

# Contents

# Acknowledgments

*The author wishes to express his appreciation to the many state fish and* game and conservation departments that supplied information and material which proved extremely helpful in writing this book. The bulletins of the California Fish and Game Department were especially helpful.

Thanks are also due to the U.S. Fish and Wildlife Service, which provided valuable information and material aiding the writer immeasurably.

Also to the editors of *Sports Afield* magazine for permission to use some of the information and illustrations that appeared in their *Sports Afield Fishing Annual*.

And finally to the editors of *Salt-Water Sportsman* magazine for permission to use some of the information and drawings that appeared in their publication.

# Foreword

*Millions of fishermen in both fresh and salt water use live or natural* baits when they seek fish. Only a small minority of anglers never or rarely use such natural baits. Sooner or later every fisherman finds that he can catch more fish, get bigger fish, and have more fun if he uses natural baits on many of his fishing trips.

But when such an angler tries to find out which baits are best, where they can be obtained, how they are kept or preserved, and how they are used, he runs into difficulties. Such information is obtained either the hard way through trial and error or bit by bit from scattered books, magazines, fishing guides, and other printed sources. Many books have been written on artificial lures and how to use them. But not many books have been devoted, as this one is, entirely to natural baits.

There is a common belief among fishermen who use artificial lures that using natural baits is too easy and requires little skill or study. But those anglers who have used natural baits for a long time soon discover that there are many things to learn about such baits. The use of natural baits often requires as much skill and knowledge as the use of artificial lures. Those anglers who have made a study of freshwater and saltwater baits and learned how to use them usually catch more and bigger fish than their fellow anglers.

There is a tendency to get into a rut when using natural baits. Most anglers stick to a few natural baits and rarely try other kinds or different ways of using them. But the most successful fishermen in both fresh and salt water know how to use a wide variety of natural baits and experiment with different ways of using them.

This has been proven in recent years by striped bass fishermen who have started using live eels, bunker, and mackerel to make some eye-popping catches of big fish. Other anglers have started using live bait fish for sailfish, marlin, and sharks. And live mullet will catch tarpon that won't even look at artificial lures. The same goes for freshwater fishing. If you want a big bass in Florida, you'll find a live shiner one of the best baits you can use.

All these recent developments in using natural baits in fresh and salt water are covered in this new book. The author hopes that this guide to the freshwater and saltwater natural baits will provide the necessary information for using these baits to catch more and bigger fish.

*Vlad Evanoff*

# FISHING WITH NATURAL BAITS

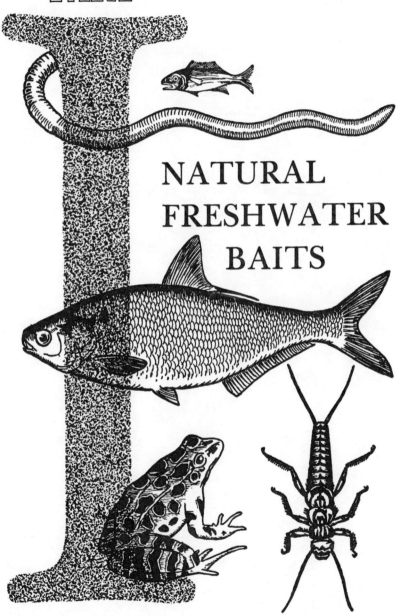

# PART I

# NATURAL FRESHWATER BAITS

# CHAPTER 1

# EARTHWORMS

*B y far the most popular natural bait used in freshwater fishing is* the earthworm. It is one of the best all-around baits that an angler can use. Most of the other live baits are limited to certain species of fish, but worms are taken by almost every freshwater fish. Add to this the fact that earthworms are found in most sections of the country, are usually easy to obtain, can be kept indefinitely, and you have the main reasons for their popularity.

The strange thing is that although worms are not commonly found in streams, rivers, or lakes, most fish will take them without hesitation if they are properly presented. Yet almost the only time earthworms find their way into streams and lakes is during heavy rains when they are washed into such waters, although a few may crawl into the water by mistake or fall in when overhanging sod banks along the water's edge break off and roll into the stream or lake.

However, whether or not the earthworm is found naturally in the stream doesn't concern the average angler too much. All he knows is that earthworms are eagerly taken by most freshwater fish, and if he uses them he can have some fine sport and bring home fish. But it is important to know some of the vital details about earthworms—their habits, and how they are found, kept, and used on the hook.

3

## CHARACTERISTICS AND HABITS

Earthworms live in many kinds of soils, but they generally prefer a rich, loamy clay soil which contains plenty of organic matter. They swallow this earth and extract the plant and animal matter from it for nourishment while the rest of the soil passes through and is expelled in the form of "castings." You can notice these small droppings around the burrow holes in almost any garden or lawn. Earthworms are usually scarce or absent in sandy or poor soils.

Earthworms do not like extreme heat, cold, or dry spells. Under any of these conditions they will usually be deep in the ground. When the ground is wet they can be found near the surface. The best time to dig worms is early in the spring or during the fall months when there is plenty of rain. During the hot summer months when the ground is dry the worms go down deep, and this is the time of year when anglers have trouble getting them.

## SPECIES

There are more than 2,000 varieties of earthworms found throughout the world, and most of them are taken by fish. But some species are scarce, while others are too small to make practical baits. The giant earthworm found in Australia is even too big, for it may reach 10 feet in length and have a diameter of one inch. In this country three kinds of worms are commonly found and used for bait.

The one usually found in bait cans is the common earthworm (*Helodrilus caliginosus*), also known as the garden worm,

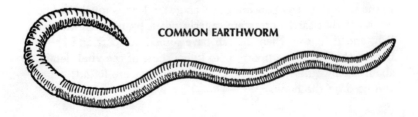

**COMMON EARTHWORM**

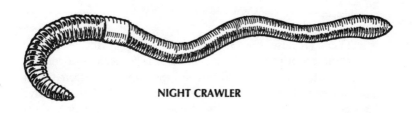

**NIGHT CRAWLER**

**MANURE WORM**

angleworm, garden hackle, and fish worm. It is found in moist, fertile soil such as in gardens, fields, and woodlands and is widely distributed throughout the United States. It may reach 5 or 6 inches in length, but most of those found average 3 or 4 inches. Its color varies, being pink, gray, yellowish, or blue, depending on where it is found. There are also many closely related species which can be used as bait.

Probably next in popularity because of its size, distribution, and availability is the night crawler *(Lumbricus terrestris)*, also known as the nightwalker, rain worm, and dew worm. It is numerous in some locations, but may be scarce or absent in others. The night crawler may reach 10 inches or more in length, but most of those found average about 6 or 7 inches. Its color is pink near the tail blending into a dark red and purple near the head. The tip of the tail usually flattens out when it is first caught.

The third worm used for bait is the manure worm *(Eisenia foetida)*, also called the fecal earthworm, stinkworm, and dung worm. This worm is widely distributed but is not too common because it is found mostly in manure, stables, barnyards, and sewage. This preference gives it a disagreeable odor and the worm exudes an unpleasant yellow liquid when handled or cut. It is a thin, small worm and reaches only about 4 or 5 inches in length. It can easily be recognized by its dark bands separated by lighter rings. It is also somewhat softer than the other worms, but it is very lively and makes a good bait.

5

There are also the "domesticated" earthworms which are bred commercially in bins or pits on a large scale and sold to fishermen and bait dealers. These are specially fed, watered, and cared for so that they grow larger and reproduce more rapidly. They are extremely hardy and will live and adapt to widely varying climates and soil conditions. They also make excellent bait and live long on the hook even underwater. These worms are usually called "red worms," "red wrigglers," "red hybrids," or similar names.

Still another commercial worm is the "African night crawler," which is now being raised by many worm farms or hatcheries and sold to fishermen and bait dealers. This worm is larger than the red worm but doesn't grow quite as large as the native night crawler. And being a tropical worm, it requires more heat than other worms, with bedding temperatures of 70 to 80 degrees for maximum production. It is also a very active worm and will escape from boxes or worm beds if there is no lid or cover to prevent this.

You can order these domesticated worms from worm farms or bait dealers in small quantities of 1,000 for fishing purposes or, if you want to raise them on a small scale, for your own use. See the classified advertising sections of such magazines as *Outdoor Life*, *Field & Stream*, and *Sports Afield* for the names and addresses of bait dealers and worm hatcheries that sell these worms.

## OBTAINING, KEEPING, AND PRESERVING

The most common method of obtaining worms for fishing is by good old-fashioned digging. This can be a simple job or a discouraging task depending on the location, type of soil, and season of the year. The common earthworm is the type usually obtained by digging and it is often found in gardens that have a rich soil. Use a garden fork instead of a shovel. The fork will not cut as many worms as a shovel will. Although worms have the power of regeneration and can grow a new tail, a large percentage of cut worms will die and can contaminate the healthy ones, so it is best to throw them away. The best time to dig worms is early in the spring or late in the fall when the ground is damp and cool, or after a heavy shower or prolonged rain which soaks the earth to a good depth. During the hot summer months when the worms are deep, you can often find them in the sod in low, damp spots around springs, ponds, or other bodies of water. Or you can get a garden hose and soak the ground with water, then dig for the worms the next day.

There are other methods for obtaining worms besides digging, such as driving a stake into the ground and rubbing the top of it with a board to produce vibrations which drive the worms out of the ground. There are also electrical devices on the market which bring the worms out of the ground when rods are pushed into the earth and the current is turned on. Then there are the various chemical solutions which are poured over the ground, then seep into the earth or into the burrows to chase the worms to the surface. You can make your own solution of mustard and water and pour this into the burrows to bring worms to the surface. After these solutions are used the worms should be washed immediately to remove the irritating substances. The trouble with most of these methods, however, is that they do not always work—and when they do, the worms are usually numerous and near the surface anyway. So it is just as simple and often quicker to dig them up.

The big night crawlers are not as easy to dig since they stay down deep during the daytime. But at night, especially in the spring of the year during heavy rains, they come out of their burrows to mate and migrate. The warm, moist, quiet nights when the ground is damp will bring them up in the greatest numbers. During the summer months when the ground is dry only a few will emerge from their burrows. But if there is a heavy shower or rain which soaks the ground they will reappear in large numbers.

The best places to look for night crawlers are golf links, gardens, lawns, parks or other spots where the grass is short and they are easy to spot. Walk softly, as they are very sensitive to vibrations, and you will be able to get close enough to grab them. They are also sensitive to strong light and if you use a flashlight, shine the beam to one side and not directly at the worm. A weak light or a red light doesn't alarm them as much as a bright, white light.

Most of the night crawlers will be stretched out with their tail sections anchored inside their burrows. Grab them near the tail end close to the burrow and hold the worm taut for a few seconds until its muscles relax and it can be pulled out easily.

The manure worm can be found in old manure, stables, barnyards, and garbage or sewage. This worm is often obtainable during the winter or early spring when the ground is frozen and other worms cannot be found. And because it lives in manure, which holds moisture well, it is also available during the hot summer months when the ground is dry and other worms are down deep.

If you run out of worms on the fishing grounds or do not have any and would like to try some as bait, you can often find a few by looking under old stumps, overturning flat rocks, boards, or decayed plants and leaves, especially in damp spots. And the damp soil along the banks of streams and lakes often contains worms which can be dug with a board or stick. You can also try pulling up weeds, clumps of grass, or sod and then searching in the roots and earth for worms.

Of course, many anglers prefer to buy their worms from bait dealers or tackle shops, but if you do a lot of fishing it is cheaper to raise your own worms either outdoors or indoors. The simplest

**WORM BOX BURIED IN GROUND**

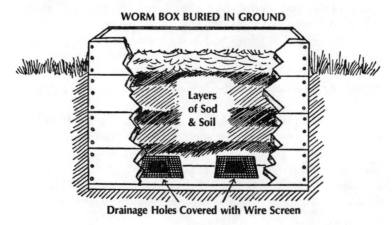

**Drainage Holes Covered with Wire Screen**

method, which entails little work or time if your ground already contains worms, is to pick a spot where you know they are present and place some wide, flat boards over it. Then empty your dishwater over this spot until the soil is well saturated. The worms will come to the top and all you have to do is lift the boards and pick them up. Ordinary water will also do the trick if the worms are numerous, but dishwater contains nourishment which will attract worms to the immediate vicinity. The water should be poured for several days in succession for best results.

However, the best method for a dependable supply of worms is to construct a worm box and sink it in the ground. Such a wooden box can easily be made using hardwoods, which will last longest in the ground. You can also coat the outside of the box with tar or wax it to help preserve it. A good-sized box which will hold plenty of worms would be about 4 feet long, 3 feet wide, and about 3 feet deep. It can be smaller or larger, depending on how many worms you want to keep. When building the box make sure that there are no cracks through which the worms can escape. A couple of holes should be bored in the bottom of the box for drainage and these should be covered with copper-wire screening.

Bury the box in a shady, well-drained spot leaving only a few inches of the top of the box extending above the ground. Then fill the box with alternate layers of sod and soil. Layers of decayed leaves can be used instead of the sod. You can also use plain moss or special preparations sold by worm farms instead of soil, but then you will have to feed the worms more often.

Finally, put a few hundred worms in the box and let them burrow into the soil. A damp burlap bag or a layer of leaves can be used to cover the soil and keep it moist. During the dry, hot summer months you may have to add some water; on the other hand, during the rainy seasons you can cover the box to prevent it from flooding. If you leave the box outdoors during the winter, cover it with a thick layer of manure or leaves to keep out the frost.

Worms can also be kept and raised indoors in wooden boxes, galvanized washtubs, metal drums cut lengthwise, big plastic containers, and similar holders. The containers can be filled with soil and some decayed leaves, rotted straw, or a small amount of manure mixed into the soil. The worms need not be fed if they are being kept for short periods of time, but if kept for a long time you can feed them vegetable shortening or lard mixed with cornmeal. Bread crumbs, chicken mash, and ground oats can also be used. This box can be kept in the cellar, garage, barn, shed, or any other place where it is cool. You should add some water from time to time to keep the soil moist.

The above methods are most suited to the angler who does considerable fishing or has to provide bait for several persons. If you just need worms for a few fishing trips you can dig or buy several hundred and keep them in smaller containers for a few months. Just place them in the containers with the soil and feed them and sprinkle some water on the soil occasionally. A few hours spent digging in the spring of the year when worms are plentiful will provide enough bait for the rest of the fishing season.

When you first remove earthworms from the soil, you will notice that they are filled with earth which they have swallowed when feeding and burrowing. They make pretty good bait fresh from the soil, but they become more attractive, livelier, and tougher if they are "scoured" before using. To do this get an earthenware crock or flowerpot and obtain some sphagnum moss from a florist or nursery. Wash the moss and wring out the excess water. Now place the moss in the crock or flowerpot. Then put the worms you intend to use on a fishing trip into the container. After three or four days in the moss the worms will get rid of the earth inside them and become almost transparent, as well as

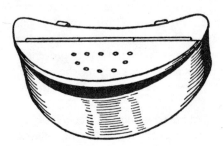

**BELT-TYPE BAIT BOX**

tough and lively. If you must keep the worms in the moss longer than a few days feed them some milk.

The ordinary tin can is still one of the most popular containers used to transport worms to the fishing grounds. It is suitable if you are still-fishing from the shore or a boat. But a trout fisherman or a wading angler must have his hands free for fishing and he needs something less bulky which he can carry on his person. A flat, tobacco can with holes punched in the cover is handy since it takes up little room and can be carried in a pocket. There are many kinds of small metal and plastic bait boxes on the market for holding worms. One of the most popular is the type that is held by the angler's belt and is curved to fit the contour of his body. It is usually made from metal or plastic and has a perforated lid on a hinge. Any of these small containers can be filled with earth if the worms are freshly dug, or with moss or grass if they have been scoured. It is important to keep the containers out of the sun as much as possible to help prevent the heat from killing the worms.

## METHODS OF HOOKING

Every angler has his own pet methods of hooking worms for the fish he is seeking. For trout fishing the worms should generally be hooked lightly under the light colored sexual collar. The point and barb should be allowed to protrude. This method usually works best in streams where the worm is allowed to float naturally with the current. Sometimes when the trout are fussy, especially in quiet waters where they can pick up the bait at their leisure, the point and barb can be covered—not because the fish can see the point and hook, but because they may feel the point and spit the bait out. The point and barb can also be buried in the head of the worm when you want a bait that will not snag the weeds or other obstructions.

Generally one worm on a hook is best for trout, but there are times when two worms on a single hook produce better results. The smaller earthworms between 2 and 4 inches are best for small and medium-sized trout, but night crawlers can be used for big

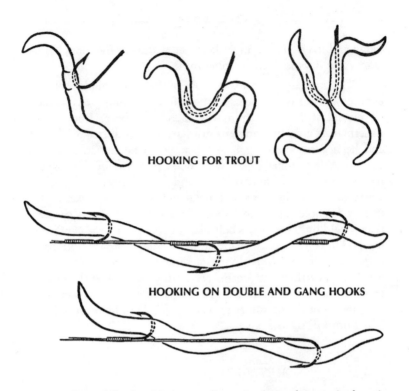

**HOOKING FOR TROUT**

**HOOKING ON DOUBLE AND GANG HOOKS**

trout. A gang hook with two or three single hooks attached to the same snell or leader is best for hooking these larger worms. It is also useful when the trout strike short, just nipping off the tail of the worm. A gang hook also holds the worm better when casting any distance, since the worm is hooked in three places and has less chance of being snapped off. Check your state fish and game laws when using more than one hook to see if it is legal on the waters you intend to fish.

For black bass, two or three night crawlers placed on a hook so that the ends are free and allowed to wriggle are highly effective. When the smaller earthworms are used, even more can be put on a hook. Large hooks in sizes No. 1 and 1/0 are best when worms are used in such numbers. A single night crawler can also be hooked near the head and cast out lightly, then allowed to drift with the current for bass.

For panfish, such as sunfish, yellow perch, and rock bass, small whole worms or half-sections of larger ones are generally

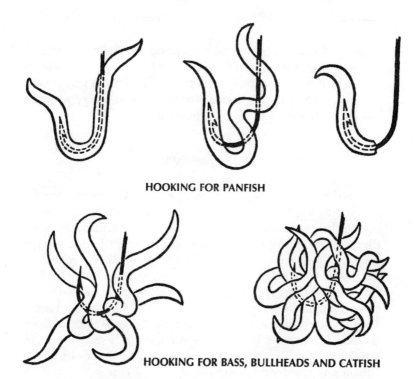

**HOOKING FOR PANFISH**

**HOOKING FOR BASS, BULLHEADS AND CATFISH**

best. They will take night crawlers, but their mouths are too small to swallow the bait and they usually nip off the ends only. Even the smaller worms are readily stolen off the hook by the panfish. The best method for such bait thieves is to loop the worm on the hook along the shank, allowing only short sections of the head and tail to wriggle.

For bullheads and catfish, several worms on a hook usually work best. These fish have big mouths and can swallow hooks baited with plenty of worms. Also the more worms you have on a hook, the more juices and liquids and blood will ooze out, helping to attract the catfish and bullhead which often feed by following up the scent of the bait.

For most fish, the livelier the worms the more strikes you will get. So the best method of hooking is the one that keeps the worms alive the longest possible time. Worms that have died or that wriggle feebly should be removed from the hook and replaced with fresh ones. Sometimes you can make the fish strike a dead or feeble worm by moving the bait up and down or from side to side to attract attention. But you can't beat fresh, lively worms on a hook if you want to catch plenty of fish. That is why it pays to dig or raise your own worms; you won't be so stingy with the bait and will always use lively, fresh worms.

## USING WORMS

Serious worm fishermen seeking trout use extra long fly rods, up to 9½ to 10½ feet in length. They like monofilament line on their reels since this helps the worm to drift more naturally. On the end of this line, they use a lighter leader, testing anywhere from 1 to 4 pounds. When the water is clear and clean the lighter leaders are more effective and will catch more fish.

These worm experts also prefer small hooks with sizes No. 8 or 6 for single-hook rigs and as small as No. 14 for gang hooks. They also carry strips of lead or small rubber-core sinkers which can be added to the leader above the hook. These will vary in weight and have to be changed according to the speed of the current and the depths being fished.

Spinning rods, especially the longer, lighter models, can also be used when worm fishing for trout. If you fish with the lighter monofilament lines such as 4- or 6-pound test, you need not use any leader. When a spinning reel has the bail left open, you can feed slack line readily in the current to give the worm a natural drift.

That is the biggest secret in worm fishing for trout. You have to drift the worm as naturally as possible in the current at the same speed as it would move without any hook or line attached. You have to avoid drag or any slowing down or speeding up of the worm. It is best to drift the worm without a sinker or weight if possible.

Worms are very effective for trout in the spring of the year when the streams are high and roily. At such times a trout is lying on the bottom and won't move very far for a bait. But if you can drift the worm right in front of a trout's nose you are more likely to get a bite. To get a natural drift and get down deep enough, you usually have to cast well upstream in fast water and as the worm moves downstream you have to feed slack line to prevent drag and keep it down as close to the bottom as possible.

Naturally, you should also fish the worm in spots where trout are apt to lie or feed. Fish the deeper pools, holes, pockets, and a deep run along the edge of the fast water. Try to drift your worm near bushes, trees, logs, overhanging rocks, and undercut banks.

Keep the worm moving with the current at all times and do not let it rest in one spot more than a second or two. If your worm acts differently or stops, lift your rod slowly and reel in any slack. If you feel the trout nibbling or a pull on the line, wait a few seconds, then set the hook.

When fishing for trout in deep, quiet pools or ponds or lakes you can let the worm settle to the bottom and leave it lying there, hoping that a fish will find it. Or you can let the worm settle to the bottom, then lift it slowly, then let it settle back on the bottom again and keep doing this as you slowly reel in the line.

When fishing for black bass you can use two or three night crawlers on a hook below a float or bobber and cast it out from shore or a boat. To cover more ground you can cast this rig about 50 or 60 feet ahead of a drifting boat. Then as you move toward the float, reel in the slack line slowly as you get closer to it. If there are no bites, when you reach the float, reel it in and cast out again and repeat the drift.

Another way to fish one big night crawler for bass on a hook is to cast the worm out without any float or weight and allow it to sink, then slowly retrieve it in a stop-and-go fashion. Try different depths and even let the worm sink to the bottom and retrieve it along the bottom very slowly.

Worms are also used for walleyes, especially when trolled behind a spinner such as the june bug. Here you can use a large single hook or a gang hook and impale the worm in two or three places.

Worms can also be used for various kinds of catfish and bullheads. A single night crawler can be used for a bullhead or small catfish or you can use a gob of several smaller worms as mentioned earlier. These can be cast out with a cane pole, bait-casting rod, or spinning rod with or without a float. But for best results the worms should be on the bottom or just above it. You can also fish the worms with a bottom rig such as a sinker and a hook on a short snell tied a few inches above the weight. This can be cast out into a river or stream and allowed to sink to the bottom. Fishing for catfish, bullheads, and eels is best at night.

When fishing for suckers in the spring, use the smallest worms you can get and impale two of them on a small No. 4 hook through the middle so that the ends wriggle. Cast this out in a pool where you see suckers or know they are present and let the worms sink to the bottom. In a quiet pool you can fish them without a sinker, but in a current you may have to add some weight to hold them on the bottom.

Then place your rod against a rock or in a forked stick and wait. Suckers take their time about swallowing or mouthing a bait, so don't try to set the hook when you see the first faint nibbles. Wait until the line starts to move off before trying to set the hook.

Worms can also be fished for carp in this manner on the bottom, but other baits are usually better for these fish. These will be mentioned in Chapter 7.

And worms are the most popular bait for various kinds of panfish. More worms are dug, raised, and used for such panfish as bream or sunfish, yellow perch, white perch, crappies, and rock bass than for any other freshwater fish. You can use worms for panfish with different kinds of tackle, but the long cane or glass pole is preferred by most anglers. A long fly rod or spinning rod can also be used. You can fish with a light float or bobber a few feet above the hook, casting it out and waiting for a bite. Or you can fish without the float, casting your worm out and letting it settle toward the bottom in shallow water near shore. But whether you use a float or not, give the worm some movement by changing the spot every so often. Just moving the worm a foot or two every few seconds will attract more fish and get more bites. Of course, once you get a bite, don't move the worm, but let the fish play with it until it swallows it and starts moving off. Then set the hook.

When fishing for rock bass in moving water in a stream, drift the worm alongside rock ledges, logs, undercut banks, brush, weeds, and into holes. Here you may need a split-shot sinker above the hook to get it down in the moving current.

Worms are also highly effective for panfish when used behind a small spinner. You can cast or troll these slowly at various depths. Use a smaller worm on the hook behind the spinner. In fact, for best results use the smaller worms in all your panfishing rather than the bigger night crawlers.

# CHAPTER  2

# MINNOWS

*N*ext *to the earthworms in popularity as bait in freshwater are* the minnows. Indeed, if they weren't somewhat harder to obtain and keep, or more expensive to buy than worms, minnows would probably be used more than any other bait. Most game fish feed on minnows to a great extent and almost all of the other freshwater fish eat them when they can get them. This is especially true of the larger fish which require plenty of food. Another factor that makes the minnow such a good bait is that when it is impaled on a hook it usually swims around energetically, attracting fish from a distance. And finally, minnows are found in most lakes, rivers, and streams throughout the country.

## CHARACTERISTICS AND HABITS

Most anglers call any small fish a few inches long a minnow. But a true minnow belongs to the family *Cyprinidae,* which includes the carps and goldfish, as well as other large fish such as the squawfish and white salmon, which may reach 4 or 5 feet in length and may weigh up to 80 pounds. And if you go by size alone you will be including the young of game fish in your bait pail, which is something no sportsman or conservationist wants to do.

Every angler who uses minnows should become familiar with the characteristics and habits of these forage fishes. Minnows have one dorsal fin, usually in the middle of the back, and it has less than ten soft rays. The carp and goldfish are exceptions,

19

having dorsal fins with more than ten rays and single spines in the dorsal and anal fins. Also, minnows have no teeth in their jaws and no scales on the head.

Minnows are found in all kinds of water from quiet ponds to the swiftest rivers and streams. Some species prefer lakes, others are found in the larger rivers, and still others frequent streams or brooks. When it comes to food, they will eat land and water insects, small fish, fish eggs, snails, algae, small crustaceans, plankton, plants, and even mud, sand, or other debris from which they can obtain organic matter.

## SPECIES

There are over 1,000 species of minnows throughout the world, with more than 300 found in North and Central America. Although most of them can be used as bait, some are more numerous and better suited for this purpose than others. The best bait minnows are those which are silvery or light in color, are active and hardy on the hook, and can stand handling, crowding, and other unfavorable conditions. The following list includes the most popular and common minnows used for bait.

## CREEK CHUB

### (Semotilus atromaculatus)

This minnow is often called the horned dace, common chub, horned chub, or just plain chub. It can be recognized by its large mouth which extends back to the eye, the black spot at the base of the dorsal fin, and the barbel just above the corners of the mouth. It has an olive-green back, steel-blue sides, and a white belly. The creek chub is a large minnow, the females reaching 5 inches and the males growing almost a foot in length. It is found in the creeks and rivers from southern Canada and in most of the eastern United States from Maine to Wyoming and south to Virginia and Missouri. It is a hardy, lively minnow which is widely used for bait. It can also be caught on hook and line with small hooks and bait and on an artificial fly.

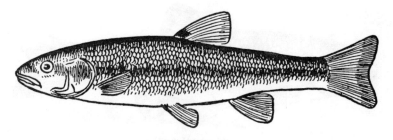

**CREEK CHUB**

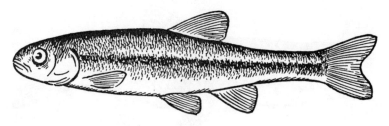

**PEARL DACE**

## PEARL DACE

### (*Margariscus margarita*)

This minnow is also called the leatherback. It has a heavy body and a blunt nose, and its color is a dusky silver mottled by darker gray scales. It is found throughout most of Canada east of the Rocky Mountains and in many of our northern states. The pearl dace prefers cool lakes, bogs, and creeks. It is a hardy bait minnow which is good for most freshwater game fish.

## THE HORNYHEAD CHUB

### (*Nocomis biguttatus*)

Also known as the jerker and red-tail chub, this is a heavy-bodied minnow with a large head and big, distinct scales. It has barbels at the corners of the mouth and the color on the body is generally olivaceous. The young have a red tail and there is a

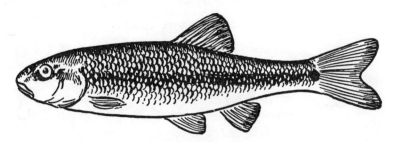

**HORNYHEAD CHUB**

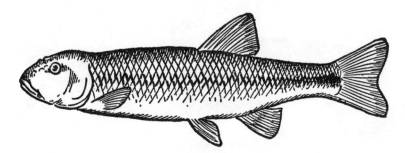

**RIVER CHUB**

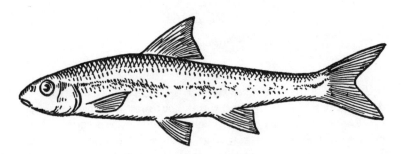

**SILVER CHUB**

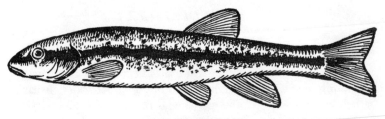

**BLACKNOSE DACE**

distinct black spot at the base of the tail. This chub prefers the larger creeks and smaller rivers with gravel bottoms. It reaches a length of 8 to 10 inches and is a hardy bait minnow which stands up well on the hook or in a bait bucket. The hornyhead chub is found from the Rocky Mountains east to the Hudson River.

## RIVER CHUB

### (Hybopsis micropogon)

The river chub resembles the hornyhead chub and is closely related to it. It also has a heavy body and large, distinct scales. But the spot at the base of its tail is not as clear or round as in the hornyhead chub. The river chub prefers the larger rivers and may reach a length of 10 inches. It is a good bait minnow for most gamefish and can readily be caught on hook and line. It is found in many of our states from the Rocky Mountains east to New England and south to Virginia and Alabama.

## SILVER CHUB

### (Hybopsis storeriana)

This minnow is also called the storer's chub and it is a silvery, attractive baitfish which may reach 8 or 10 inches in length. It is a slim minnow with a short, broad back that is greenish in color. The silver chub frequents large, silty rivers and lakes. It lives well in captivity and is active on a hook. It is found from the Red River drainage in Canada to the southern shore of Lake Ontario and southward to Alabama, Oklahoma, and Wyoming.

## BLACKNOSE DACE

### (Rhinichthys atratulus)

Also known as the striped dace, slicker, and brook minnow, the blacknose dace is a fairly small minnow rarely reaching more than 3 inches in length. It is a slim minnow with a dusky back and black spots all over and a dark streak or stripe on the side of

23

the body from the snout to the tail. This minnow prefers the cool, clear brooks and is often found in trout streams. The western form ranges from the Lake of the Woods region south to Nebraska and through most of the tributaries of the Great Lakes to the northern part of the Ohio River system. The eastern form, which closely resembles the western dace, is found from Quebec southward, east of the Appalachian Divide to Virginia.

## REDBELLY DACE

### (*Chrosomus eos*)

The northern redbelly dace reaches 3 inches in length and is dark bronze in color with two distinct lateral bands running from head to tail. It is found in bog ponds and sluggish creeks in many parts of Canada and most of our northeastern and north-central states. A southern form, the southern redbelly dace, is found from Iowa to the southern parts of Wisconsin and Michigan to Pennsylvania and south to Alabama and Oklahoma.

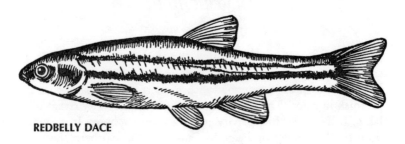

**REDBELLY DACE**

**GOLDEN SHINER**

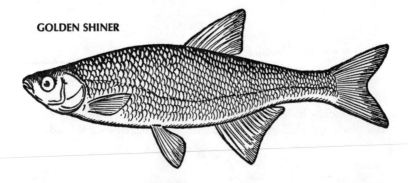

## GOLDEN SHINER

### (Notemigonus crysoleucas)

This shiner is also called the roach or bream. It has a flat, wide body and small, upturned mouth. The scales are distinct, fairly large, and pale gold in color. It is found from North Dakota to southern Ontario and south to Oklahoma and Arkansas. Another form, the eastern golden shiner, is found from New Brunswick, Quebec, and the St. Lawrence River southward east of the Appalachians to Virginia. Still another form is found in our southern states and is especially plentiful in Florida. The golden shiners make good bait and may reach 12 inches in length in our northern states and 18 inches in our southern states. They prefer the shallower lakes, ponds, sluggish rivers, and streams with vegetation and have been raised successfully in artificial ponds. They can be caught readily on tiny hooks baited with worms or insects.

## COMMON SHINER

### (Notropis cornutus)

This minnow is also known as the silversides, skipjack, redfin shiner, and just plain shiner. It has a steel-blue back, large, silvery scales, and white belly. It is found in the cooler creeks and streams and in some lakes and ponds, ranging from Canada south to Colorado, Kansas, Missouri, and from the Rockies east to New England. It is a popular bait minnow, but less

**COMMON SHINER**

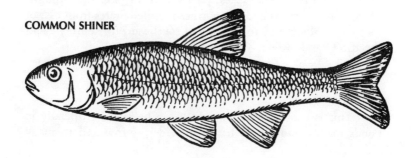

hardy than many other species. It reaches a maximum length of about 8 inches. Another form, the central common shiner, is found from the southern Great Lakes area south to Alabama and Oklahoma. There are many other shiners which are related to the common shiner, such as the emerald shiner, spot-fin shiner, river shiner, spottail shiner, blackchin shiner, and blacknose shiner. Most of these shiners make attractive baits, although they are more delicate than most of the other minnows.

## BRASSY MINNOW

### (Hybognathus hankinsoni)

This minnow is also known as the grass minnow and has a blunt head, small mouth, and short, rounded fins. The scales are large, are brassy in color along the sides, and come off easily. It is found through most of the Great Lakes region and from Montana to southern Ontario southward to Colorado, Nebraska, Iowa, and southern Michigan. It prefers small creeks and bog waters and is found occasionally in lakes.

## FATHEAD MINNOW

### (Pimephales promelas)

Also known as the blackhead minnow and tuffy minnow, this bait fish is one of the easiest to raise artificially in small ponds. It can be recognized by its robust body, short, rounded head, and blunt snout. The color of this minnow is usually dark brown to olive with a copper or brass tinge. It is a small minnow reaching only about 3½ inches in length but is popular for bait because it stays alive and active on a hook for a long time. It is found naturally in small lakes, ponds, and silty streams throughout southern Canada and the northern United States from east of the Rocky Mountains to Maine and southward to Kentucky and the Rio Grande River.

## BLUNTNOSE MINNOW

### (Hyborhynchus notatus)

This is another minnow which can be raised artificially in ponds readily and which has been widely introduced to many

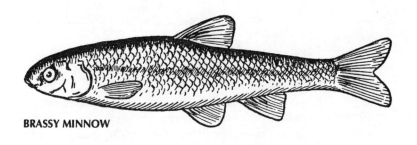

**BRASSY MINNOW**

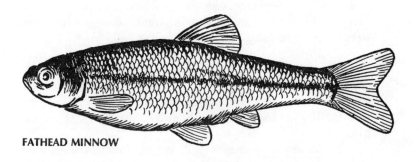

**FATHEAD MINNOW**

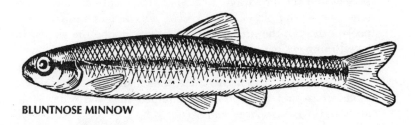

**BLUNTNOSE MINNOW**

waters. Its natural range is from Winnipeg through the Great Lakes region to Quebec and southward to Virginia and the Gulf States. Here it prefers the larger, clearer lakes and firm-bottomed streams. It is a long, slim minnow, olivaceous in color with a dark spot at the base of the tail. It reaches about 4 inches in length.

## CARP AND GOLDFISH

These two members of the minnow family are often used as bait when young, but it is a practice that should be discouraged.

In fact, many states prohibit their use. Carp and goldfish are prolific fish and when introduced into lakes and rivers they soon crowd out the more desirable food and game fish. They feed on vegetation and root up the bottom, dirtying the water and destroying plant life. This usually creates unfavorable conditions for game fish and results in poor fishing for these species. Of course, where carp and goldfish are already present in a lake or river, there can be no harm in using them for bait in these waters. But they should not be used as bait in strange waters. Check your state laws before using carp or goldfish as bait.

The above list is far from complete; it includes only the most popular and common minnows. There are many other species which can be used for bait, but those which are most numerous in your locality are the easiest to obtain and usually make the best bait.

Minnows can be caught in almost any brook, stream, river, or lake. The best place to look for them depends on the species present and the formation of the shoreline, depth of water, current, and hiding places. Some species will be found in the quiet pools, others in the riffles, and still others among the weeds. In lakes, minnows tend to congregate in the shallow coves and near feeder streams or brooks emptying into the lake. They usually come closer to shore at night. Piers, docks, and other spots where table scraps and other food are dumped into the water often attract minnows in large numbers.

## CATCHING, KEEPING, AND PRESERVING

The most efficient method of obtaining minnows quickly and in large numbers is by means of a seine. But before a seine is used, make sure that it is legal in the water you intend to try. Most states have laws specifying the waters where seining is allowed and regulating the length, mesh, and width of the seine used. Seines from 4 to 100 feet long may be used, depending on the body of water and the persons available for seining. The short seines are popular in small brooks, streams, and ponds and can be

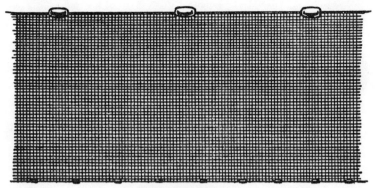

**MINNOW SEINE**

operated by one man. The larger seines are best for rivers and lakes and are operated by two or more men. In shallow water two men can use seines by wading, and in deeper water two rowboats can draw the seine. The general procedure is to start some distance away from shore and to draw the seine toward land, forming a half-circle so that the two ends of the seine touch land and cut off the escape of the minnows. Another way is to anchor one end on shore and swing the other end around until it touches land.

When the haul has been completed there will be an assorted catch of various sizes of minnows and many other species of water life in the seine. Don't remove the seine from the water to the shore. Form a bag with the seine and float it out to deeper, cleaner water. Then the big minnows which are to be used for bait should be dipped out with a small hand net and placed in the bait pail. The small minnows and other species in the seine should be carefully returned to the water. Too many bait seiners haul the net to shore, pick out the minnows they want and then dump the rest on dry land to perish. This not only destroys valuable minnows, but will also kill any young gamefish or pan-fish present in the seine, not to mention various water insects and crustaceans which are important fish foods.

Another method used in catching minnows is the "drop" or "umbrella" type net, which is usually square in shape and has lines attached to each corner for lifting. There are many types and designs on the market which can be bought cheaply. Or you can easily construct one using wire, line, and cheesecloth or mosquito netting. It can be any size from 3 to 10 feet square. The smaller

**MINNOW DROP NET**

ones are best because they can be worked by hand and do not require supports or pulleys as do the larger ones. There are small portable types on the market which have a collapsible frame that takes up little space when folded.

These drop nets are lowered to the bottom in shallow spots or to a depth of a few feet in deeper spots where minnows are known to be plentiful. Then soaked bread, crumbled crackers, or oatmeal are thrown above the net and permitted to sink into it. After the minnows have gathered over the net to feed on this stuff, it can be lifted quickly to catch them.

Still another method widely used to catch minnows is traps. These can be bought in almost any tackle store and come in a variety of shapes, sizes, and materials. Most of them are either round or rectangular and are made of wire or glass, but there are others made from plastic or cloth mesh. They all work on the same principle. There are one or more funnel entrances which make it easy for the minnows to enter but hard to escape the trap. The traps are set in a stream or lake where minnows are plentiful, and are baited with bread or cracker crumbs. In streams the funnel entrance should face downstream and a shallow hole should be dug in the stream bottom to hold the trap. For best results the trap should be examined about every hour or two to prevent any minnows from escaping after the food is gone. If you use more than one trap you can catch a good supply of minnows in a short time. Here again, it is best to check with your state

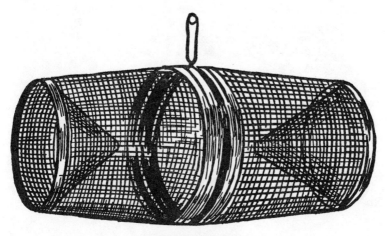

**WIRE MINNOW TRAP**

laws, for some states limit the size and number of traps which can be used.

Some of the larger minnows can also be caught on hook and line using small No. 16 or 18 hooks baited with bits of worm or doughball. The doughball bait can easily be made by mixing flour with water and kneading it into dough. Or you can soak some bread and then squeeze out the excess water to make bait. But the hook and line method is a slow one at best, and is usually used only when a few extra-large minnows are needed.

Of course, if you can't obtain minnows in any other way, or if you need them in a hurry, you can always buy some from a fishing tackle store, a bait dealer, or boat livery which carries them. But if you do a lot of fishing with minnows, it is cheaper to catch your own bait.

After the minnows are caught, if you are going fishing soon, they can be transferred to a pail or bait bucket. If the weather is cool, an ordinary pail will sometimes serve to hold minnows for short periods of time and carry them short distances. When you get to the lake or stream, you can place the pail in the water in a shady spot just deep enough to submerge it about three-quarters of the way.

But if you are traveling long distances or fishing from a boat, a special minnow bucket is much better. There are many types and sizes on the market. The old standby is the metal type

**MINNOW BUCKET**

holding about 2 to 4 quarts of water. Those having a perforated inner liner which floats in the water are popular. In recent years more and more of these minnow buckets and containers are made of plastic or styrofoam. Actually, all you need is one of those styrofoam food or drink holders with a tight cover. This can be filled with cool water; the water will stay cool for many hours and keep the minnows alive. To provide oxygen you can drop in one off those tablets sold for this purpose every so often. There are also many kinds of bait buckets and minnow buckets which have built-in air pumps and devices for providing oxygen and keeping the water cool.

The important things to remember when handling, transporting, and keeping minnows are not to crowd them and to keep the water cool and rich in oxygen. Also, when transferring minnows from one container to another, make sure that the water temperature in the new container is close to that in the first one.

For short trips the water can often be aerated by dipping up some of it from the minnow bucket with a dipper or cup and pouring it back from a height several times. For longer trips and in hot weather you can place some ice on top of the minnow bucket and allow the water to drip into the container as it melts. Or you can place the minnow bucket in a box or tub and surround it with cracked ice.

To keep minnows in large numbers for future use you will need large tanks or small pools which have a constant supply of cool, well-aerated water entering under pressure from above the water level. The drain or outlet should be near the bottom of such a tank or pool to permit stagnant water and wastes to leave. City water or any other water with too much chlorine should not be used unless the excess chlorine is removed by filters or other means.

Minnows can also be kept for long periods of time in live boxes or carts. Such a box can easily be made to accommodate a good supply of minnows. Don't make it too small or too large, however. The minnows thrive better if they have plenty of room, but on the other hand, too large a box is heavy and unwieldy. One about 26 inches long, 20 inches wide, and about 12 inches high is a good size. Build the wooden frame this size, then cut boards to cover the top of the box and nail them in place. Now cut out a door in the center of this wooden top and fasten it on with a pair of hinges. Cover the rest of the frame with quarter-inch mesh wire screening on all sides and the box is ready to use.

If the water in the lake or stream is clean, cool, and flowing, the live box can be kept close to shore. But if the water is warm or rough, minnows will live better if you sink the box in deeper water where it is cooler and cleaner, where there is no wave action to toss the minnows around.

Springs are good places to keep minnows: the water is clean and cool during the summer months; and during the winter it doesn't freeze too readily, enabling the angler to keep minnows for ice fishing.

**MINNOW LIVE BOX**

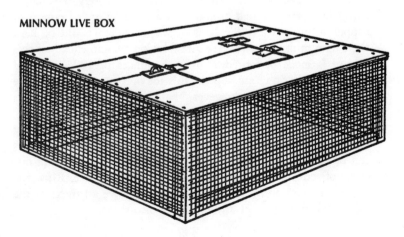

When keeping minnows for any length of time it is best to keep those of approximately the same size together in the same tank. If you are keeping minnows for only a few days, there is no need to feed them. But if you are holding them for a week or more you can feed them every two or three days to keep them healthy. Some of the foods used for minnows include oatmeal, bread, cornmeal, crackers, finely ground meat or fish, and various commercial preparations. It is important not to overfeed the minnows because the leftover food will decay and contaminate the water.

To keep minnows free from disease, you should not overcrowd them or handle them roughly. If the film that covers the fish is removed or the skin is broken by careless handling, the minnows may become infected by bacteria or fungus. The fungus shows up as a white fuzz on various parts of the body and spreads all over until the minnow dies. It occurs most often when the water is warm. As soon as any minnows develop this fungus they should be removed from the tank and placed in a different container where you can try to treat it. One solution recommended is ⅛ ounce of malchite green in 15 gallons of water. The minnow should be dipped in this solution for ten seconds. This treatment can also be given to healthy minnows that have been exposed to the disease in order to prevent the fungus infection.

Another disease in minnows is fin rot, which may be caused by several kinds of bacteria. In this disease the fins or tail of the minnows degenerate until they are destroyed entirely. To control this disease dip the sick minnows in a solution of 6½ ounces of copper sulphate to 100 gallons of water. They should be kept there for a minute or two. Another solution recommended for this disease is made of formalin, using 8 ounces to 100 gallons of water; the minnows are kept in this for one hour. If the disease has progressed too far, however, these dips will not help much and the minnows should be destroyed.

One of the best ways to prevent diseases is to sterilize at regular intervals the tank or box in which minnows are kept. This can be done by scrubbing the containers with a solution of one quart of sodium hypochlorite to 250 gallons of water. Rinse the containers with fresh water afterward to remove all traces of the solution before you put any minnows into them.

Although live minnows are generally best for fishing, there are times when minnows are difficult to obtain and dead or preserved minnows must be used. For certain kinds of fishing, like trolling and casting and retrieving, dead minnows often serve just as well as live ones. Many anglers would like to know how minnows can be preserved for future use.

Minnows can be kept for a few days by placing them in layers in a container and covering each layer with salt. Although they will turn hard and shrivel somewhat, as soon as they are used in the water they will soften up again. Minnows can also be kept for a few weeks in a jar with strong brine.

However, the best method of keeping minnows indefinitely requires the use of formaldehyde. One formula calls for a solution of 1 percent formalin and 99 percent water in an airtight jar. A mayonnaise or Mason jar will do. The minnows are placed in this solution. Seal the jar and watch the solution for any signs of discoloring. If this happens, make up a fresh solution and, after washing the minnows, place them in it. If you find the minnows too stiff you can use less formalin. If they are too soft you can add a bit more formalin. You may have to change the solution two or three times before it remains clear. Some anglers also add from 5 to 10 percent glycerin to keep the minnows soft.

Another method of preserving minnows, one which helps to eliminate the objectionable formalin odor, calls for 1 part formalin, 6 parts glycerin, and 40 parts water. The minnows are kept in this solution for four to six weeks and then are removed and transferred to a strong brine which will remove the formalin odor. Some anglers keep the minnows in a formalin solution but add a few drops of rhodium oil to kill the odor.

You can, of course, freeze some minnows and then use them for bait. However, they tend to get soft after they are thawed out and they do not last as well as minnows preserved in brine or a chemical solution.

## METHODS OF HOOKING

The size of the minnow used depends on the fish being sought. Minnows from 1½ to 2½ inches are best for panfish.

35

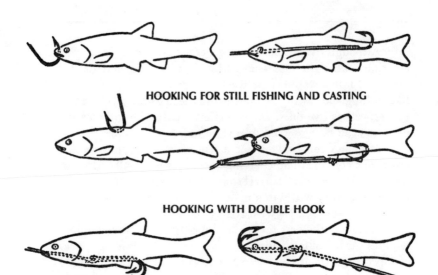

**HOOKING FOR STILL FISHING AND CASTING**

**HOOKING WITH DOUBLE HOOK**

**METHOD OF SEWING MINNOW ON HOOK**

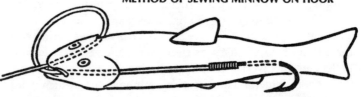

Trout minnows usually run from 2 to 3 inches. For bass, the minnows can run from 2½ to 5 inches, while for pike and muskellunge or lake trout minnows from 4 to 10 inches are not too big. If you are looking only for big fish, it is best to use the larger minnows. But if you just want to catch fish, no matter what size, use the smaller ones, for a big fish will take a small minnow but it is difficult for a small fish to mouth and swallow a big minnow.

There are many ways of hooking a minnow, depending on the fish sought, the water being fished, and the method of angling being used. For still-fishing, minnows are usually hooked through the back, side, or belly if used alive. The most popular way is to run the hook through the back just in front of or behind the dorsal fin, being careful not to strike the backbone. This method is good if the minnow is just being lowered into the water or is being cast only a few feet. For making longer casts, hooking through both lips is better.

Several other methods may be used in hooking minnows for casting and trolling. One simple method is to run the point and barb of the hook into the minnow's mouth, then out through one of the gill openings and into the back behind the dorsal fin. Another method calls for the use of two hooks with one of them tied to the leader or snell about 2 inches above the other; one hook is run through the minnow's lips and the end hook is inserted into the minnow's back, near the tail. In both these methods a slight bend can be produced so that the minnow will spin or revolve when retrieved, drifted, or trolled.

Another method calls for the use of a double hook. A large needle is needed to pull the leader end through the minnow's mouth and out of the vent. Then a double hook is tied to the end of the leader and the shank is pulled into the bait's body. The minnow's body rests between the two hooks, the points of which face upwards. There is a variation to this method which calls for the double hook at the head of the minnow. Here the needle to which the leader end is tied is first inserted into the vent and pushed through the minnow's body until it emerges from its mouth. A double hook is then attached to the leader end and the shank is pulled back into the bait's mouth, causing the head of the minnow to rest between the two hooks.

Still another head-first method can be worked out with a single hook by sewing the minnow on the hook and leader. Here the entire hook is pushed through the minnow just above the tail and a few inches of the leader are pulled through. Then the leader is wrapped completely around the minnow twice and the hook is forced through the body again under the forward part of the dorsal fin, after which the point of the hook is worked through the bait's gills and out of its mouth. Finally the slack in the leader is tightened up until the bend of the hook rests against the minnow's mouth with the point clearing the head enough to hook a striking fish.

In rigging a minnow so that it will have a permanent bend which will cause it to spin or wobble when moved through the water, each angler has his own pet method. One of the simplest is

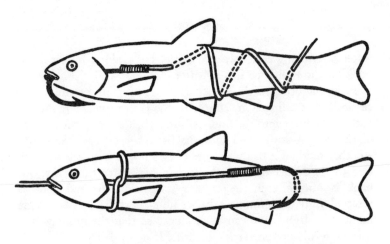

**TWO WAYS TO SEW A MINNOW ON THE HOOK**

to run your hook into the minnow's mouth and out of the gill opening. Then tie a half hitch around the minnow's body just back of the head and insert the hook midway between the dorsal fin and the tail. Finally, tighten up on the leader, putting a bend into the minnow, and secure the half hitch.

Another way to get a permanent bend or curve in a minnow is to run your hook into the minnow's mouth and out of the gill opening and then pull through about 4 inches of leader. Then run the hook into the minnow's mouth a second time and out through the opposite gill opening. Next you insert the hook into the minnow's body along the side near the tail and bring it out on the same side. Now pull on the leader against the hook, creating the bend or curve you want in the minnow. Tighten up on the slack leader loop alongside the bait's head to keep the bend in place. See the illustrations in this chapter showing how the sewing of these minnows is done.

There are also many types of minnow gangs and rigs on the market which hold the minnow in place, and these can be bought in most fishing tackle stores. Some have spinners attached to give them an added attraction. The thing to remember when using minnows is that movement and flash attract game fish and this must be brought about by the activities of the live minnow itself or the manipulation of the dead minnow by the current or the angler.

## USING MINNOWS

Minnows make a first-rate bait for trout, especially the bigger "cannibal" trout which feed mostly on such minnows or small fish. You can still fish with live minnows in pools or holes in streams and rivers, or in lakes near shore when trout come into shallow water in the spring and fall. Here a live minnow can be cast out with a light spinning outfit and allowed to swim around naturally to attract the trout. If there is a current, you may have to add a split-shot sinker or two on the leader above the hook to get it down into deeper water. When fishing in lakes from a boat, you can lower the minnow toward the bottom. Here if the minnow doesn't go down by itself you may also have to add a light sinker or weight.

But in most trout streams and rivers you'll get better results if you use a dead minnow sewn on a hook as described above and let it have plenty of action and movement in the current. If the minnow has the proper bend or curve it will wobble in a crippled manner, thereby attracting big trout. Here you can cast upstream and across and let the minnow tumble at various depths until you find the one where the fish are lying or feeding. Usually the biggest trout will be close to the bottom, so you should try to get your minnow down deep. You can cast it into rapids or riffles and let it drift into a pool. Or cast it along the edges of the fast water and let it drift through pockets and eddies and under cut banks, log jams, and rocks.

You can also cast the dead minnow across and downstream and then retrieve it in short jerks. Here the minnow will travel closer to the surface, but by casting more upstream you can let it get down deeper before starting the retrieve. Or you can cast directly downstream to the lower end of a rapid or run, then retrieve it slowly against the current. You can pause or stop reeling every so often and let the minnow stay in one spot, or even let it drop back a bit so that it acts disabled.

In the quiet pools or in a lake you can cast the dead minnow out as far as possible. Then let it sink to the bottom, after which you can reel it back slowly with some rod action or jerks to make it look alive.

When fishing for lake trout you can do the same thing by casting the dead minnow out from shore in the spring, when these fish are in shallow water, and retrieving it with some rod action. However, most of the year the lake trout are in deep water and here you can fish a live minnow on a bottom rig with a sinker on the end of the line and a hook with a minnow on a leader about a foot or so above the weight. Let this rig down until you feel the sinker hit bottom, then let the minnow swim around by itself, but every so often lift and lower the rod to give the minnow some added action and to prevent it from hiding in the rocks.

Minnows can also be used for black bass in many ways. Here you can use almost any fishing tackle when still-fishing. A cane pole, glass pole, fly rod, or spinning or bait-casting outfit can all be put to use. Add a float or bobber on your line a few feet above the hook or to reach the depth you want. Usually fishing a minnow about a foot off the bottom or off the weeds is most effective. You may need a small clamp-on or rubber-core sinker on your line between the bobber and the hook to get the minnow down to this depth.

In deeper water you can still-fish with a live minnow by eliminating the float or bobber. Here you can cast out your minnow and let it sink toward the bottom. You may have to add a light sinker on your line above the hook to achieve this. Then when the minnow reaches bottom you can reel it in a few feet, then let it sink back again, reel in, sink back, and so on until the retrieve is completed.

Still another way to use the minnow for large-mouth bass is to drift in a boat and let a minnow, hooked through the lips, trail in the water. Here you should let out about 30 to 50 feet of line. When there is no wind or the boat isn't moving fast enough, you can slowly row or paddle it along a shoreline. A variation of this method is to add a float or bobber above the minnow and then cast it out about 50 or 60 feet in the direction in which the boat is moving. As the boat approaches the float you reel in the slack line but without disturbing the float or bobber. In other words, let it stay in one spot. When the boat gets up to the float you reel it in and cast out once more well ahead of the moving boat and repeat.

In any of these methods it is important to give the bass

plenty of time to swallow the minnow before trying to set the hook. A bass usually grabs a minnow crosswise in its mouth. Then he swims away and stops to turn the minnow around to swallow it head first. Then he will start moving again and this is the time you should set the hook.

Live minnows can also be used for pickerel in much the same ways described above for black bass. You can also hook a minnow through both lips and cast it close to lily pads, weeds, or into shallow coves and along the shorelines. This can be done without a float and you can slowly reel in the minnow with stops or pauses along the way. As soon as you get a bite, lower the rod and give some slack line. Then when the pickerel starts moving away, set the hook.

You can also use live minnows to catch walleyes in lakes near shore at night. Here you can use a float or bobber so that the minnow is suspended just off the bottom. Cast this out and let it lie in one spot for a few minutes. If you get no bites, reel it in a few feet and let it stay in that spot for a while. Keep repeating this until the bait is near the boat or shore. In deeper water you can use a bottom rig with a sinker on the end of the line and a hook on a short leader about 18 inches above this weight. If this is fished from a slow-moving or drifting boat you don't need any more action. But if you are fishing from shore or an anchored boat, try casting this rig out, let it lie in one spot a while, then reel it in slowly a few feet, let it lie, reel in, and so on.

In stream or river fishing for walleyes, minnows can be drifted through the deeper channels, holes, and below rapids, falls, or dams. Or you can add a minnow to the hook of a jig and cast it into these spots. You can also troll a minnow behind a spinner, slowly and down deep, for the walleyes. Walleye fishing with minnows is most effective early in the morning, toward dusk, and during the night. But you can also fish in the daytime on an overcast day or in deeper water.

Minnows both dead and alive can also be used to catch catfish. Channel catfish in rivers go for live or moving dead minnows and they should be drifted into deep holes, around snags, fallen trees, logs, below riffles entering a pool, and below falls and dams. Dead and live minnows can also be fished with a

41

sinker on the bottom rig in rivers or lakes for most catfish. Here you can cast the rig out, let it sink to the bottom, and let it lie in one spot. One trick here is to take a fresh minnow and step on it to mash it a bit before putting it on the hook. The blood and scent flowing out of the mashed minnow attracts catfish from a distance to the bait.

Small minnows can also be used for the various kinds of panfish. They are especially good for crappies when these fish are spawning near shore in the spring. Look for them around lily pads, hyacinths, stumps, sunken brush, and trees. Then hook a 2-inch minnow with a small No. 8 hook and fish it with or without a float. If you do this with a float or bobber, use a very small, light one which is pulled under easily. Crappies tend to bite gently, mouthing the minnow and moving into the depths with it. Don't strike too early or you'll pull the minnow out of their mouth. Let the bobber or float disappear and then set the hook gently and play them carefully for they have paper-thin mouths and the hooks tear out easily.

Other panfish which will take tiny live minnows are the yellow perch, white perch, white bass, and the larger bluegill sunfish.

# CHAPTER 3

# OTHER FRESHWATER BAIT FISHES

*T*his section includes the fishes that are not true minnows but that are often used for bait. Many of the methods described in Chapter 2 for capturing, keeping, and transporting minnows can be applied to the fishes in this group. Likewise many of the methods described for hooking minnows are also suitable for most of these fishes.

## SUCKERS

The sucker family is a large one, with some 100 species found in North America. They are closely related to the minnows and are often mistaken for them when young. However, most of them can be distinguished by the thick, fleshy lips and by the ten or more rays in the dorsal fin. They live on the bottom of lakes, rivers, and streams. Most of them ascend smaller streams and brooks to spawn in the spring. One of the most widely distributed species is the common white sucker *(Catostomus commersonii),* which is found east of the Great Plains from Canada to Georgia. Some of the other suckers are the sturgeon sucker, the hog sucker, the spotted sucker, and the chub sucker. The sucker family also includes the buffalo fish, the quillback and the red horse. The buffalo fish may reach 3 feet in length and a weight of 60 pounds and some of the other suckers often reach several pounds. But only the young ones from about 3 to 12 inches are used for bait.

43

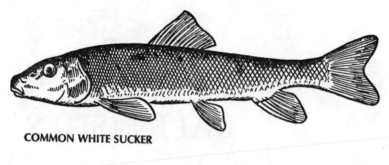

**COMMON WHITE SUCKER**

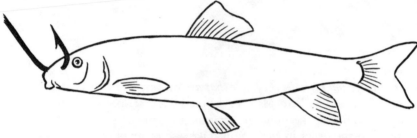

**HOOKING AND HARNESSING SUCKER FOR CASTING**

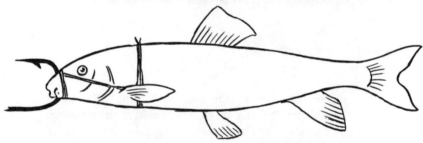

Suckers about 3 or 4 inches long make a good bass bait. Those from 4 to 8 inches can be used for pike and lake trout. Small whole suckers or chunks can also be used for catfish.

You can catch some of the larger suckers on hook and line, the hook baited with tiny earthworms and lying on the bottom. Seines and nets can also be used to catch them. You can also try snagging a few with lures or treble hooks.

Big suckers up to 10 or 12 inches can be used to catch muskellunge. You can use a live sucker by still-fishing it under a float or bobber. Hook the sucker in the back with a 5/0 or 6/0 hook and let it out about 40 or 50 feet from the boat. When a musky takes the bait and starts moving away with it, follow the float or bobber by rowing slowly after it. Keep doing this to give the musky plenty of time to swallow the sucker. When the float stops moving, stop the boat and wait. When the float starts moving away again, set the hook.

You can also use dead suckers for muskellunge by tying a harness with a big hook to the sucker's head and then casting it repeatedly with a stiff rod and working it along the surface to act like a crippled fish. When a musky rises and grabs the sucker you must give him some line so that he can bore down deep and take the bait with him. Then you have to give the musky plenty of time to swallow the sucker before setting the hook. Depending on the individual fish, this may take anywhere from a few minutes to an hour or more.

## STONE CATS, MAD TOMS, AND BULLHEADS

These small members of the catfish family are used as bait for many game fish. The stone cats and mad toms can be recognized by their small size and by the fact that the adipose fin is continuous along the back and joins with the tail fin. In the other catfishes the adipose fin and tail or caudal fins are separated. The stone cat *(Noturus flavus)* is one of the larger members and may reach 10 to 12 inches. It is found east of the Rockies, from Canada south to Virginia and Texas. The mad toms, which belong to the genera *Schilbeodes*, usually run from 3 to 5 inches and there are several species such as the tadpole mad tom, freckled mad tom, common eastern mad tom, slender mad tom, brindled mad tom, and mountain mad tom. Most of these small catfishes are found in the riffles under stones in creeks and rivers, although some prefer the quieter water with weeds. They can be caught in shallow water by striking the flat stones with another rock to stun the fish; when the rock is turned over they can be picked up with a small dip net. After they are put in a bait pail they will revive in a short time. Care should be taken in handling these stone cats and mad toms, for their sharp spines have poison glands at the base which can cause a painful wound.

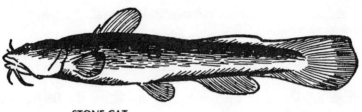

**STONE CAT**

**BLACK BULLHEAD**

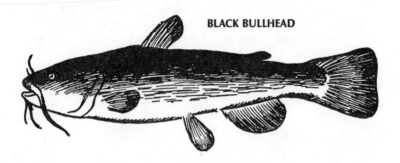

The bullheads, which grow larger than the stone cats and mad toms can also be used for bait when young (from 2 to 5 inches in length) for black bass, walleyes, and other game fish. They are also used (from 5 to 10 inches) for the larger catfishes, especially on set or trot lines which remain in the water for a long time.

Three species, the black bullhead, the brown bullhead, and the yellow bullhead, are commonly found in many parts of the country. The bullheads prefer the quieter streams, rivers and ponds, and lakes with muddy, weedy bottoms where they can be caught on hook and line using worms for bait. They are especially active at night and when the water is muddy from recent rains. The stone cats, mad toms, and bullheads are very hardy baits and will live for a long time in bait pails, in tanks, or on the hook. Several fish can often be caught on a single bait.

The smaller stone cats, mad toms, and bullheads can be used as bait for black bass. The stone cats are highly effective for small-mouth bass in creeks and rivers where these small catfish are normally found. Here you can cast them into an eddy or pool and let them swim around naturally in the depths. Or you can cast one into a riffle or rapid and let the current take it into pockets, behind rocks and boulders and other spots where small-mouth bass lie. In lakes you can fish stone cats, mad toms and small bullheads under a float or bobber just like minnows.

The larger bullheads up to a foot or more in length can also be used for pike and muskellunge. Here it's a good idea to first clip off the sharp spines with a pair of cutting pliers or shears. Then use a two hook rig consisting of two treble hooks tied a few inches apart. The front or forward treble hook should pierce the back of the bullhead just behind the head, while the second treble hook should be impaled through the back, closer to the tail.

## LAMPREYS

Although lampreys look like small eels and are often called "lamprey eels," they are not related to eels at all but fall into a special primitive class lower than the other fishes. The true eels have jaws, while the lampreys have a circular funnel-shaped mouth lined with horny spines. This round sucking mouth fastens to the side of a fish and rasps a hole through which nourishment is obtained. Not all of the several species of lampreys are parasitic and harmful to fishes, but one of the most destructive is the sea lamprey, which may reach 2 or 3 feet and is really a saltwater species. It lives along the Atlantic Coast but ascends rivers to spawn. It has become landlocked in some lakes, where it causes great damage to freshwater fishes. Two other lampreys which are strictly freshwater species and are also harmful to fishes are the silver lamprey and chestnut lamprey. Two of the harmless species are the Michigan brook lamprey and the American brook lamprey.

Lampreys make good bait for game fish and are especially favored for black bass and walleyes. But because of the harmful habits of the parasitic lampreys they should not be used for bait in

**AMERICAN BROOK LAMPREY**

waters where they are not already present—this to prevent their spreading. The lampreys that are usually used for bait are found buried in the mud bottoms of streams and rivers. To obtain them, dig in a few inches of water near shore, dumping the mud on the bank and then searching through the mud for the lampreys. They make a tough but slippery bait and are often used behind a spinner for walleyes. They can also be used for sturgeon in some rivers when fished on the bottom. To hook them, run the hook through one of the holes or gill openings just behind the head and let the point of the hook come out through the opposite side.

## DARTERS

These small fishes look like minnows but belong to the perch family. They have a long, slim body and the males are brightly colored during the spawning season. They lie on the bottom of streams or lakes, resting on their large pectoral fins. When disturbed, they dart forward a short distance and come to rest on the bottom again. In size they usually range from 1 to 8 inches but average about 2 to 4 inches. One of the most popular darters used for bait is the log perch (*Percina caprodes*), which is also known as the sand pike, stone pike, and zebra fish. Various species are found in many parts of the United States, and they can all be tried for bait. Although they are somewhat dark in color and do not live too well in tanks, they are hardy on the hook. They can often be caught by dip nets and seines or by using tiny hooks baited with bits of worm. Black bass, walleyes, and other fish will take them.

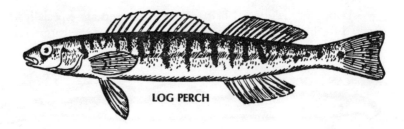

**LOG PERCH**

## YELLOW PERCH

Small yellow perch are sometimes used as bait for black bass, walleyes, pike, and muskellunge. Some anglers cut off the sharp dorsal fin to make the bait more attractive. An old favorite lure used in skittering for pickerel is a strip cut from a perch's belly with two of the ventral fins left attached. If you run out of bait while panfishing, you can cut up a yellow perch into small cubes and use these to catch other yellow perch, crappies, and sunfish. Even the eye of a perch can often be used as bait.

However, the yellow perch is another bait which should be used with caution. They have ruined many a stream, river, and lake when introduced deliberately or by accident. Such waters have often become overpopulated with stunted yellow perch, causing a depletion of game fish. Of course, where yellow perch are already present it is safe to use them for bait, but check your state laws to see if it is legal.

## SUNFISH

Small sunfish will sometimes take black bass, pike, and muskellunge. They also make a good bait for big catfish fished on or near the bottom. Sunfish used for game fish must be quite small, however, since their width makes them difficult for the fish to swallow. Cutting off the sharp spines of the dorsal fin will make them more attractive baits and easier to swallow. There are many species of sunfishes and most of them can be used for bait.

## ALEWIFE AND GIZZARD SHAD

These members of the herring family are occasionally used as bait, although they are delicate and do not stay alive too long on the hook or in a bait pail. The alewife (*Pomolobus pseudoharengus*) is really a saltwater species but ascends freshwater streams and rivers along the Atlantic Coast to spawn. In some of the lakes, however, they have become landlocked and are present the year

49

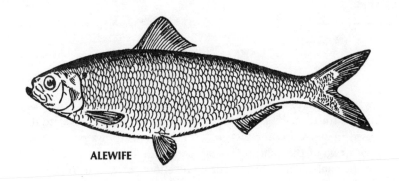

ALEWIFE

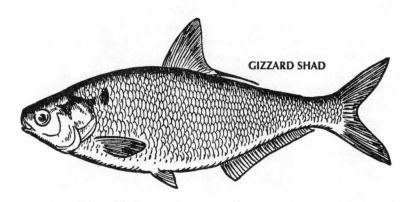

GIZZARD SHAD

round. The alewife has a deep, flat body and may reach 6 inches in length.

The gizzard shad (*Dorosoma cepedianum*) also has a deep, compressed body but it can easily be recognized by the long, thin last ray of the dorsal fin. It is found in the larger bodies of water from Minnesota to New York and southward to Mexico and the Gulf Coast. Gizzard shads have become very numerous in some man-made lakes and reservoirs, and serve as an important food supply for the game fishes. They may reach up to 16 inches in length but the average is much smaller.

If you catch a live alewife or gizzard shad where you are fishing, you can hook it gently through the back, then cast it out and let it swim around in the water either on a plain line or with a float or bobber a few feet above the hook. This is a good way to use them for black bass. When using an alewife for lake trout, use a rig with a sinker and lower this down to the bottom. When fishing for catfish use a small, whole gizzard shad or cut a big one into chunks and fish this on the bottom with a sinker.

## KILLIFISHES

These small fishes include many species, some of which are found in fresh water while others frequent brackish and salt water. The fresh species include the eastern banded killifish, the western banded killifish, the northern starhead top minnow, and the blackstripe top minnow.

Another good killifish is the caledonia *(Fundulus seminolis)*, which is found in freshwater swamps, river, and lakes with sandy bottoms. They are plentiful in Florida where they are popular as bait for black bass. They can be caught with seines along sandy shores; or you can use a tiny hook baited with a small piece of worm and fish this close to the bottom.

The common killifish or mummichog *(Fundulus heteroclitus)* is a brackish or saltwater species which is found along the Atlantic Coast and in the Gulf of Mexico. See Chapter 15 for full details about this killifish. The reason it is included here is that it is readily taken by many freshwater game fish and is one of the hardiest and easiest bait fishes to keep and use. It will live for a long time when packed in cool, damp seaweed, moss, or grass without water. Because of this and since it lives long on a hook, the killifish is used despite the fact that killifish in general are rather dark and dull in coloring. They grow up to 5 or 6 inches in length, although the average found is between 1½ and 3 inches.

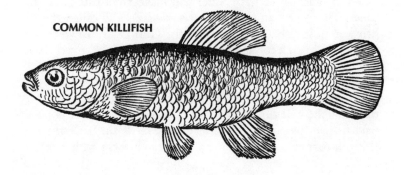

COMMON KILLIFISH

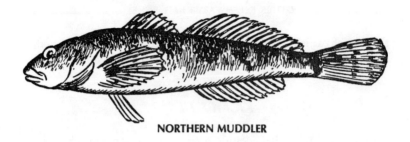

**NORTHERN MUDDLER**

## THE SCULPINS OR MUDDLERS

These small, bottom-dwelling fishes with large, flattened heads and winglike pectoral fins are sometimes used as bait. They are rather drab in color and usually try to hide under a stone or in the weeds when on a hook. But they are hardy baits and are often effective for big trout and other game fish. There are several species of sculpins and one of the most popular is the muddler *(Cottus bairdii)*, which is also called the common sculpin and miller's-thumb. It is usually found in streams but also lives in lakes with boulder-lined shores. The muddlers usually remain hidden during the daytime under stones and can be caught at night in the shallow riffles by using a flashlight and dip net. During the daytime you can often catch them by turning over the stones in narrow, shallow riffles and chasing them downstream into a scoop trap made from wire screening.

## SMELT

The smelts, although primarily saltwater species, are often found in brackish or fresh water and make good bait for many fishes. The American smelt *(Osmerus mordax)*, also called the ice fish and frost fish, is found from the Gulf of St. Lawrence to Virginia. This is a common smelt in the tidal creeks, rivers, bays and even fresh water. It ascends freshwater streams and rivers to spawn and has become landlocked in many freshwater lakes.

This smelt reaches 13 or 14 inches in length, but most of those caught will run from about 6 to 8 inches. It is a popular food fish and is often sold in fish markets. If they are running thick in narrow streams you can often catch them with a net or

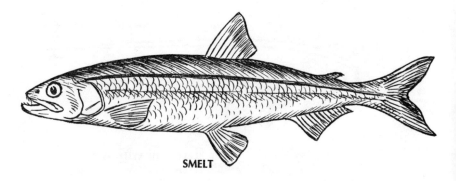

**SMELT**

seine. They also bite well on a small hook baited with worms, tiny shrimp, or pieces of fish.

Smelts are tender fish and die quickly after being removed from the water or put on a hook, so most of them are used dead. They make an excellent bait rigged on one or two hooks behind a spinner and trolled for ~~bass~~, walleyes, ~~pike, and lake trout~~. A whole smelt can also be sewn on a hook and trolled for landlocked salmon close to shore or around the mouths of streams and rivers entering a lake where smelt often congregate before their spawning run.

## BOWFIN

The bowfin *(Amia calva)* is also called the dogfish, mudfish, grindle, and scaled ling. It is found from the Great Lakes and the Mississippi Valley to Virginia, Florida, and Texas. It is most

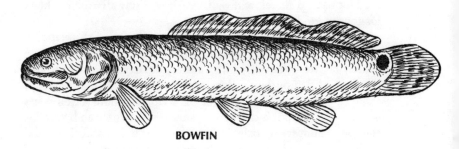

**BOWFIN**

**BELLY STRIP WITH FINS**

plentiful in the muddy, weedy, quiet waters of rivers, canals, and lakes. During spawning time in the spring the bowfin come into streams and can be caught in large numbers. They will bite on hooks baited with worms, minnows, or cut-fish and will often hit slow-moving lures fished deep. You can keep them in bait cars, tanks, or ponds for long periods of time and feed them fish scraps.

Bowfin up to a foot or so in length make a good bait for pike and muskellunge. They are a very tough bait which will stay alive on a hook for a long time. You can hook them with a large single hook or a treble hook through the back and cast them out into spots where pike and muskies lurk. Don't let them swim down to the bottom, however, since they may hide in the weeds or mud.

There are quite a few other small fishes which can be used as bait at times. The mudsucker or long-jawed goby *(Gillichthys mirabilis)* is a small Pacific Coast saltwater fish which is popular with freshwater anglers. The common eel is often cut up and used as bait for big catfish, and young eels can be used for many game fish. The mud minnow *(Umbra limi)* is a hardy bait which can be used for bass, pickerel, and walleyes. It will stay alive on the hook for long periods.

And finally strips cut from almost any large fish including the game fishes themselves can often be used as bait. These are usually cut from the belly into a variety of sizes and shapes to suit the type of fishing being done and the fish sought. In general, though, the longer and narrower the strip, the more action it has when moved through the water. Another bait that can be used is the eye of almost any fish. Fish are more or less cannibalistic and the eye of a brook trout, for example, has been gouged out and used to catch other brook trout.

Of course, it is impossible in a book of this sort to include every fish that is used for bait. There are many bait fishes which are only of local importance, being found in limited areas and used only by the natives in that spot. And local fishing conditions can make a bait deadly in one area and practically useless in another. When fishing strange waters you can't go wrong by listening to the advice offered by the local anglers and bait and tackle dealers.

# CHAPTER 4

# WATER INSECTS

*I*nsects that spend most or part of their lives in the water are eaten by many freshwater fishes. Some water insects are so small that they are eaten only by minnows and young game fish and they are too small to use as bait, but others are large enough to interest the bigger fishes and these often make excellent baits.

Insects go through either three or four distinct states of development from the egg to the adult. The immature water insects known as "nymphs" are in the second of *three* stages: egg—nymph—adult. They resemble the adult insect in the shape and hardness of their bodies. The immature states of dragonflies, damsel flies, mayflies, and stone flies, are called nymphs.

The immature insects known as "larvae" go through *four* stages of development: egg—larva—pupa—adult. The larvae usually do not resemble the adult too much and have soft bodies The immature stages of caddis flies, hellgrammites or dobson flies, and the true flies are called larvae.

Water insects differ so much in size, structure, and habits that general rules cannot be laid down for obtaining, keeping, and hooking them. Some are delicate, while others are hardy. Some insects live in clear, running water, while others prefer stagnant, quiet waters. Some live under stones or logs, while others are found in the mud or among water plants. These individual characteristics and habits will be dealt with in detail in this chapter.

57

There are two devices which can be used to catch many of the water insects. One is a section of wire screening 2 or 3 feet square reinforced by a wooden frame. An old window screen will serve the purpose nicely. The other is a small dip net made from cloth with fine mesh.

## HELLGRAMMITES

The hellgrammite (*Corydalis cornutus*) is one of the most popular water insects used for bait. There are quite a few insects called hellgrammites, but the larval form of the big, winged insect known as the dobson fly is the true one. Hellgrammites are known by different names in various parts of the country —alligator, water grampus, conniption bug, helldiver, snipper, clipper, flip-flap, crawler, and many others.

The adult dobson fly is a big insect with a wingspread of 4 inches. The female fly lays several thousand eggs on branches, rocks, or other objects overhanging a stream. When the eggs hatch, the tiny larvae drop into the water and live there for almost three years, hiding under the rocks in the rapids or riffles and feeding on other insects. When a hellgrammite is fully grown (at least 2 years and 11 months) it crawls out on land, hides under a log or stone for about a month, and is transformed into the adult dobson fly. Then the cycle is repeated all over again.

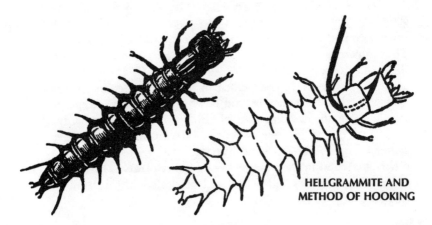

**HELLGRAMMITE AND METHOD OF HOOKING**

A fully grown hellgrammite may reach 3 inches in length, but most of those found in streams and rivers will run from 1 to 2½ inches. It is a long, black or dark brown creature with six legs and a pair of appendages on each segment of its soft body. It also has a pair of nippers which can inflict a painful bite, and two tiny hooks on the end of the tail section.

Hellgrammites are most numerous in the fast water of streams and rivers, where they can be caught by turning over the rocks while a wire screen or net is held below the rocks. Although one man can easily hold the screen with one hand and lift rocks with the other, two people are even better. Then one man can turn over several rocks at a time while his companion holds the screen below them. The fast current will sweep the hellgrammites onto the screen, where they will hang on for a while. It is also worthwhile to examine each stone you lift or turn over to see if any hellgrammites are clinging to it.

Hellgrammites can be kept for a long time in running water while being fed ground meat to prevent cannibalism. They will also live for weeks in a cool cellar in a box or container having decayed leaves or rotten logs. These should be kept damp but not too wet. Small containers or boxes filled with leaves, grass, or weeds can be used to carry hellgrammites when fishing. They will live all day if you keep the container out of the sun and sprinkle the leaves with water occasionally.

The hellgrammite is a tough bait which will stay alive on a hook for a long time. You can often catch several fish on one bait. The best way to hook hellgrammites is to run the hook under the hard collar just behind the head. Some anglers break off the two tiny hooks at the end of the tail so that the bait cannot grasp the bottom and hide under a rock or log. Hellgrammites can also be hooked near the end of the tail. They will take black bass, trout, walleyes, sunfish, yellow perch, rock bass, and other fish.

The larva of another insect closely related to the hellgrammite resembles it somewhat. It is known as the fish fly (*Chauliodes pectinicornis*). But it does not reach the size of the hellgrammite and it prefers quieter waters, where it lives among the water plants on the bottom. It can also be used as bait for many of the same fishes that take the hellgrammite.

## USING HELLGRAMMITES

When fishing hellgrammites for small-mouth bass, cast them into riffles and rapids of rivers and streams, especially where the water flows into an eddy or pool. This is where the bass will be looking for them. Cast up and across stream and let the hellgrammite drift down naturally. You may have to let out some slack line every so often to accomplish this. When your line straightens out at the end of the drift, retrieve the hellgrammite very slowly for a few feet, then let it drop back again. Keep repeating this until the bait has been completely retrieved.     .

Most of the time the bass will grab the hellgrammite and swallow it so the hook can be set immediately. But other times the fish may hit with short pecks and fail to get hooked. Only experience and practice will give you the feel and know-how which will tell you when to set the hook in this case.

In lakes you can fish the hellgrammite from a boat and work rocky bottoms for small-mouth bass. They will also take large-mouth bass at times, but are not as good for these fish as for the small-mouths. You can cast the hellgrammite out and let it sink to the bottom. Then raise it off the bottom with your rod tip, and then let it sink again toward the bottom. Keep doing this until it is brought in up to the boat. Then cast it out into another spot and repeat the process.

The smaller hellgrammites can be fished in the same way in streams and rivers for trout, but here again they are not quite as good as for small-mouth bass. The very small hellgrammites do make very good baits for yellow perch, sunfish, and rock bass.

## DRAGONFLIES AND DAMSEL FLIES

These insects are readily recognized in the adult stage when they are seen flying over the water or resting on a plant. The dragonfly is especially numerous and is called by many names such as darning needle, mule killer, snake doctor, and snake feeder. Although they look somewhat alike, the dragonfly is not as delicate or fragile as the damsel fly. Also, it holds its wings at

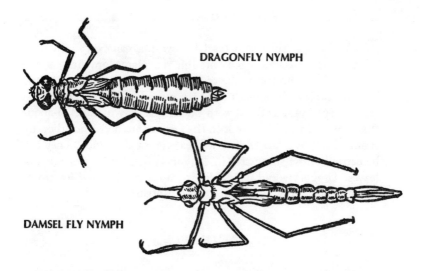

DRAGONFLY NYMPH

DAMSEL FLY NYMPH

right angles to the body when at rest, whereas the damsel fly folds its wings vertically and holds them at an angle over the abdomen. There are many different species of dragonflies and damsel flies in this country and they vary in coloring and size.

However, it is the nymphs of the dragonflies and damsel flies which we are mainly interested in, and these are eaten by many freshwater fishes. The dragonfly nymphs have broad, flat bodies and the abdomen is usually wider than the head. The damsel fly nymphs have long, thin bodies and the abdomen is usually narrower than the head.

Dragonfly nymphs are called "perch bugs" or "bass bugs" in various parts of the country. They live in ponds, lakes, and the quieter sections of streams in the mud, vegetation, and debris on the bottom. They usually crawl very slowly using their legs, but can shoot forward fast by expelling water from the tail end of their bodies. The nymphs spend from 1 to 3 or more years in the water feeding on other water insects. When they are fully grown they crawl out of the water up a plant stem, rock, or tree, where the insect splits down the back and emerges from the skin, head first. In the beginning it is very soft, but in less than an hour the wings and body harden and it flies away to spend the rest of its life catching insects on the wing and laying eggs in the water —from which tiny dragonfly nymphs will hatch to repeat the cycle.

The dragonfly and damsel fly nymphs can be caught with seines or dip nets dragged through the plants growing in the water. Or you can use a rake to bring up the debris found on the bottom and search through it for the nymphs. Dragonfly nymphs can be kept in tanks filled with water, but only nymphs of about the same size should be kept in the same container, since they are cannibalistic and larger ones will eat the smaller ones. They can be carried on a fishing trip in containers filled with wet moss or leaves. Dragonfly and damsel fly nymphs can be used for trout, black bass, yellow perch, and other panfish.

## CADDIS FLIES

These small insects resemble moths in the adult stage, but they have tiny hairs on their wings instead of scales as the true moths do. It is their larvae which are used as bait. These are known as stickbaits, stickworms, reedamites, caseworms, barnacle, caddis worms, or caddis creepers, depending on the kind of case they make and where they are found. For there are a great many species of caddis flies found in the streams and lakes of the country. Each species builds a special kind of case. Some use tiny sticks, sand, or leaves which they cement together with a secretion from their mouths. The larva or worm is a whitish-looking grub with six legs and a dark head which builds the case around itself for protection. Those with portable cages drag them around when moving from one place to another. But others build sta-

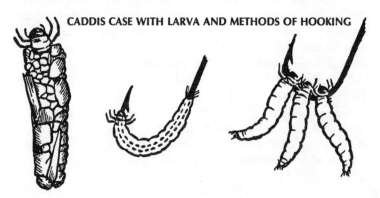

CADDIS CASE WITH LARVA AND METHODS OF HOOKING

tionary cases which are firmly attached to rocks. Caddis larvae feed on vegetation and animal matter and those species which are the largest make the best baits. They can be found in the quieter sections of streams and the weedy shorelines of lakes. If you watch the bottom of a stream or lake closely you can usually spot the caddis larvae crawling very slowly around on the bottom or among the vegetation. They can easily be picked up.

The caddis larvae can be kept in a tank or aquarium if the water is cold. If the water is warm or the tank is overcrowded with the larvae, it should be cooled and aerated. Caddis worms tend to be cannibalistic in captivity, so it is better to catch a fresh supply instead of trying to keep them for any length of time. They will live for quite a while in a container filled with wet moss or leaves.

Caddis larvae are a favorite food of trout, which eat them together with the case. They can also be used for bluegills, perch, and other panfish. Although fish eat them with the case, they make a more attractive bait if they are removed from their protective covering. This can easily be done by splitting open the case or using a pin or point of a hook to pick out the small worm. To hook one, you can use a small, short shank hook and thread the larvae on it, covering the bend and allowing the point to protrude slightly from the head of the bait. Sometimes two, three, or four caddis worms impaled on a single hook bring more strikes than a single larvae.

For trout let the caddis larvae drift with the current in a brook, stream, or river at various depths. But since they are found on the bottom, that is where the trout will be looking for them, so let the bait roll along the stones. Caddis larvae can be used at any time of the year for trout, but are especially effective in the spring and when streams are low and clear.

For panfish such as sunfish and perch use a couple of caddis larvae on a small hook with or without a float above the bait.

## MAYFLIES

These delicate insects are eaten by many freshwater fishes both as adults and nymphs. The adults are easily recognized by

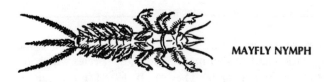

the two pairs of delicate, net-veined wings, the three pairs of long legs, the slim abdomen, and the two or three hairlike tails. Trout fishermen who imitate the mayflies when tying dry flies know the adults as shad flies, fish flies, and drakes.

However, it is the immature or nymphal stage of the mayfly which is used for bait. There are many species of mayflies found in the streams, rivers, ponds, and lakes of the country. The nymphs vary widely in size and shape. Some prefer the clear, rocky streams where they cling to the stones in riffles. Others burrow in the silt and mud of streams and lakes. Still others swim around freely in the shallows. Most of the mayfly nymphs are too small and delicate to make practical baits, but some of them reach very good size and these can be used.

One of the largest is the nymph of the burrowing mayfly, which is often called a "wriggler" or "seahorse." There are several kinds of burrowing mayfly nymphs and some reach close to 2 inches in length. They can be recognized by their jaws, which have two pointed tusks, their six pairs of large, bushy gills along the abdomen, and their three fuzzy tails. These nymphs live in the mud which is slightly porous in depths from a few inches to 40 feet of water. But they are most numerous in water from about 2 to 10 feet in depth. Where they are plentiful you can notice their burrow openings or "blow holes" in the mud bottom. To get the nymphs, the mud can be scooped up with a shovel and washed out in a small box with a wire-screen bottom. Some anglers make a special combination shovel and bucket out of ⅛- or ¼-inch mesh of wire screen attached to a long handle. They scoop up the mud and slosh it around in the water to leave the insects exposed for the picking. You can also buy these nymphs from bait dealers in some areas. They are very popular for bluegills when fishing through the ice in the winter. Mayfly nymphs can also be used for trout, crappies, perch, and other panfish.

The nymphs can be kept in tanks of cold, well-aerated water. The bottom of the tank should be lined with dead leaves, leaf mold, or moss to allow the nymphs to hide. They can be transported to the fishing grounds in damp moss if the weather is cool.

## STONE FLIES

Although at first glance the stone fly nymph resembles the mayfly nymph, there are differences if you examine them closely. The stone fly nymph is flat and has two tails instead of the three usually found on mayfly nymphs. The stone fly nymphs also have longer antennae protruding from the head than do the mayfly nymphs. The stone fly nymphs usually prefer the fast-running streams, where they can be found clinging to the undersides of stones. They vary in size depending on the species, but some of the larger ones can be used for bait. They can easily be gathered by lifting stones from the fast-running water and examining the undersides. These nymphs are often called "hellgrammites," but this tends to confuse them with the true hellgrammite of the dobson fly mentioned earlier. Stone fly nymphs can be kept in cold-running water for future use.

The adult stone flies resemble the nymphs in body shape and structure, but they also have cellophanelike wings which fold flat in a horizontal position over the body. They are poor fliers and are usually seen crawling over the rocks and weeds along the shores of

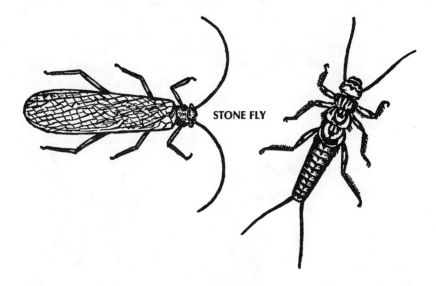

STONE FLY

streams. They can also be used as bait for trout being fished on or near the surface. But it is the nymph itself which is most widely used as bait for trout. They have also been used for whitefish.

The nymph can be hooked through the collar just behind the head. Another method is to thread the nymph tail first on a short shanked hook, following the curve of the hook and allowing the point and barb to penetrate to the head of the nymph.

## USING NYMPHS

Nymphs are very tender and soft and are difficult to keep on a hook, especially if you try to cast with them. However, the larger, tougher nymphs will stay on a hook fairly well. If the nymphs are small, try putting two or three on the same hook. Tiny No. 12 or 14 hooks of light wire are best for hooking nymphs.

When using nymphs for trout, it is best to let them drift naturally with the current. A fly rod is good for such fishing and the upper part of the leader and fly line can be coated with a solution to make it float. Then as the nymph drifts you can keep an eye on the leader where it enters the water. If the line twitches or stops, that usually indicates a bite and you should then set the hook.

In ponds and lakes and the quiet pools of streams or rivers you can fish a nymph by casting it out as far as you can and letting it sink to the bottom. Then start retrieving it very slowly with short twitches along the bottom.

For fish such as sunfish, crappies, yellow perch, white perch, and rock bass you can fish one or two nymphs on a small hook suspended under a light float in spots where these fish are found.

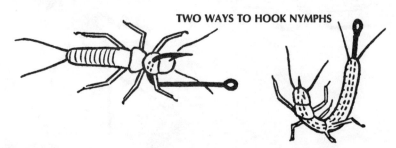

TWO WAYS TO HOOK NYMPHS

CRANE FLY LARVA

## CRANE FLIES

There are many species of these delicate flies, which look like overgrown mosquitoes and are often called "daddy longlegs" and "gallinippers." They do not bite as mosquitoes do and they are too fragile to be of any use as bait. But their larva, which look like overgrown, translucent maggots, are often used as bait. These are called "leatherjackets" and "waterworms." Some of the larger ones may reach almost 2 inches in length. They may be brown, white, or greenish in color and are found in streams among the decaying leaves, debris, and water plants. The larva has a tough skin, but if it is pierced the liquid drains out, making an unattractive bait. However, it has a small hard head which it withdraws into its body when disturbed. This head can be pulled out and the hook can be inserted through it. Or you can use thread to tie the larva to the hook. It can be used for trout, bluegills, perch, and other panfish.

When you are gathering the above insects from any stream or lake, great care should be taken to see that you don't disturb the bottom and vegetation too much. When you turn over stones searching for insects, put them back again the way you found them. If you use a screen or net, don't dump the debris that accumulates in it on dry land. Pick out the insects you want to keep and then wash the rest off into the water. In this way, you will save hundreds of tiny insects which are hidden among the debris or are too small to be noticeable. If dumped on dry land, much of this stream life will perish. Some states have laws regulating the taking of water insects from trout streams. They usually do allow the angler to take insects for his own use as bait. The small number of insects removed by anglers rarely hurts the trout streams, but if a great many are taken by bait dealers when they gather them to sell, then much harm can be done.

67

# CHAPTER 5

# LAND INSECTS

$T$*he insects found on land outnumber those that are found in the* water, and many of them are eaten by fish if they fall or are blown into the water. Heavy rains and floods also wash land insects into streams, rivers, and lakes. Like the water insects, the land insects go through either three or four stages of development from the egg to the adult. There are so many land insects that general methods cannot be laid down for obtaining, keeping, and hooking them, and they vary even more than water insects in size, structure, and habits. Each insect must be dealt with individually. Although most land insects can be used for bait, only the larger and more popular ones can be considered here.

## GRASSHOPPERS

There are many kinds of grasshoppers found in the fields which can be used as bait. Most of them are the short-horned grasshoppers, which are considered locusts and include many species. Those that belong to the genus *Melanoplus* are commonly used, but there are many others which also make good bait. It is up to the angler to find out which are most numerous in his locality and which attract the most fish. A few, such as the big gray-brown or smaller red-brown flying kind, are too hard to catch in any numbers and do not seem to appeal to the fish. Others, such as the green long-horned grasshoppers and the katydids, are somewhat delicate and hard to keep on the hook.

Grasshoppers are most numerous and reach the biggest size in the late summer and early fall months. During the daytime when the sun is high, they are quite active and hard to catch. But at night or early in the morning, when the grass and weeds are damp and the air is cold, they can be picked up more easily. If you must catch them during the daytime you can use a small butterfly net or fly swatter to pin them down against the grass. You can also try spreading a wool blanket on the grass and then chasing the grasshoppers so that they land on the blanket. Here their legs get tangled in the wool and they can be caught.

As you catch the grasshoppers, keep them in a cloth bag through which air can enter. Tie the opening with a string and you can allow one grasshopper at a time to emerge when you need it. A cigar box makes a good container for grasshoppers and other insects. Cut out a small square on the top and cover it with wire screening to allow air to enter. To remove the insects or put them in the box one at a time, a small hole should be bored in the cover of the box and covered with a small sliding door which can be cut out of a sheet of metal. A couple of screws will hold the door in place and keep the hole covered until it is slid open. A handful or

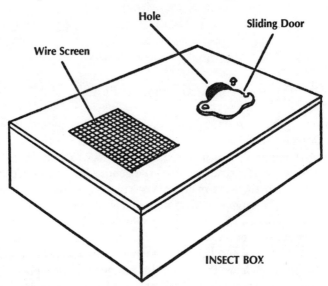

INSECT BOX

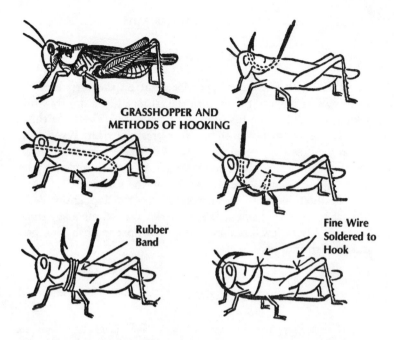

**GRASSHOPPER AND METHODS OF HOOKING**

Rubber Band

Fine Wire Soldered to Hook

two of grass or clover will keep the insects in the box content and alive during the fishing trip.

There are several ways of hooking grasshoppers. One method is to run the point of the hook into the grasshopper's back about a half-inch from the front of the head and then bring the point of the hook out at the top of the head between the eyes. Another method is to run the point of the hook into the grasshopper's back at the neck and bring it out at the underside and then run it again into the abdomen. Still another way is to run the point into the front of the head between the eyes and push the hook through most of the hopper's body, letting it come out near the tail end of the abdomen.

Of course, the above methods tend to kill the grasshopper rather quickly and many anglers prefer other methods. Some solder two pieces of fine wire to the shank of the hook and wrap these around the grasshopper. Others use a thin rubber band and slip several turns around the body of the grasshopper just in front of the two hind legs. Then the hook is run under the rubber bands. Or they tie the grasshopper to the hook with fine cotton or nylon thread.

## USING GRASSHOPPERS

You can use a grasshopper for trout on the surface of the water by just letting it drift with the current like a dry fly while it kicks and stirs up a fuss on top of the water. The same thing can be done for small-mouth bass in a stream or river. If you want to fish the grasshopper below the surface, you can add a split-shot or two on the leader above the hook and in streams and rivers let the hopper drift with the current below the surface.

In quiet pools or in lakes you can cast the hopper out, let it sink, then retrieve it slowly in short jerks. Or you can add a small float or bobber a few feet above the grasshopper and fish it for bass and panfish in a pond or lake.

## CRICKETS

The larger dark brown or black field crickets which are found in the grassy fields are popular as bait for many freshwater fishes. There are several species of field crickets, but the one usually caught and used is the common black field cricket (*Gryllus assimilis*), which is one of the largest. Crickets, like grasshoppers, are most numerous and are the largest during the late summer and early fall months. They can be found under stones, hay piles, and under wheat, corn, or rye stacks. You can also attract crickets by using stale bread as a lure. After they are caught they can be kept in the same types of containers as those used for grasshoppers. If you are keeping them for several days you can feed them grass, moist bread, or lettuce.

But catching crickets in large numbers is quite a chore and many fishermen prefer to raise their own. Experiments at the Alabama Polytechnic Institute have shown that the common black field cricket can be easily raised in large numbers. Metal or plastic cans such as garbage cans, lard cans, metal drums with tops removed, and similar containers can be used. The can should be kept indoors in a garage, basement, barn, woodshed, or empty room. If the building is screened, the top of the can can be left open. But if it is not, a piece of window screen should be used as a

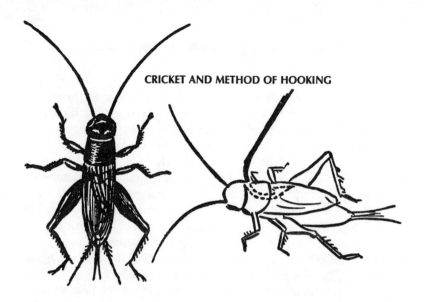

CRICKET AND METHOD OF HOOKING

cover to keep out spiders, ants, and other insects or animals which can harm the crickets.

The container which is used should be sandpapered on the inside for about 8 or 10 inches from the top. Then this area is coated with floor wax and polished to keep the crickets from climbing out. Next, from 4 to 6 inches of fine, clean, damp sand is spread on the bottom of the can or container. It must feel damp to the touch in order for the crickets to lay their eggs in it. To provide cover for the young crickets a layer of from 4 to 5 inches of excelsior or straw should be spread over the sand.

Now the container should be stocked with an equal number of male and female crickets. The females can be recognized by the long tube protruding at the tail end which is used to deposit eggs. From 20 to 50 crickets may be needed to stock the can, depending on its size. Poultry laying mash has proved to be one of the best foods for crickets. A small tray or saucer should be filled with the mash and placed inside the container. To supply the crickets with water, a small glass jar fountain such as those used by poultrymen is good. The saucer holding the water on the bottom should be filled with cotton to prevent the young crickets from drowning.

The crickets will thrive during the warmer months and produce from 200 to 500 young, depending on the size of the container and your original stock. During the colder months, if you want the crickets to grow and reproduce, suspend an electric light bulb to within 5 or 6 inches of the excelsior in the can. It takes the crickets about three months to reach maturity if the heat is maintained at around 80 degrees Farenheit. The eggs usually hatch in 15 to 25 days and the young crickets become large enough to use as bait in about a month.

You can also buy a stock of crickets from some commercial bait farmers. They will also supply information on the care, keeping and feeding, and breeding of their particular kind of crickets. You can obtain names and addresses of such bait farmers in the classified section of the outdoor magazines.

Crickets are rather delicate and are hard to keep on a hook. Small, fine wire hooks should be used and the hook should be run under the collar either with the point toward the head or away from it. They can also be hooked like the grasshopper, running the hook from the back through the neck, then out on the underside and into the abdomen. You can also use the hooks with the wire soldered to the shank or can tie the cricket to the hook with fine cotton or nylon thread.

## USING CRICKETS

Crickets can be used in much the same way as grasshoppers. But because these baits are more delicate, you have to be careful when casting them or when pulling them through the water, especially in fast currents. A long cane pole or fly rod is best for fishing with crickets, since you can just flip out the line with the bait and it will land softly on the water. When using crickets for trout or bass you can set the hook almost immediately, since they are small and are quickly mouthed or stripped off the hook. When fishing for bluegills or other panfish you can wait a second or two for these fish with small mouths to engulf the bait.

## COCKROACHES

Although cockroaches are repulsive to many people, others find that they make good bait for panfish. They can be found in

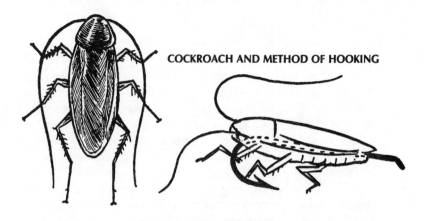

COCKROACH AND METHOD OF HOOKING

warehouses, garbage pails, and dumps, where they are especially active at night. They are fast runners and are difficult to catch but can often be caught in good numbers in traps baited with raw potatoes, apples, or bread soaked in water. They can also be raised in containers similar to those used for crickets. Two species, the German cockroach or Croton bug *(Blattella germanica)* and the American cockroach *(Periplaneta americana)*, are best for raising.

The containers used should be covered with cheesecloth or wire screen to prevent the roaches from escaping. Some oil or vaseline smeared near the top of the container will keep them from getting out when it is opened. Roaches will eat many foods, such as fruits and vegetables. A mixture containing 50 percent whole ground wheat, 45 percent dried skim milk, and 5 percent dried baker's yeast is recommended as a stock diet. This mixture is moistened with water, then allowed to dry. Cockroaches drink plenty of water and this can be supplied in the same type of glass jar fountain as used for crickets.

Roaches are also delicate and should be threaded on a hook tail first with the hook running the full length of the body, and the point and barb penetrating up to the head. They can be used in much the same ways as crickets. For bluegills, other sunfish, and panfish, use them a few feet below a float or bobber.

## MAGGOTS

These larvae of flies are another bait which is repulsive to many people. But the reason may be mainly that they are usually associated with manure, garbage, or decaying flesh. If the maggots are properly cleansed they can be handled with little trouble. The best maggots for bait are the larvae of the housefly, the stable fly, and the blowfly. The housefly maggot is smaller than the other two and is usually found in garbage; the stable fly maggots are found in manure, whereas the blowfly maggots live in decaying flesh.

To obtain blowfly maggots, you can hang a piece of meat or dead animal outdoors to attract the adult flies. They will soon lay their eggs on the meat and these will hatch into tiny larvae. In about three or four days the maggots will reach their full growth and then you can knock them off with a stick into a container filled with cornmeal or bran. This will dry and scour the maggots and make them more pleasant to handle. Maggots can be hooked and used for trout, whitefish, and panfish in the same ways as caddis larvae described in Chapter 4.

## MEALWORMS

These yellow and brown larvae of the beetle are considered pests because they spoil grains in mills, grain stores, grain elevators, feed bins and other places where these foods are stored. But mealworms are also used as food for various pets and as bait for panfish. They can be found where grain is stored or can be bought from pet shops, aquarium dealers, and bait dealers.

The mealworm may reach an inch in length, and two species, the yellow mealworm *(Tenebrio molitor)* and the dark mealworm *(Tenebrio obscurus)*, are commonly found. They can be raised in large quantities in washtubs, boxes, or plastic garbage cans with smooth inside walls and a cover of wire screen or cheesecloth to prevent the escape of the larvae and adults and to prevent other insects or animals from entering. A layer of chicken mash or other grain meal is spread to a depth of ¼ inch on the bottom of the container. Then a layer of burlap is used to cover this food. Then more mash is sprinkled over the burlap and this is covered with another layer of burlap. Several alternate layers of feed and burlap should be built up to provide food and hiding places for the larvae. This box will need a sprinkling of water each day, or some raw carrots or potatoes should be placed in the container to provide the necessary moisture. Then you can stock the container with several hundred mealworms. These will turn into adults, which will lay eggs to provide more mealworms, and some of the adults can be removed to other boxes to start new cultures.

Mealworms make a good bait for trout, bluegills and other sunfish, yellow perch, and crappies. They are especially popular for use while ice fishing but are good the year round. Hook and use them the same way as caddis larvae described in Chapter 4.

## GRUBS

Although the adult beetles are eaten by fish and can be used for bait, it is the larvae which are more commonly used for this purpose. The big white grubs of the june bug and the Japanese beetle are found in the ground, where they feed on the roots of grasses, shrubs, trees, and other plants. There are many kinds of beetles and some of their grubs live in rotting stumps, logs, and posts, under the bark of trees, and in animal dung. They can be kept in the same substances in which they are found.

Many grubs make good baits for trout, bass, and panfish. They are rather delicate and lose their body liquids if pierced by a hook or squeezed too hard. So hook them with a fine wire hook through the head or tie them to the hook with fine thread.

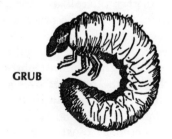

**GRUB**

## CATALPA WORM

This caterpillar is the larva of the sphinx or hawk moth. It may reach a length of 3 inches and has a smooth body which is dark brown or black on the back and green along the sides. They are also known as "catawbies" and are found in catalpa trees, which is their only source of food. The trees may produce two or more crops of worms a year from May to September. The worms can be picked off the tree and kept dormant in a refrigerator for a few weeks until they are ready to be used. Some anglers turn them inside out with a stick or nail before using them as bait. But they can be used as they are for big fish such as bass or can be cut in half for bluegills and other panfish.

## CATERPILLARS

There are many other caterpillars of the butterflies and moths which can be used as bait. Those with short hairs are generally not as good as those with smooth bodies. Also, those with hairs can be irritating to the skin and should be handled carefully. That great pest the European corn borer, which does so much damage to corn, is a caterpillar which can be used for bait. It is found on the leaves, under the husks, and in tassels of the corn during the summer months. During the late fall and in the winter they can be found in dry stalks which remain in the fields. They make good panfish baits during the summer, and in the winter for fishing through the ice for bluegills.

Another caterpillar which attacks corn, and also cotton, tomatoes, tobacco, and other crops, is the corn earworm, which can also be used for bait. The green caterpillars found on cabbage leaves are used by some anglers. Another small green caterpillar is found during the summer months on oak trees. It can be obtained by shaking the branches over a cloth or paper. Most of these caterpillars, if large, can be used for bass. Smaller ones can be used for trout and panfish.

Caterpillars usually have thin skins and should be hooked through the tougher head or tied to a hook with thread. Hooking them deep through the body will cause the body fluids to seep out and kills them quickly.

The pupae of moths, which are usually enclosed in cocoons, and those of butterflies, which are naked, can also be used as bait. This is the resting stage of the insect in its transformation from the larva or caterpillar to the moth or butterfly. Those with cocoons should be removed from the silk covering before using.

## GALL WORMS

The larvae found in the galls or swellings on the stems of plants can be used for bait. These are usually the larvae of flies, moths, or wasps. A popular bait is the small white larva found in the gall on the stem of the goldenrod plant. These gall worms make good winter bait for bluegills, since they can be obtained easily when other baits are scarce. The galls can be collected in the fall or early winter and stored in a cool, dry place until needed. Split open the gall with a knife and your bait is ready for use.

## CICADA

The cicadas, harvest flies, and seventeen-year locusts are sometimes used as bait for trout, bass, and catfish. These are the big insects with transparent wings, blunt heads, and large eyes. There are many species and they appear almost every year. But some species appear only at intervals every so many years. The males can be located easily when they sing loudly and shrilly while clinging to a tree, post, or plant. But catching them is another matter; you have to sneak up quietly and make a quick grab.

CICADA

You can hook a cicada through the body and then throw or cast it on the water, where it will flutter around creating a big disturbance and hopefully attract a big trout or bass. You can also drift it underwater with a weight above the hook. Or you can hook two or three of them on a big single hook and fish them on the bottom for catfish.

## WASPS, BEES, AND HORNETS

The adults of these stinging insects can be used as bait but few anglers have the courage to tackle the job of obtaining them and then using them. The small larvae or grubs found in the combs or nests of bees, wasps, hornets, and yellow jackets are less of a problem if you can raid the nests without disturbing or encountering the angry adult insects. You can use these small grubs for trout, sunfish, and other panfish.

Of course, there are many other land insects which have not been mentioned here which also make good baits. If you see anything that flies, crawls, or hops and looks big enough to tempt a fish, give it a trial and most of the time you will find that the fish will take it. One of the best things about land insect baits is that they are so varied and numerous that there is almost always some kind of bait available. This comes in handy if you run out of bait and would like to continue fishing. A search in the grass, weeds, shrubs, decaying logs, under the bark of dead trees, and under stones generally produces some kind of insect which can be used for bait.

# CHAPTER 6

# OTHER FRESHWATER BAITS

*T*his section will deal with the miscellaneous baits that do not readily fall into the groups considered so far.

## CRAYFISH

This small crustacean is easily recognized since it looks like a miniature lobster. It is also called the crawfish, crawdad, craw, and crab. There are some 100 species found in the swamps, brooks, creeks, lakes, and rivers of the country. Some grow larger than others but most of them fall between 2 and 5 inches in length. Some prefer the riffles of streams, others are found in the quieter pools, and still others live in ponds and lakes. Some even live in burrows which they dig in wet fields or river banks and hillsides. But most of them, no matter where found, can be used as bait.

Crayfish are more or less scavengers, feeding on a wide variety of plant and animal matter. They are active at night, when they leave their hiding places under stones or their burrows to come out into shallow water to feed or molt. This molting is necessary because the crayfish has a hard shell which does not allow it to grow; it must be cast off to make room for the expanding tissues. Just before the crayfish gets rid of its hard shell it is known as a "peeler." After it casts it off, it becomes a "soft-shell," and when the new shell starts to harden a day or so

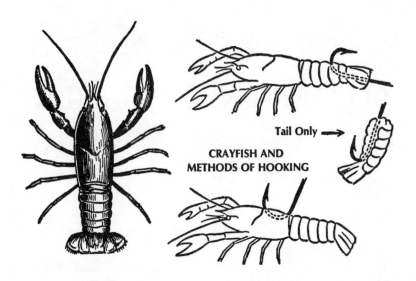

**Tail Only** ➜

**CRAYFISH AND
METHODS OF HOOKING**

later it is called a "paper-shell." Then when the new shell hardens completely, it becomes a "hard-shell" again. Crayfish make good baits in all their various stages but are best when they are soft-shelled.

Crayfish can be caught by hand, with dip nets, or with seines. You can usually find them in the water in the daytime by turning over stones or searching through the weeds. Sometimes they can also be dug out of their burrows in clay or sand banks. But the best time to catch them is at night, using a flashlight and dip net or seine. Some anglers also use minnow traps or specially constructed wire traps with funnel entrances, baited with dead fish or meat. These can be left overnight and checked in the morning. However, the majority of the crayfish caught by this method will be hard ones.

Anglers are always searching for a method that will turn hard-shelled crayfish into soft ones. But the only foolproof method is to let nature take its course and help it along a bit by feeding the crayfish so that they grow faster and molt more often. Crayfish will live in minnow ponds, pools, and tanks supplied with running water. Here you can feed them pieces of meat or dead fish and have some soft-shell crayfish on hand when you need them. If you have several ponds or tanks, you can be sure that some crayfish will be molting. And since the smaller ones grow faster and shed more often, it is best to stock the tanks with small and medium-sized crayfish. Always remove the excess food and dead crayfish from the pools or tanks immediately to protect the live ones and prevent contamination. It is also wise to separate the crayfish according to size, since the larger ones will often attack and cripple or kill the smaller ones. The soft-shelled crayfish should also be removed from the tanks as soon as possible to prevent them from being killed or eaten.

If soft-shelled crayfish are to be used soon, they can be kept in a container filled with damp moss. But if they are to be kept for several days, they should be placed with the moss in a refrigerator or icebox, where they will stay soft for a few days. The cold will prevent the shells from hardening, but after the crayfish are removed from the ice or cold they should be used immediately. Hard-shelled crayfish can be carried in a container filled with damp moss or grass. Here, too, always keep the hard-shelled crayfish separated from the soft-shelled ones.

Crayfish are used for many freshwater fishes and are especially good for small-mouth bass. The hard-shelled crayfish are generally hooked through the tail, with the point and barb facing either up or down. Some anglers also hook them through the back, but since bass and other fish usually swallow the crayfish tail first, the tail method of hooking is more popular. Some anglers also break off the big pincers to make the bait more attractive and easier to handle. The tails of hard-shelled crayfish make excellent baits, too. These can be broken off and used as is or peeled and then threaded on the hook.

The soft-shelled crayfish are much harder to keep on the hook and usually have to be lashed on with fine cotton or nylon thread; rubber bands can also be used to hold them on a hook. Or you can solder two pieces of fine wire to the shank of the hook and use these to tie the crayfish down.

## USING CRAYFISH

When using crayfish for big trout, small-mouth bass, or walleyes in streams or rivers, use a spinning outfit and cast the crayfish out into the current, letting it drift downstream into pockets, eddies, holes, and pools.

When fishing in quiet pools or lakes cast out the crayfish, let it sink to the bottom, and then pull it back slowly along the bottom. Or you can let the crayfish sink to the bottom and coil some slack line on a flat rock or the bottom of the boat. Thus when a fish picks up the crayfish and moves off it will have plenty of time to swallow the bait without feeling the pull of the line.

You can also fish the crayfish on the bottom with a sliding sinker rig or a bottom rig. This is a good way to fish for catfish or freshwater drum. But channel catfish often prefer a moving bait; when fishing rivers for them let the crayfish drift under banks, rocks, ledges, logs, and other spots where they like to lie. The same thing can be done when using small crayfish for rock bass in quiet flowing streams.

## FROGS

These amphibians are another bait popular with many anglers, especially those seeking big fish. There are many species of frogs that can be used as bait, but four kinds are used more than any others. The bullfrog *(Rana catesbiana)* is one of the largest. It is light gray-green and sometimes brown-green above, and yellow-white underneath. The bullfrog is usually found in the larger shallow ponds and lakes. It is sought a great deal for food and is scarce in many areas. For most fish, only the younger, smaller bullfrogs make practical baits.

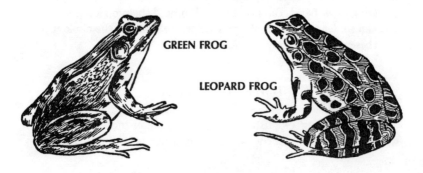

GREEN FROG

LEOPARD FROG

Another frog is the green frog *(Rana clamitans)*. This is often confused with the bullfrog, but it has a dark greenish-brown back and vivid green head and shoulders. The throat is bright yellow and the belly a creamy white. It is found in the same places as the bullfrog and in many other fresh waters.

One of the frogs most widely used as bait is the leopard frog *(Rana pipiens)*. This frog has a ground color of rich green which is sometimes brownish and the familiar spots on the back which are irregular and edged with light bands. It lives in the grass along streams, brooks, ponds, and springs, but it often travels far inland and is found quite a distance from water at times.

Another frog that is widely used for bait is the pickerel frog *(Rana palustris)*. This resembles the leopard frog, but it is mostly brown, with dark yellow or orange inside its hind legs and on the lower abdomen. The spots are square instead of irregular like those on the leopard frog. While it also prefers the shorelines of lakes, brooks, streams, and ponds, it rarely ventures as far away from water as the leopard frog does.

Frogs can be caught by hand if you are fast enough, or with a long-handled dip net. Look for them in the weeds growing in the water and in the grass along the edges of lakes, ponds, streams, and swamps. The best time to hunt them is at night, when you can use a flashlight to blind or confuse them and they will usually remain in one spot until disturbed. Some of the larger frogs can even be caught on a hook baited with a worm or a piece of red cloth and dangled in front of them.

Frogs can be kept in a live box made of wire mesh partly submerged in the water and filled with some rocks so that they can come up to breathe and rest. They will also live in a container or tank kept in a cool spot and filled with a few inches of water. Here, too, some rocks or a board should be placed on the bottom to allow the frogs to leave the water. They will eat worms and insects that are alive and moving. Worms and strips of meat will often be taken if dangled in front of them.

The usual method of hooking frogs is through both lips with the hook entering underneath and coming out on top. They can also be hooked through the front or hind leg or in the crotch. There are also many frog harnesses on the market which do not

85

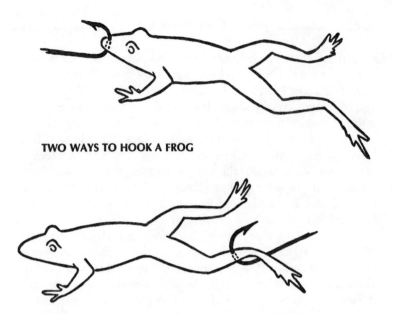

**TWO WAYS TO HOOK A FROG**

injure the frog, and some even have weed guards so that the angler can fish the frogs in the weeds and lily pads.

Before catching or using frogs check your fish and game laws, since many states have regulations governing the taking and using of these baits.

The tadpoles which are the young or immature frogs can also be used for bait. They can be caught by hand or with a dip net in shallow water near shore where they are usually found.

## USING FROGS

Small frogs can be used to catch big trout, especially along meadow streams where such frogs are commonly found. They are especially effective when fished for big brown trout in the evening around dusk, when frogs become more active and the big trout look for them.

For bass, pike, and muskellunge you can fish a frog on the surface, where it can kick up a fuss while swimming and attract these fish. Fish the frog close to shore around lily pads, hyacinths, and weed beds, where frogs are usually found. When fishing among lily pads let the frog swim around and even up on top of a pad. Then wait a while and pull it off the pad and let it swim around in an open spot. It's a good idea to hook your frog with a weedless hook when fishing among such lily pads and weeds.

You can also fish a live frog below the surface for large-mouth bass, small-mouth bass, and walleyes. Here you can add a couple of split-shot sinkers or a clamp-on sinker on the leader above the hook to take the frog down to the bottom.

When using dead frogs you have to give them some rod action to make them effective. You can let the frog sink down deep and then slowly retrieve it with regular jerks or sharp lifts of the rod tip. You can also hook a dead frog through the lips and cast it out and then retrieve it on top of the water in short jerks. Frogs can also be skittered on the surface for pickerel or bass using a long cane or glass pole. Here you keep the frog on top and draw it across the lily pads, through the open spots, varying your speed until you find the one the fish want.

Dead frogs can also be fished with a bottom rig for catfish. Here you can use pieces of a big frog or a whole small frog. Cast it out with a sinker to hold it on the bottom where catfish prowl.

Tadpoles can be used for trout or bass. If you hook one through the base of the tail and cast him out, he'll head for the bottom. Don't let the tadpole hide in any rocks, weeds, or mud that may be on the bottom. If necessary, when he reaches the bottom lift the rod slowly so that he can swim around and be seen.

## TOADS

Small toads also make good baits at times. The trouble is that they are usually difficult to obtain in any quantities, but there are times when they are very numerous and swarm all over the place. They can also be found in gardens at night when they come out to feed. Toads are used for black bass and catfish.

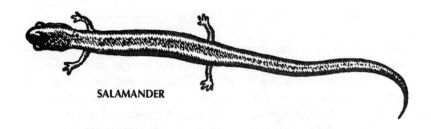

SALAMANDER

## SALAMANDERS AND NEWTS

These lizardlike creatures are amphibians, like frogs, and may be found in the water or on land. There are many species, some of them, like the hellbender and mudpuppy, reach a foot or more in length. However, most of them grow to only a few inches. They live in brooks, springs, lakes, and streams, or on land in moist places. They are active at night, and during the day they hide under logs, stones, in moss, holes, and the overhanging banks of streams. Others can be found in the riffles of streams under rocks, logs, and other debris. They can be caught by hand or with seines. Grab them near the head or midsection because many salamanders and newts have tails which break off easily. They can be kept for short periods of time in containers filled with damp moss and placed in a cool spot. For longer periods, tanks or aquariums with running water are best. They can be fed insects, mealworms, earthworms, and small bits of meat or fish.

## USING SALAMANDERS

Salamanders may be hooked through one of their hind legs, at the base of the tail, or just under the skin. But care must be taken when casting them since they are rather delicate. The smaller salamanders and newts can be used for trout and bass. For trout cast the salamander into a riffle entering a pool or into the pool itself and let it drift naturally or swim around. But keep it off the bottom where it can hide in the rocks, weeds, or debris. They can be used the same way for small-mouth bass in streams and rivers.

For bass in lakes or quiet pools you can cast the salamander out and let it sink to the bottom, then slowly retrieve it back, along the bottom, to shore or to the boat.

88

The larger salamanders, such as the hellbender and the mudpuppy or waterdog, are excellent as bait for pike and muskellunge. Here a good way to hook the salamander is to tie a couple of wraps of line around its body just behind the front legs. Then insert a 5/0 or 6/0 hook under the loops of line. Or you can just insert the hook through both lips of the hellbender or mudpuppy. Cast this bait into a pike or musky hangout and let it swim around below the surface at various depths.

## LEECHES

These are the familiar bloodsuckers which are found in most ponds, streams, and lakes. There are many species and they vary in size and color. But they can easily be recognized by their wormlike shapes and the fact that they have sucking discs at each end of their bodies. Not all of them suck blood; some feed on tiny animals and plant matter.

Leeches can sometimes be caught in traps similar to the minnow type, which are baited with fresh meat or coagulated blood. They can also be caught with a seine or dip net. Leeches usually remain well hidden, but if you stir up the water by wading through it and kicking up the mud and weeds they'll often come out. When they attach themselves to the bare skin they can be removed by pulling hard. These aquatic worms can be kept in an aquarium or other container filled with water. They will live for a long time without food, so there is no need to feed them.

Leeches are especially good baits for trout, bass, and walleyes, and for channel catfish during the summer and early fall months. They can be fished in much the same ways as worms. Or you can hook a leech behind a spinner and cast or troll it slowly.

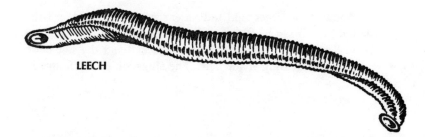

**LEECH**

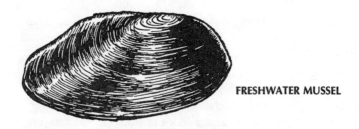

FRESHWATER MUSSEL

## CLAMS AND MUSSELS

There are many species of freshwater clams and mussels found in the streams and rivers. They are also found in some lakes. They lie partly buried in the mud, sand, or gravel bottom and can easily be gathered by hand in shallow water. In deeper water you may have to feel for them with your bare feet or dive down and dig them out. To take them in larger quantities, large curved hooks with four prongs are dragged along the bottom to catch between the shells and bring them up. Some states have regulations governing the taking of clams and should be consulted for size limits, seasons, and the number of clams and mussels you can take.

Clams can be kept for quite a while in a live box submerged in the water; for short periods you can keep them in containers filled with water. To open them just hit them hard against a hard object and crack the shells to remove the soft meat. Or you can insert a knife blade between the halves of the shell and cut the hinge muscle.

Clams and mussels are good for catfish, carp, buffalo, and suckers, and will take panfish at times. Even bass have been caught on them. For catfish the soft meat from the clams is allowed to sour before using. It can be placed in a jar with sour milk and allowed to stand for several days.

## SNAILS AND SLUGS

Some of the larger land and water snails can be used for bait. The land snails can be found under stones and logs and in damp places. The snails hard shell must be cracked and the soft body removed before using it for bait. The slugs which are found in

SLUG

gardens, cellars, and damp places look like snails without the complete shells and these can also be used for bait. They are used mostly for trout, black bass, and panfish.

## SHRIMP

The small saltwater shrimp and prawns are sometimes used for trout, bass, white perch, and smelt. Although these small crustaceans live in salt and brackish water, they can be used in fresh water. They can be caught in saltwater bays along the weedy shores using a fine-mesh seine. They will live best in a wire cage suspended in the water, but they can also be kept in a container lined with cracked ice on the bottom. Cover the ice with burlap and fill the container with wood shavings or sawdust. Then place the shrimp inside and lightly cover them with shavings or sawdust.

A similar small shrimp is found in fresh water, and these are also used at times for bass and panfish. These small shrimp and prawns are not very large baits, so sometimes two or three of them on a hook are better than only one.

## MICE

Not too many anglers use mice as bait since they are not always easy to obtain when needed. And the average angler doesn't care to handle or bait a hook with these rodents. But they sometimes make effective baits for big, wily trout, black bass, pike, or muskellunge which do not fall for other bait and lures. The mice used are usually the common house mouse and the field mouse, but there are many other small mice which can also be used. Mice can be caught in the regular wire cage traps which take them alive. These can be bought in almost any hardware store. Field mice can often be caught under stacks of wheat, rye, or oats which have been standing for some time. Here you can often find a nest of young mice and these also make good bait, especially for catfish. Mice are usually hooked under the skin or are tied on with wire or thread. Gloves should be used in handling them for they will often try to bite. Mice can easily be raised in quantities in wire cages. Some excelsior for nests, and straw or wood shavings for bedding is needed. The only additional requirements are fresh water to drink and foods like cereals, bread, mash, fruits, and vegetables.

When using mice cast them out and let them swim around on top of the water. They work best near shore or under trees or brush where they are apt to fall into the water. In a stream or river you can put the mouse on a small board or log and let him drift downstream with the current while you let out slack line. Then when the board or log reaches a spot where big trout or bass lie, pull the mouse off and let him swim around on top of the water kicking up a fuss and making ripples which attract the fish.

## SNAKES

Like mice, snakes will never make popular baits due to the average person's dislike or fear of them. But fish such as black bass, pike, and muskellunge do take them at times. Of course, another reason why they are unpopular is that most people can't tell the difference between the harmless and poisonous species, and therefore avoid them all. This is the safest policy, but if you can recognize the poisonous snakes there is no danger in using the harmless kinds. The ribbon snakes, green or grass snakes, the smaller garter and water snakes, and many other kinds of harmless snakes can be used for bait. The green snake rarely bites, but the garter and water snakes will often attempt to bite, so grab them behind the head. Snakes will live for quite a while in almost any container. They'll eat insects, frogs, toads, earthworms, or small fish, depending on the species. Snakes can be hooked under the skin or near the base of the tail, near no vital parts.

To use snakes for bass, pike, or muskellunge, cast them out and let them swim around on top of the water. They will move and live for a long time and while swimming they will create a disturbance on the surface which will attract fish from great distances.

# CHAPTER  7

# PREPARED BAITS

*T his chapter deals with the various formula and recipe baits, but* it also includes some baits which have not been covered so far and which do not readily fall into the previous sections.

## SALMON EGGS

Salmon eggs are a very popular bait for steelhead trout, especially during the winter months when other lures or baits fail to interest the fish. They are also used for other trout where it is legal, but since many states prohibit the use of salmon eggs for game fish it is best to check your local game laws before using this bait.

Salmon eggs are sold in many tackle stores and can be purchased in small jars, but many anglers do not consider the packed eggs to be as good as those taken from a freshly killed salmon or steelhead trout. Eggs taken from fish that are ready to spawn are big enough to be used singly. But those from fish in which the eggs are not ripe are small in size, and these are usually used in clusters of a dozen or more eggs. The egg sacs taken from the female salmon or steelhead trout can be cut with scissors into "gobs" of any size bait you wish to use. The membrane which is attached to the eggs helps to hold them in place, but they still wash off easily or fall off the hook when cast. Therefore many anglers tie them on the hook with thread, or loop the leader over them, or enclose them in small bags of cheesecloth, mosquito netting, or a similar mesh. Commercial packers are reluctant to reveal the various processes they use to preserve and color their eggs. However, by using the following methods and experimenting a bit, you can find the one which gives the best results. If you get fresh eggs from a freshly killed fish which you plan to use soon, you can merely harden them by sprinkling them lightly with salt or borax, then roll them up in paper and place them in a refrigerator.

To prepare eggs for a longer period of time, get fresh, large, firm eggs, which separate readily from the membrane. Split open the egg sacs and pour hot water over the eggs to separate them from the membrane. The process can be helped along by running the eggs lightly over a wire mesh screen. But don't use so much hot water that it damages the thin membranes enclosing each egg.

Now put the eggs in a solution of 1 part sugar to 3 or more parts of salt—as much as 9 parts salt can be used. The brine solution should test 80 or 90 percent by salinometer. Aniline dyes can be added to the eggs to give them a red coloring. Stir the eggs every so often with a wooden paddle as they soak in the solution from 20 to 30 minutes to cure, color, and harden them. Properly cured eggs will not be too hard, brittle, rubbery, or shrunken. Finally the eggs are drained and packed in airtight jars. If the jars remain closed, the eggs will keep for a long time in a cool place. However, in warm climates a solution of 5 percent formalin can be added. Another preservative which is often added is 1 percent sodium benzoate.

The same process can be used to preserve cluster eggs, but these are merely washed in ordinary cold water before being placed in the brine solution, and they are allowed to cure in the solution somewhat longer than single eggs before being drained and packed in jars.

Another method which can be used to preserve salmon eggs is to keep them in a salt solution strong enough just to barely float the eggs until the slime is cut. Then they should be drained, put in glycerin, and kept in airtight jars in a cool place. When these eggs are to be used, they should be drained of the glycerin and placed in separate tightly covered containers. Once the eggs have been removed from the glycerin they should not be put back in it.

## HOOKING AND USING SALMON EGGS

There are many ways of hooking salmon eggs, depending on the size of the eggs and the fishing being done. When using large single eggs, small short-shanked hooks from about size No. 10 to 14 are used. The bend and shank of the hook is buried in the egg and often even the eye of the hook is pushed into the egg with a toothpick or stick.

Clusters of eggs can be wrapped around the shank and bend of a single hook or treble hook with fine, red-colored silk or cotton thread. Some anglers enclose the cluster around a single or treble hook with a small piece of cloth netting and tie it above the hook to form a small bag.

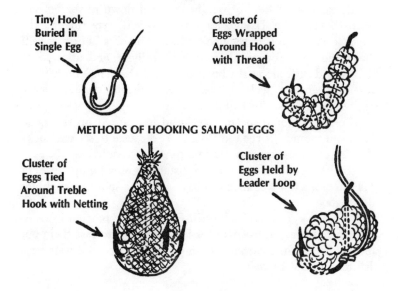

**Tiny Hook Buried in Single Egg**

**Cluster of Eggs Wrapped Around Hook with Thread**

**METHODS OF HOOKING SALMON EGGS**

**Cluster of Eggs Tied Around Treble Hook with Netting**

**Cluster of Eggs Held by Leader Loop**

One of the most popular methods is to tie up two or three dozen clusters in small sacks in advance. Use 3-inch squares of cheesecloth or other netting which is red in color. The egg cluster is placed in the center of the square and the corners of the netting are gathered in and tied with red thread to form a small sack. Such enclosed clusters of eggs can be put on a hook by running the point into the sack just below the tie, then burying the bend in the eggs and allowing the point and barb to protrude from the netting. Some anglers don't use any netting, but run their leader through the eye of a hook, and then make a sliding tie on the shank forming a loop which tightens around the cluster of eggs.

When using a single salmon egg you get best results if you use no weight on your leader or line but let the egg drift naturally in the current. This is best done fishing with a long fly rod and using a short line so that the current doesn't make your leader or line pull the egg too fast or too slow through the water. In other words, try to make the egg drift as if it had no line attached. This means you will have to fish each spot very carefully and quietly because you will be working close to the fish at all times.

When fishing a cluster of eggs for steelhead in a river you usually need some kind of weight to get it down to the bottom where these fish lie. Using a long, thin "pencil" type sinker and a 2-foot leader from it to the hook is best. This should be cast well above the spot you think contains steelhead and allowed to bounce and drift along the bottom toward the fish. You have to develop a sense of "feel" or "touch" when fishing the eggs, since steelhead often take the bait gently. Any strange hesitation, pull, stop, or throb could mean a steelhead has picked up the eggs. Then you should lift the rod tip a short distance to set the hook.

To cover the most water in a river you should cast the eggs out to different spots and varying distances. Moving upstream or downstream a few feet after you have worked a spot thoroughly is also a good idea.

Salmon eggs can also be still-fished on the bottom in rivers and lakes. Here you use a sinker heavy enough to cast them out and hold them in a current. Then you settle back and wait for a fish to pick up the bait.

## DOUGHBALLS

Doughballs are used for carp, buffalo fish, and catfish, and there are hundreds of formulas used in preparing them, depending on the individual angler's ideas and preferences. The basic ingredients are flour, cornmeal, water, and some kind of sweetening or flavoring. Some of the more commonly used formulas are listed below. You can experiment to find out which one gives the best results in your local waters.

The first recipe will provide one or two anglers with enough bait for a whole day's fishing under normal conditions. Pour 1 cup of water into a pan, add 2 teaspoonfuls of sugar, and bring the water to a boil. Then add 1 cup of cornmeal and about ¾ of a cup of plain flour to the water. Stir this mixture over a low flame for about 5 minutes. Then place a cover on the pan and put it in a larger pan filled with water (or use a double boiler). The mixture should be cooked for about half an hour. Then stir the mixture once more to test its consistency. If it's too thick you can add a little water, and if too thin you can knead more flour into it. Finally, roll the whole mixture into a large ball and when it cools it is ready to use. Just pinch off as much as you need to make the doughball.

Another recipe uses ½ cup of plain flour and ½ cup of cornmeal, a pinch of salt, and enough water to form a smooth dough. Mix these ingredients thoroughly and then drop the dough into boiling water and keep it there for about 20 minutes. Then take it out, let it cool, and it's ready to use.

Another recipe calls for 1 cup of cornmeal, ½ cup of plain flour, and 2 teaspoonfuls of sugar. Add enough water to mix this into a dough. Form the dough into balls somewhat smaller than you use for bait, since they will expand after they are cooked, and drop the doughballs into a kettle of boiling water. Keep them there for about 15 or 20 minutes until they are firm and rubbery, and then drain off the water. When it cools the bait is ready for use.

Another recipe calls for 1 cup of plain flour and 2 cups of wheat bran, with water added to form a stiff dough. After knead-

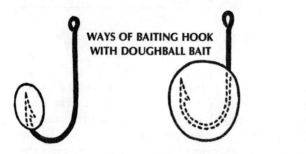

**WAYS OF BAITING HOOK WITH DOUGHBALL BAIT**

ing it thoroughly, roll the dough into small balls and cook them in boiling water for 15 or 20 minutes. Then drain off the water and the bait is ready to use when it cools.

Still another recipe requires 2 large potatoes which are peeled and grated, ½ teaspoonful of salt, 1 tablespoon of cornmeal, and enough flour to make a stiff batter. Roll into balls of the size desired and drop them into boiling water to cook until they float.

The carp is supposed to have a sweet tooth and many anglers also add sugar, honey, molasses, or corn syrup to the dough.

Absorbent cotton, cornstarch, or white of egg are often added to the doughball recipes to help hold the bait together on the hook. But if the doughballs are properly prepared these extras are not really needed. In fact, the best doughball bait clings to the hook well, but is still soft enough to mold easily. Doughball bait will keep better on a fishing trip if it is wrapped in wax paper or tinfoil. To keep it longer, wrap it in the paper or foil and put it in a refrigerator.

The size of the doughball formed around a hook depends on the size of the fish present and the way they are biting. With small fish, or on days when large fish prefer small baits, only a pinch of the dough is molded around the point and barb of the hook. If the fish are large and biting strongly the dough can cover the point, barb, and bend of the hook to about halfway up the shank. When the fish are large, or when you are fishing in a current, or when the bait will be left overnight or longer, the whole hook can be covered up to the eye, forming a pear-shaped doughball. These larger doughballs also are heavy enough to cast, and you need not use a sinker when fishing in quiet pools or lakes.

## OTHER CARP BAITS

Other baits used for carp include whole grains, such as wheat, rye, and barley, which are soaked until they soften. String several of these on a thin wire hook. Vegetables such as potatoes, carrots, and parsnips can be boiled until half done and then used as bait. About five or six kernels of fresh-cut sweet corn can also be used. Or you can buy canned corn or canned peas and use these. Dried green peas, lima beans, and other beans can be soaked, parboiled, and then used for bait. Some anglers even swear by small pieces of marshmallows or gumdrops as bait. Even ordinary moss, found on rocks or in the water, has been rolled into a ball and placed on a hook for carp and sturgeon.

## BREAD

Fresh bread and rolls or biscuits can be used as bait for carp and other freshwater fish. If the bread is freshly baked all you have to do is pinch off a piece and knead it or roll it between your fingers to the desired size. If the bread is old or stale, you can soak it in water, then squeeze out the excess water and knead the bread until it is the right consistency.

For panfish such as sunfish, a small ball of bread placed on the point and barb of the hook is sufficient. You can fish this with or without a float or bobber but it's a good idea to move it every so often to get the attention of the fish and make them take it.

A larger ball of bread or a pear-shaped bait on a hook can be used for bullheads, catfish, or carp. Here it is best to cast out the kneaded bread and let it sink to the bottom and rest there without giving it any movement. Various scents and flavors mentioned in the doughball section above can be added to the bread.

Bread can also be used as "chum" to attract minnows, panfish, or carp to an area. Here you simply break up the loaves or slices into small pieces and scatter them on top of the water. To make them sink faster you can soak them in water first.

## CHEESE AND STINK BAITS

These baits have a strong odor which is suppposed to be irresistible to catfish and attract them from a distance. Like the doughball bait, there are many recipes and formulas for these baits.

One recipe calls for equal parts of Limburger cheese and hamburger meat. A little hot water is added and mixed in well. Now work in enough plain flour to make the bait stick well, and the bait is ready to use. Almost any ground meat or fish can be used with the Limburger cheese and it doesn't have to be fresh. In fact, the riper the meat and the more rancid the cheese, the better the bait.

Another formula uses ½ pound of strong cheese grated fine and mixed with about 4 cups of plain flour. Water is added to make a stiff dough. Form doughballs of the size desired and let them stand and dry out for a couple of hours. Then drop them into boiling water and let them cook for 20 or 30 minutes. Take them out, let them dry again, and they are ready to use.

Minnows, pieces of fish, or chunks of meat can be placed in a jar and allowed to stand in the sun for a few days. When this bait becomes really "ripe" it is ready to use. The same thing can be done with freshwater mussels or clams, and here many cat-fishermen add sour milk.

Another stink bait calls for placing minnows or other small fish in a large jar or can and then allowing them to decompose until only an oil substance remains. Then small pieces of sponge are soaked in this mess until they absorb the odor and the sponge is placed on a hook. After a while these sponge baits may lose some of the strong odor and should be removed from the hook and put back into the container to absorb more of the stink.

Another method calls for making the same smelly solution as above and then mixing it with flour to make a stiff dough. You can mold the bait around the hook in any size you want.

Various scents are often added to the stink and cheese baits. Oil of rhodium, oil of anise, asafetida, and rotten eggs have all been used. For those anglers who don't like to bother making stink and cheese baits, there are quite a few preparations on the market which can be bought already prepared. These are sold in most fishing tackle stores. There are also scents that come in tubes or bottles which can be spread on baits to lure catfish and other fish.

## BLOOD BAITS

Chicken blood that has congealed is a good bait for catfish. This blood can usually be obtained from a poultry market or chicken processing plant. The usual procedure in preparing chicken blood for bait is to obtain a bucket of fresh blood and pour it into a tightly woven cloth bag. This is allowed to hang for a few hours so that the plasma (the colorless liquid) will drain off. The blood left inside will thicken and can be cut up into chunks or strips of the size desired for bait. This bait can be kept for a week or two if placed in a jar in the refrigerator.

To make a tougher chicken bait, pour the fresh blood onto a layer of chicken feathers or cotton. After the blood congeals, hang it up to drain and when it hardens you can cut it into strips.

Other anglers add a couple of tablespoons of powdered waterproof glue to a jar of warm chicken blood to toughen it. The mixture is stirred thoroughly to dissolve the glue, after which the blood is poured into a pan to cool and harden. Still other anglers use alum to toughen the blood.

Plain chicken blood will stay on a hook for a while and a treble hook will hold it better than a single hook. You can also use a short piece of string which can be tied to the line just above the hook. Wrap the string several times around the chicken blood and tuck the end under the barb of a hook. Strips of the tougher chicken blood will stay on a single hook if you run the hook through the strip two or three times.

The congealed blood from other poultry such as turkeys, ducks and geese can also be used for bait, as well as the blood from cattle, pigs, and other animals.

## MEAT BAITS

Fresh or decayed meats from various animals make good catfish baits. Beef and pork are usually used. And beef, pork,

103

rabbit, lamb, and chicken livers are also effective. These meat baits can be cut into thin strips or chunks and will stay on a hook quite well. Chicken entrails and those from other animals can also be used for catfish. Many of the above baits will also take eels, especially when used at night.

## OTHER CATFISH BAITS

There are few natural baits which the catfishes won't take at some time or another. Almost all the freshwater and some of the saltwater baits covered in this book are eaten by catfish. Many of the larger fish such as carp, eels, and the various panfishes can be cut up and used for bait. Small animals such as mice, rabbits, birds, and chicks can all be used. The larger of these can be cut up into smaller chunks, and the smaller ones can be used whole.

Sometimes catfish will take berries and fruits, particularly the mulberry. Even small chunks of white laundry soap have caught them. Most expert catfishermen take a wide variety of baits with them and try them all to find out which ones are being taken most readily.

## PORK RIND AND PORK CHUNK

Although these baits are usually used in the same way as artificial lures or together with such lures, they are really a natural bait, being obtained from an animal. And since many anglers would like to know how to prepare and preserve these baits, they will be included here.

The tough pork rind can usually be obtained from a butcher who sells salt pork if you ask him to save it for you. A very sharp knife or razor blade will cut the rind into strips of any size or shape you desire. Before you do this, make sure that all the excess fat has been scraped off the rind. Then put your strips in a brine solution strong enough to float a potato. Keep them there for about two or three days, then remove and bleach them by soaking them in a dilute hydrochloric or acetic acid solution until they

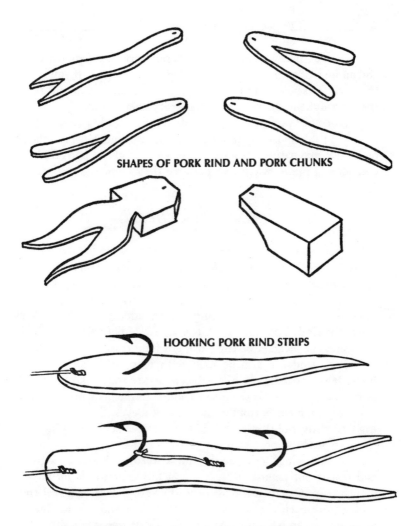

**SHAPES OF PORK RIND AND PORK CHUNKS**

**HOOKING PORK RIND STRIPS**

turn white. Finally, pack the strips in airtight jars containing a little glycerin and a solution of 10 to 20 percent formalin. A solution of 1 percent sodium benzoate in water can also be used instead of the formalin. You can also use ordinary rubbing alcohol or even a heavy brine solution to preserve the pork rind. Some of these solutions are good only for short periods of time, whereas others preserve the pork rind indefinitely. Some stiffen the rind, others keep it soft. A little experimenting will tell you which one is best suited for your purpose.

Pork chunks are also made from salt pork, but here the rind and an inch or so thickness of the fat are also utilized. If you keep the pork for several days in a solution of formalin, you will find that it toughens the pork and makes it easier to cut.

Of course pork rind strips and chunks already prepared can be bought in almost any tackle store. But most anglers have their own ideas about the best size, shape, and weight of pork rind or chunks and prefer to cut and preserve their own.

## USING PORK LURES

Every freshwater angler should carry pork rind and use it in various ways. You can use a plain strip of pork rind on a single or double hook and troll it slowly at various depths, giving it occasional rod action. Or you can cast a small strip with a fly rod to likely spots, or with a spinning rod by adding a small sinker above the rind. You can also skitter a strip of pork rind on top of the water for pickerel or bass, using a long cane or glass pole.

Pork rind can also be used with many different kinds of lures. It is especially effective when added to the hook of a spoon or behind a spinner. It can also be added to the hook on a jig and bounced along the bottom for bass and walleyes. Sometimes adding a tiny sliver of thin pork rind to the treble hook on a plug can make it produce more strikes.

When using pork chunk, run a weedless hook through it and cast it out among lily pads, hyacinths, or weeds for largemouth bass. Cast it right into the thickest growth and reel the pork chunk back across the top of the water and weeds. When you come to an opening among the pads or weeds you can slow down your reeling a bit. Hold your rod high when using pork chunk in this manner.

# CHAPTER 8

# RAISING BAIT for PROFIT

*At one time, not too long ago, all the live baits used for freshwater* fishing were obtained as needed by anglers and bait dealers. But with the increasing demand for such baits, more and more people are starting to raise baits to sell. Some baits have become scarce in many areas because of this increasing demand, and bait dealers find that they no longer can obtain enough to satisfy this need. And even when baits are plentiful, gathering, digging, trapping, and seining can be quite a time-consuming chore.

The shortage of some baits has caused many states to pass laws regulating the taking of bait, thus making it still more difficult for the bait dealer to obtain a supply for his customers. Another reason for raising your own bait is that you always have a supply on hand, even during the seasons when baits are scarce or difficult to obtain.

Many fishing tackle dealers, and those who rent boats or own fishing camps, find that it pays to carry a variety of baits in order to attract more customers. Anglers will patronize the boat livery or tackle store that can also sell them live bait when they need it. Since such tackle stores and boat liveries cannot always depend on bait dealers for bait, they find it pays to raise their own if they have the space and facilities.

Many people, too, are discovering that the live-bait business can be highly profitable. Although more and more bait dealers are springing up all over the country, there is plenty of room for others, either as full-time bait business or part-time suppliers and retailers. During the fishing season in many areas the demand for bait is so great that the dealer can sell out his supply in a short time. Furthermore, demand for live baits is bound to increase, since more and more people are taking up fishing. Then, too, many people are moving from the country to the suburbs or cities where they cannot obtain their own bait and they must depend on the bait dealers.

Most important of all, however, is the fact that the bait business can often be started on a shoestring—especially when it comes to raising worms. This requires a smaller investment of money, material, and time than many other ventures. But, like most businesses, it requires knowledge—knowledge of the baits to be raised, methods of breeding, keeping, handling, and distribution. And, of course, it requires some work. However, one advantage is that you can always start off on a small-scale or part-time basis and find out if it is profitable in your area and whether you like the work or not.

No doubt, the easiest bait to raise and one which requires the least investment of time and money is the earthworm. They can be raised indoors or outdoors. Earthworms are very prolific, and so by starting off with a few hundred worms you will have thousands in a matter of months and then millions, depending on how big a business you want and how much time, space, and money you can devote to it.

There are many so-called worm ranches, farms, or hatcheries in various parts of the country where you can buy a breeding stock of prolific and lively worms to start your own business. These worm farms have been raising worms for years and have experimented with methods and species of worms to find out which are most prolific, hardiest, and make the best fish bait. Many of these worm farms provide free literature with each purchase of worms, or sell booklets which will tell you all you need to know to raise worms in large numbers. Look in the classified advertising sections of outdoor magazines such as *Field & Stream*, *Outdoor Life*, and *Sports Afield* for their addresses.

You can start raising worms on a small scale indoors in a basement, garage, shed, barn, or other building. Here all you need are small wooden propagation boxes which can be stacked on top of one another with air spaces between them. Or you can easily construct a pit or two indoors or outdoors from concrete or cinder blocks. Or you can make some wooden pits or bins indoors or outdoors under some protective cover. Even washtubs have been used to raise the worms successfully.

Then you can fill these boxes, pits, or bins with compost or bedding. For this you mix a 50-50 mixture of manure and peat moss. You can use cow, horse, sheep, or rabbit manure which has been aged for some time. Or you can buy manure in bags such as those sold in garden supply stores. Soak the peat moss for a day or so before adding the manure. Then mix the two thoroughly so that it is moist but not too wet.

To this basic mixture you can add other organic materials and foods such as kitchen and garden scraps, leaves, grass clippings, skins and remains from fruits and vegetables, meat scraps, milk or cream, and similar waste materials.

To make the worms grow fast and big, you should also feed them with poultry feeds, meal, ground grain feeds, and similar poultry or cattle foods. Spread these thinly on top of the bedding or into shallow trenches, but do not mix them deep into the bedding because they may create heat.

You can obtain a starting batch of worms from one of the worm hatcheries or farms. They can be bought as "breeders," which will help you get off to a faster start since all these worms are big and mature and ready to reproduce. But you can also start with "pit-run" worms, which are cheaper. Pit-run worms contain quite a few large worms but also many smaller worms and egg capsules. However, they will grow fast and in two or three months will catch up to the larger sized worms.

If you want additional, detailed information on raising worms commercially, I strongly recommend the book *Raising Earthworms for Profit* by Earl B. Shields, which can be ordered directly from Shield Publications, P.O. Box 472, Elgin, Illinois 60120. It sells for $2.00. The publisher will also send you a free list of other books on raising earthworms which can be ordered from them by mail.

After you have started raising worms in quantities, you will want to sell them. If you live in a locality near good fishing waters, you can often sell your worms profitably direct to anglers. A sign or two in front of your place or along a well-traveled road is usually all you need. If you are some distance from the fishing waters or highways, you can sell your worms to tackle stores, boat liveries, or bait dealers. Or you can advertise in the outdoor magazines and sell your worms by mail to anglers and to others interested in starting their own worm business. And don't forget nurseries, farmers, and gardeners who want to improve their soil.

Raising minnows for bait is usually a more involved and expensive proposition than raising worms. But the demand for minnows is great and most minnow hatcheries have no trouble selling their stock. More and more states are regulating commercial netting of minnows, so that fewer and fewer bait dealers are depending on minnows seined from public waters. Many of them now raise their own minnows or depend on minnow hatcheries to supply them.

Minnows can be raised fairly cheaply if you have a natural pond or two which is suitable for their propagation. Otherwise you will have to invest quite a bit of money to construct the necessary ponds and obtain the equipment and materials needed for a large-scale operation. Raising minnows in large numbers requires a knowledge of the best species, the construction and selection of the right ponds, the proper breeding, feeding, control of disease, handling, transportation, and other information.

You should start minnow propagation on a large scale with minnows that are hardy, are fast-growing, and actually spawn and reproduce in a landlocked pond. Some of the best ones to raise are the bluntnose minnow, fathead minnow, creek chub, golden shiner, and the redbelly dace.

Whether you raise your minnows in natural or artificial ponds will depend on your locality, the type of soil, and the amount of money you intend to invest. If you can buy or rent natural ponds you will not have the high cost of pond construction to face. But artificial ponds usually produce better and offer bigger profits.

But for artificial pond construction you need the right kind of soil, such as clay, to keep the cost down. On sand or gravel soil it will cost you more to build the pond, since such soils do not hold water as well as clay bottoms.

Also, when selecting a site for pond construction you have to consider the water supply. It should be dependable at all seasons of the year, should have the proper temperature, and should be only moderately hard. Usually springs and artesian wells are the best source of supply; they are dependable, easily controlled, cool and clean, and free from pollution. But ponds have also been successful where the water source was a stream, river, or lake.

You have to stock the pond with the correct number of brood fish. And it is important to choose a species that is hardy and can be handled, raised, and transported. The minnow should also grow fast and reach bait size in a short time.

A pond also has to be fertilized to produce a food chain for the minnows. Various organic fertilizers have been used to start such a cycle and provide food for the minnows. Otherwise you will have to feed them artificially with such foods as ground meat and fish, fish meal, bone meal, cooked cornmeal or oatmeal, maggots, and similar foods.

When the minnows reach bait size they must be harvested by means of seines or nets. They must be sorted or graded, then held in tanks or transported to bait dealers, boat liveries, tackle shops, and other places where they are sold.

Of course, there is a lot more to this than the steps mentioned above. There are the various diseases and parasites you have to watch out for and combat, weed control, predators and pests which can injure or kill your minnows.

Frogs are popular baits in many localities, but they are difficult to raise artificially and most of those sold are caught in either wild or private ponds. These ponds can be improved to allow a greater number of frogs to breed, live, and reach fishing size. This usually consists of making an irregular shoreline or constructing small islands, encouraging plants and attracting insects for the frogs to eat.

Crayfish can be propagated in ponds similar to those used for minnows. They can often be raised in the same pond with minnows. If the pond is a large one or consists of several small ponds, you can raise large numbers of crayfish and have plenty to sell for bait. And with large numbers of crayfish present you can also have a good supply of soft-shell crayfish on hand, because some of them will always be shedding during the summer months. You can even speed up this process by feeding the crayfish well so that they grow faster and shed their shells more often. Crayfish bring good prices and are always in demand during the fishing season, especially in areas where small-mouth bass are caught.

The water insects such as nymphs and hellgrammites are difficult or impractical to raise artificially, and you will have to obtain your own bait from streams and lakes or buy them from bait dealers.

Some of the land insects such as crickets and cockroaches are easily raised in large numbers. Mealworms can be raised for fishing and can be sold to pet shops and aquarium dealers. Then there are the various prepared baits such those used for catfish, carp, and other fish, which can be made up and packed in cans or jars and sold retail, or to bait dealers, or through the mail.

In recent years more and more of the natural baits have been dried or dehydrated or preserved in special solutions and sold in jars, plastic bags, or other containers. They, of course, are dead and not quite as effective for some fish as live baits, but they are convenient to buy and use, and more and more anglers are using them.

Before you start raising or selling natural baits, it is important to check your state fish and game department for laws on the subject. Many states regulate the taking, selling, and distribution of natural baits when done on a commercial scale. Some states also require special permits and licenses which must be obtained before you can catch or raise bait for sale.

PART

# NATURAL
# SALTWATER
# BAITS

# CHAPTER 9

# SEA WORMS

*T*he sea worms head the list as the most popular baits used in saltwater fishing, especially along the North Atlantic Coast, where many millions are used yearly. Although sea worms are dug commercially at scattered points along the coast, most of them come from the state of Maine. Some are also dug in Canada. Sea worms dug in Maine are shipped to many points along the Atlantic Coast and are even flown by plane to the Pacific Coast.

One of the reasons for the popularity of sea worms as bait is that most tackle stores and bait dealers along the seacoast carry them throughout the fishing season. Sea worms also stay alive for long periods and are handy to keep and carry. But no doubt the main reason sea worms are a favorite bait with anglers is that most saltwater fishes will take them.

There are many kinds of sea worms which can be used for bait, but since some kinds are scarce or too small to make practical baits, the field narrows down to the sea worms that are dug commercially and show up most often in tackle stores and bait dealers. Other kinds rarely appear in tackle stores but are numerous enough in certain localities to be obtained by anglers and used for bait. The ones that the average saltwater angler is apt to encounter will be dealt with in this chapter.

## CLAM WORMS

The group of sea worms most numerous in numbers and species are the clam worms, which belong to the genus *Nereis*.

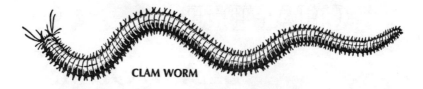

CLAM WORM

They are also called sandworms and muck worms along the Atlantic Coast, and mussel worms, pile worms, and rock worms along the Pacific Coast, depending on the species and where it is found. Numerous species are found in many parts of the world but only a few are important as bait to saltwater anglers. The clam worm can be easily recognized by the body, which is rounded on top and flat below. There are distinct segments along their dark, iridescent backs which vary in color from a reddish-brown to green and blue. Their undersides are lighter in color and may be pink, orange, or red. Along the sides they have two rows of orange or red appendages or "legs" which are used in breathing and swimming.

One of the most common species of clam worm is *Nereis virens*, which is also one of the largest, sometimes reaching 18 inches or more in length. It averages between 5 and 10 inches. It is found along the Atlantic Coast from New York northward as far as Labrador. This popular bait worm prefers muddy and shelly sand where it lives in burrows. It also lives under rocks between low- and high-water marks. At night it often emerges from its burrow and can be found lying on the flats or swimming in shallow water. It has black jaws which it uses in capturing other worms on which it feeds. This is the worm that is usually sold for bait under the name of "sandworm." It is also found along the Pacific Coast, but is not as numerous there.

Another worm closely related to the one above is *Nereis limbata*, also called the sandworm. It resembles *Nereis virens* except that it rarely reaches more than 6 inches in length and has light yellow jaws instead of black ones. It also prefers sandier soil than the other sea worms. This worm is found from Maine to South Carolina.

Another similar worm which is sometimes used for bait is *Nereis pelagica*, also called the muck worm, which is smaller than the two sandworms. The female rarely reaches more than 5 inches, while the males are only 2 inches long. It is reddish-

116

brown in color and the body is widest in the middle. It prefers hard bottoms and is found under stones, among mussels, and on shelly bottoms. It is found along the Atlantic Coast from Virginia to Greenland, but is most numerous north of Cape Cod.

The most common species of clam worm found along the Pacific Coast is *Nereis vexillosa*, also known as the mussel worm and pile worm. It may reach 12 inches in length but most of those found run from 3 to 6 inches in length. This popular bait is widely distributed along the Pacific Coast from Alaska to San Diego. It lives among mussels, barnacles, rocks, gravel beaches, and wharf piles.

The giant clam worm of the Pacific is *Nereis brandti*, which may reach 3 feet or more in length, but it is not as plentiful as the one above. It is found in sandy mud and under mussel beds from Puget Sound to San Pedro.

## BLOODWORMS

Next to the clam worm in popularity is the bloodworm, also called the white worm, beak thrower, four-jawed worm, and proboscis worm. Other marine worms are often called bloodworms, but the name is usually associated with the worms belonging to the genus *Glycera*. This worm is easily recognized by its smooth, round body and many narrow, faintly visible segments tapering on both ends. When disturbed it shoots out a long proboscis equipped with four tiny black jaws on the end. In color, bloodworms vary from light pink to red, often with a purplish tinge. Several species are found in the mud flats along the Atlantic and Pacific Coasts. Some may reach a foot or more in length, but most bloodworms average from 6 to 8 inches.

The two kinds of bloodworms usually found along the Atlantic Coast are *Glycera dibranchiata* and *Glycera americana*. They are found from the Carolinas to the Bay of Fundy. On the Pacific

BLOODWORM

Coast the two species usually encountered are *Glycera rugosa* and *Glycera robusta*. But they are not too plentiful and bloodworms from the Atlantic Coast have been flown to the West Coast to supply the demand of saltwater anglers.

## RIBBON WORMS

Another worm sometimes used for bait is the ribbon worm, also called the proboscis worm and tapeworm. However, it should not be confused with the real tapeworms, which are parasites sometimes found in men and animals. The ribbon worm is a marine worm which lives in the sand and mud near low-water mark. It can easily be recognized by its long, flat, body which in some species may extend several yards in length. When disturbed it shoots out a long proboscis which is used in burrowing and capturing its prey. There are many species of varying lengths, colors, and widths, but those belonging to the genus *Cerebratulus* are the ones mostly used for bait. The ribbon worm *Cerebratulus lacteus,* which is yellowish-white or flesh-colored, is commonly found along the Atlantic Coast from Maine to Florida. Fully grown and stretched out it may reach 20 feet in length and a width of an inch, but most of those found do not exceed 4 or 5 feet. Related species are also found along the Pacific Coast. Ribbon worms are very fragile and should be handled carefully. Even then, you'll find that they often break up into small sections. They are usually used for flounders, but can also be tried for other saltwater fish.

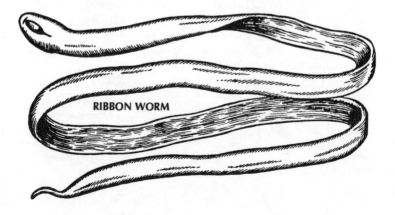

RIBBON WORM

LUGWORM

## LUGWORMS

This ugly worm is also called the burrowing worm. It is found living in sand or mud flats, in a U-shaped burrow with two openings to the surface. These can be located by looking for the pile of castings around the mouths of the burrows. At low tide the lugworms sometimes emerge and crawl around along the surface. Lug worms have black, brownish, or olive-colored skins which are rough and covered with tufts of hairlike gills. The head part is larger and thicker than the rest of the body and is filled with a yellowish liquid making it a messy bait. Lugworms may reach a foot in length but most of them run from 4 to 8 inches. The most common species along the Atlantic Coast is *Arenicola marina,* which is found from Rhode Island southward. On the Pacific Coast, *Arenicola claparedii* is the one usually encountered. Lugworms are also found in European waters and are more popular as bait there than in this country. They can be used for many of the same fish caught on the other marine worms.

Of course, there are other sea worms which can be used as bait. Any good-sized worm you can find can be tried, and chances are that it will catch fish. And in a pinch you can even use earthworms or night crawlers which are found on land for many fish found in brackish and salt water. These include flounders, eels, white perch, smelt, and tomcod. You can also try earthworms or night crawlers behind a spinner to catch striped bass.

## OBTAINING, KEEPING, AND HOOKING

Most saltwater anglers buy their sea worms from tackle stores, bait dealers, or boat liveries, since they do not have the knowledge, equipment, time, or energy to dig their own worms. And time and energy are two requisites when digging sea worms, for it can require several hours of back-breaking work to dig enough worms for a day's fishing. But in some areas and during

119

certain years the worms are plentiful and can be obtained fairly quickly. Then again, when plenty of worms are needed, you can save some money by digging your own.

The equipment needed to dig sea worms is simple and inexpensive. A pair of boots, a garden fork or clam hoe, and a box or pail to keep the worms in will put you in business. During the summer months boots are not essential; an old pair of sneakers can be used, if you don't mind getting your legs covered with mud and muck.

Learning to locate the best places to dig for sea worms will take a little time and experience. Of course, the best way to find out the productive flats is to watch where the other worm diggers gather and go there too. But such flats may have been overworked and you are better off if you seek mud flats that haven't been dug recently.

Clam worms and bloodworms prefer a mixture of shelly sand and soft mud, where they can be found living in their burrows. Sometimes the entrances of these burrows can be noticed. The worms may be anywhere between low- and high-water marks. A good time to dig sea worms is when the tide is about half out to when it is half in again. The most favorable tides usually occur during the full moon and new moon, since they are extra low and expose a larger area. Try different spots on the mud flats until you locate a colony of worms. Then stay there and dig systematically until the whole section is turned over.

Clam worms and bloodworms occur in the same mud flats, but the bloodworms will be just a few inches under the surface, while the clam worms may be a foot or more beneath the surface. This means that you will usually have to dig twice in the same spot to reach the clam worms.

Clam worms can also be obtained on dark nights, when they emerge from their burrows and lie exposed on the mud flats. For this you will need a flashlight or, better yet, a headlight to spot the worms. They are sensitive to vibrations and strong lights so you have to walk softly and grab them quickly. They also swarm at times in shallow water, especially during the spawning periods, but at this time they are extremely soft and not fit for bait.

Other kinds of sea worms can be found among seaweeds, under stones, and among mussels and barnacles. The ribbon worms or tapeworms are often found on the same mud flats as clam worms or bloodworms, especially where soft clams are plentiful. Lugworms prefer sand or a mixture of sand and mud, and the best place to dig is where there are burrow openings with castings around them.

Sea worms are usually easier to obtain during the spring and fall months when the weather is cool. During the summer months they burrow deep to escape the heat. They do the same thing when there is too much rain, for they dislike fresh water.

One word of caution about digging sea worms. Some states and towns along our coasts have laws and regulations regarding the digging of sea worms. Some of these require that you be a resident of the state or area or that you have a special permit. Find out what the laws are in your area before you attempt to dig sea worms.

Although most sea worms are rather delicate and die quickly, they will live for several days and even up to two weeks if properly cared for. Sea worms cannot tolerate too much heat, dryness, or fresh water. For best results they should be kept in rockweed, sea moss, or sea lettuce, which is moist but not too wet. The worms should be kept in a cellar or other cool spot. An icebox where the temperature is around 40 degrees is a good place to keep them for several days. The worms should not be allowed to bunch up, and most dealers who handle large quantities of worms have trays which can be turned over each day to keep the worms separated. If the rockweed dries out it can be wetted down with salt water until it is moist. But fresh water should never be used since it will kill the worms. Likewise, worms of each species should be kept in separate containers. Bloodworms and clam worms are deadly enemies and often attack one another. And finally, all dead sea worms should be removed from the containers as soon as possible.

On a fishing trip most saltwater anglers keep their worms in the small paper boxes in which they are sold. The worms usually stay alive for a day or so in such boxes. If you have a lot of worms and expect to keep them for more than a day, a large wooden box

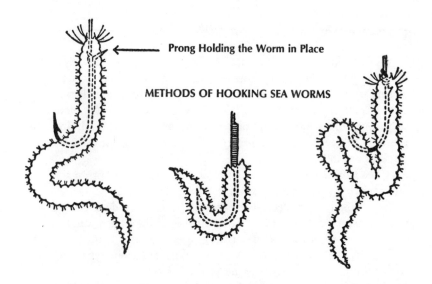

Prong Holding the Worm in Place

METHODS OF HOOKING SEA WORMS

or tray with plenty of moist rockweed is better. The styrofoam food and bait containers are excellent for keeping the worms for long periods. The containers should always be kept out of the sun and in the coolest spot that can be found.

Many anglers would like to know if sea worms can be propagated or raised like earthworms, so that they can reproduce and be available in large numbers. Unfortunately, it is difficult or impractical to provide the type of conditions and food the sea worms require to live and reproduce. So the sea worms must be obtained from the tidewater flats where they are found naturally.

There are many methods used in hooking the sea worms, depending on the kind of worm used, the type of hooks or rigs, and the fish sought. The clam worms or sandworms which are used whole for fairly large fish can be hooked in back of the head, then threaded along the shank until almost half of the worm covers most of the hook, leaving the point and barb exposed. Hooks with sliced shanks are often used to keep the worm from sliding down the hook. Some anglers also use special hooks, wrapping a prong on the hook shank which extends out at an angle near the hook eye. Then the worm's head is impaled on the prong to hold it in place.

If the fish are nipping off the tail end of the worm without getting hooked, the worm can be looped and hooked through the

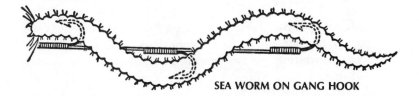

SEA WORM ON GANG HOOK

tail once or twice. Or you can use a gang hook which holds the worm in two or three places. These tandem hooks are also used for holding worms used in trolling behind a spinner.

Sometimes two or three sea worms on a hook bring more strikes, especially when the fish are large. For small fish with small mouths, pieces of worm from 1 to 3 inches long are usually best. Almost any fish found in salt water will take clam worms. They are often used for striped bass, tautog or blackfish, scup or porgies, weakfish, flounders, eels, croakers, corbina, and other fish.

Bloodworms can be hooked by some of the methods used for clam worms but they have one disadvantage. They do not live long or look attractive if they are cut up into sections. The blood or other liquids ooze out and leave just the skin of the worm if it is cut. For best results the worm should be placed on the hook whole. When used for striped bass, several bloodworms on a hook are much better than just one. The hook should be impaled through them just once near the middle of the body so that the

HOOKING SEVERAL SEA WORMS

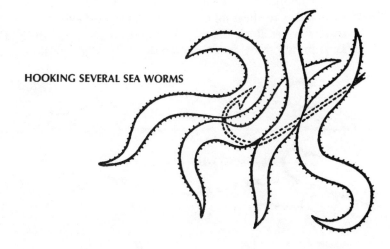

ends wriggle. Bloodworms can be used for most saltwater fishes, but are best for striped bass, flounders, weakfish, northern and southern whiting, porgies or scup, blackfish or tautog, croakers, and spot.

## USING SEA WORMS

For such fish as striped bass and weakfish the best way to use a whole sandworm is to hook it once through the head. You can do this quickly by running the point of the hook into the sandworm's mouth and then out about an inch below the head. In this way the worm swims or drifts around naturally and the body has plenty of wriggle and movement. Of course, this eventually kills the worm, so some anglers prefer to attach the worm to a hook with a couple of thin rubber bands wrapped around the worm's head and the shank of the hook.

One way to fish a whole sandworm is to anchor the boat and let the worm drift on a free line into holes, channels, along drop-offs and other likely spots. If you want to keep the sandworm at a certain level you can add a small, light float at the correct distance above the hook. When fishing in this manner it's a good idea to chum with grass shrimp, minced clams, or ground fish to attract stripers, weakfish, and other fish up to the boat.

You can let out a whole worm from a drifting boat and trail it behind as the boat moves along. This is most effective in fairly shallow water along the shore and over sand and rock bars. The same thing can be done from a boat by trolling very slowly and

HOOKING WHOLE SANDWORM

Rubber Bands

letting the worm out some distance. Here you may find that you need a weight or have to use wire line to get the worm close to the bottom.

A whole worm can also be used on a bottom rig with a light sinker of about one or two ounces and a 3-foot leader to hold a 2/0 or 3/0 hook with the worm. The leader can be tied about a foot above the sinker. Then you can let this out in a strong tide from an anchored boat or you can drift and let the sinker bounce along the bottom. While you are drifting, keep raising and lowering your rod slowly every so often to give your worm an up-and-down action. Striped bass and other fish will often grab the worm as it drops or sinks. From an anchored boat this same lifting of the rod every so often will enable you to "walk" the worm close to the bottom, giving it better action and also letting you cover more territory.

A whole sandworm can also be used when surf fishing for striped bass or weakfish. Here you use a regular surf bottom rig and cast it out to likely spots. In certain areas and at certain times of the year striped bass prefer bloodworms to sandworms. Then you should impale two or three or more whole bloodworms on a hook. Do this by running the hook only once through the worm so it lives longer and the ends can wriggle.

Both sandworms and bloodworms can also be trolled behind a spinner on tanden hooks. Here the Cape Cod, willow-leaf, and june bug type spinners which revolve at slow speeds are best. In shallow water and when the fish are feeding near the surface, you can troll the worms on monofilament line without any weight or sinkers. But in strong currents and when you want to troll the worms close to the bottom, you have to add trolling weights or use wire line to get them down.

When fishing for bottom species such as flounder, blackfish or tautog, porgies, sea bass, kingfish or the whitings, croakers, and spots, use smaller pieces of worm. You can cut a big sandworm into three or four sections. A bloodworm can be cut in half or into three sections. It all depends on the size of the fish that is running and how big a mouth it has.

When using sea worms, the thing to remember is that when the worms die on the hook and lose their color and flavor or juices they also lose most of their effectiveness as bait and should be replaced with fresh worms. It's true that sea worms are often difficult to obtain and expensive to buy, but the angler who usually catches the most fish is the one who uses fresh worms and is not afraid to use plenty of them. The stingy angler who cuts his worms into tiny pieces and keeps the dead worms on his hook for long periods of time is only reducing his chances of catching fish.

# CHAPTER 10

# CLAMS, MUSSELS and OYSTERS

*R*ight behind the sea worms in popularity as bait for saltwater fish are the clams. These bivalve mollusks are numerous in numbers and species along the Atlantic and Pacific Coasts, where they are found living in the mud and sand of beaches, inlets, bays, and the ocean. They are sought not only for bait, but also for food, and great quantities are shipped annually to various parts of the country to supply fish markets, restaurants, roadstands, canneries, bait dealers, and fishing boats. Although there are many species of clams which can be used as bait, only those which are commonly used in fishing and are easily obtained can be dealt with here.

## SURF CLAM

The surf clam *(Mactra solidissima)* is the largest bivalve found along the Atlantic Coast, sometimes reaching a length of 7 inches. It is also called the skimmer clam, hen clam, ocean clam, sea clam, and giant clam. This clam lives in the sand in the surf along the ocean but is also found in deeper water of up to 60 feet or so. Large quantities are dredged up to a mile offshore by commercial fishermen. The surf clam has a heavy shell and a powerful foot, which it uses to dig into the sand. In color the shell varies from yellowish white to gray or brown. These large clams are found from Labrador to North Carolina, but they are

**SURF CLAM**

most numerous from New England to New Jersey. A smaller variety *(Mactra solidissima similis)* is more commonly found south of Cape Hatteras in southern waters. The surf clam or skimmer is the one usually sold for bait along the North Atlantic Coast and it is also used for food to some extent.

Surf clams can be bought from bait dealers, boat liveries, and tackle stores in many areas. They can also be found by wading in shallow water at low tide along the sandy beaches, where they can be noticed partly exposed in the sand. A few live clams can often be picked up lying high and dry on the beach at low tide. After a storm large numbers of them are often washed up on the beach and can be gathered for future use. Surf clams are a favorite bait for striped bass, cod, haddock, sea bass, tautog or blackfish, scup or porgy, flounders, and almost any other fish found in the ocean.

## PISMO CLAM

The Pismo clam *(Tivela stultorum)* of the Pacific Coast is somewhat similar to the surf clam of the Atlantic Coast in that it is a large clam and prefers the surf-swept sandy beaches. It is found from Half Moon Bay near San Francisco to Mexico but is most numerous in California at Pismo Beach. It may reach 7 inches in length but most of the clams found run under 6 inches. It has a thick, heavy, shiny shell which varies from pale brown to dark brown in color. Some Pismo Clams also have lines and stripes forming patterns on the shell.

The Pismo clam is highly valued for food and millions are dug each year for this purpose, mostly by individuals, since commercial digging or selling of the clams is strictly regulated. Large numbers of the clams are also used for bait. Because of this great demand for bait and food, laws have been passed to protect the Pismo clams, which are in danger of becoming extinct in many areas. These laws have established open and closed seasons, protected areas, a bag limit, and minimum size. A sport fishing license is also required to take the clams. Check the California game laws before you start digging Pismo clams for bait. If you dig out of season, take more clams than the law allows, or use smaller clams than the minimum size limit, you can be subject to a stiff fine.

Pismo clams can be obtained by digging on sandy beaches at low tide on the exposed flats or in water 3 or 4 feet deep. By probing with the fork you can feel when you strike a clam; then it can be uncovered. Sometimes you can notice the siphons of the clam slightly exposed at low tide. On dry sandy beaches with the flats exposed at low tide, you may notice the holes and mounds of sand which often reveal the location of the clam. Another way to obtain the clams is to drag rakes with long handles either by hand or by boat. Storms and heavy tides also wash the clams out of the sand and leave them stranded high and dry where they can be picked up. Whichever method is used in obtaining the clams, care should be taken with undersized clams which cannot be legally kept. The law states that these should be returned to deep water or the hole from which they are removed. Too many careless diggers toss these clams on the sand high and dry where they soon die.

Pismo clams are usually used for corbina, surf perch, croakers, and flounders, but will also catch many other fishes found in Pacific waters.

## HARD-SHELL CLAM

The hard-shell clam (*Venus mercenaria*) is the common clam of the Atlantic Coast which is sold in fish markets and served in restaurants. It is also called the hard clam, round clam, littleneck clam, cherrystone clam, and quahog, depending on its size and

**HARD-SHELL CLAM**

where it is found. The hard-shell clam when fully grown may reach 5 or 6 inches in length, but most specimens are 3 inches or less. It may be white, gray, or yellowish on the outside with a violet border along the inside edge of the shell. The hard-shell clam is found from Maine to Florida in the sandy and muddy bottoms of bays, sounds, and other tidal waters. There are several related species and varieties of this clam found along the Atlantic and Gulf Coasts.

Millions of pounds of hard-shell clams are taken annually by commercial fishermen, mostly by dredging with tongs and rakes in fairly deep water. The angler can always buy his hard clams at a fish market or one of the roadside stands which sell the clams along the Atlantic Coast. They can also be obtained in shallow water by digging with clam hoes, rakes, or forks in the sand and mud bottoms where the clams lie just under the surface.

Although the hard-shell clams are more commonly used for food than for bait, they can be used for cod, haddock, striped bass, porgies or scup, croakers, blackfish or tautog, flounders, and many other saltwater fishes.

## SOFT-SHELL CLAM

The soft-shell clam (*Mya arenaria*) is another clam that is more popular as food than as bait. It is also called the soft clam, long clam, longneck clam, mud clam, sand clam, steamer clam, nannynose, and squirt clam. The soft-shell clam may reach 5 inches in length but most of those found are about 2 or 3 inches. This clam is easily recognized by its long siphon or neck and the oval-shaped shell which is dull gray or chalky white. It is usually

130

**SOFT-SHELL CLAM**

found buried in muddy bottoms about a foot below the surface between high- and low-water marks. Soft-shell clams are found from the Arctic Seas to North Carolina but are most common north of Cape Cod. Maine is noted for its soft-shell clam flats, and millions of pounds are dug and sent to many fish markets, restaurants, and roadside stands to be eaten as steamers, as fried clams, or in clam chowder. These clams are also found to a certain extent along the Pacific Coast from British Columbia to Monterey, California. They are not native to this area, but were introduced to Pacific waters from the Atlantic many years ago.

Soft-shell clams can be obtained on the tidal flats, where they lie buried, by digging with a clam hoe or garden fork. They can be located easily since they squirt a jet of water into the air if a person walks over the mud flats where they are present. You can also look for the mounds of mud and broken shells left by clam diggers working their earlier. The best time to dig them is during low water, especially during the full moon and new moon phases when more flats are exposed. You can also buy soft clams by the bag or bushel in fish markets, seafood roadside stands, and lobster pounds.

The part of the soft clam that makes the best bait is the tough siphon which stays on the hook fairly well. The dark skin can be peeled off to make a more attractive bait. Soft-shell clams will catch tautog or blackfish, eels, porgies or scup, flounders, and many other saltwater species.


## RAZOR AND JACKKNIFE CLAMS

There are many species of these long, cylindrical-shaped clams found along both the Atlantic and Pacific Coasts. Some are narrow and shaped like old-fashioned razors with square ends.

131

**RAZOR CLAM**

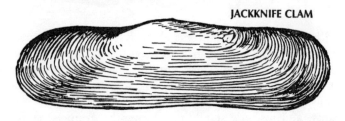

**JACKKNIFE CLAM**

Others are wider with shells that are rounded on the ends. A few razor clams may reach 10 inches in length, but most of them average between 2 and 6 inches. These clams live in the sand and mud flats and ocean beaches where they lie buried beneath the surface.

Razor and jackknife clams are not used too often for bait, since they are not too easily obtained, and are sold as bait only in a few areas. The most commonly used is the jackknife clam (*Tagelus californianus*), which is found from Santa Barbara to Mexico and is used by anglers in Pacific waters.

Most of the razor and jackknife clams obtained by anglers or sought for food by clams diggers are obtained in shallow water or during low tides when the sand and mud flats are exposed. These clams live in burrows or holes up to 18 or 20 inches in depth extending vertically downward in the mud or sand. Often they will lie only a few inches below the surface. But if disturbed they can move with amazing speed toward the bottom of their burrows and may even dig deeper to escape capture.

You can locate razor clams in the wet sand or mud by looking for their "shows" or holes or a dimple in the sand. They also reveal their presence by squirting water into the air

You can dig razor and jackknife clams out of the damp sand or mud with a small, narrow bladed shovel if you work fast, making several scoops until you reach the clam, then grabbing it by hand. Some anglers also use special spears with an arrowhead on the end which they thrust into the burrows of the jackknife clams. The spear is pushed until the arrowhead passes the clam, then it is twisted and the clam closes on the shank of the spear and is pulled to the surface.

You can also obtain razor clams by means of a clam gun. This is a 2-foot section of steel tubing about 4 or 5 inches in diameter. The bottom of this tube is open; the top is closed, but has a hole drilled in it, and a handle welded on it. To use the gun you look for a blow-hole or "show" indicating there is a clam below the surface. Then you quickly shove the pipe or tube into the sand around the hole. Next, stick your finger into the hole on top of the tube and pull up on the handle. This will remove a core of sand and the clam. The extreme low tides at full moon and new moon are best for such clamming because more beds are exposed.

It is also claimed that if you sprinkle some salt over the burrow in the mud or sand where the razor clams are living, they will come to the surface.

Before you go out to dig razor clams, check state and local laws, especially along the Pacific Coast where most states have regulations on the number and size of the clams you can keep. They may also close certain areas to digging for certain periods of time.

Razor clams are thin-shelled and crack or chip easily, so you have to handle them carefully. They can be kept on ice or in a cool spot until used. Or you can remove the clams from their shells and pack the meat in salt-brine for future use. You can also freeze the meat.

Razor clams are not as common along the Atlantic Coast but if you can obtain them you can use them for such fish as flounders, porgies, blackfish or tautog, and sea bass. Along the Pacific Coast you can use them for spotfin croakers, yellowfin croakers, surf perch, rockfish, flounders, corvina, and other species which feed on the bottom.

## OTHER CLAMS

There are many other kinds of clams which can be used for bait if they can be obtained in sufficient numbers and are large enough to make practical baits. Some of them are numerous enough to be sold for food but others are rarely dug by commercial clam diggers and can be obtained only by individual amateur diggers. The angler who wants to dig his own clams should check local and state laws to see if there are any regulations governing the taking of these shellfish. Clams are protected in certain areas by open and closed seasons or areas, size limits, and bag limits. You may have to be a resident of the area or need a special license or permit to dig clams.

## MUSSELS

These bivalves are familiar to all who go down to the ocean or bay at low tide, where they can be seen clinging to the rocks, piles, mud flats, and any other object below high-water mark. Mussels may be black, blue-black, brown or olive-colored, depending on the species and where found. One of the commonest mussels is the edible mussel (*Mytilus edulis*), also called the Atlantic mussel, blue mussel, and sea mussel along the Atlantic Coast, and known as the bay mussel along the Pacific Coast. It may reach 3 inches or a bit more in length, but most of those found are from about an inch to 2 1/2 inches long. The edible mussel ranges from the Arctic seas to North Carolina along the Atlantic Coast, and is also found in Europe and along the Pacific Coast, where it was introduced from the Atlantic many years ago.

Along the Pacific Coast the large sea mussel (*Mytilus californianus*), which ranges from Alaska to Mexico, is commonly found attached to rocks between tide marks along the surf. These mussels, also called "big mussels," may reach 8 inches in length but average 3 to 4 inches.

**EDIBLE MUSSEL**

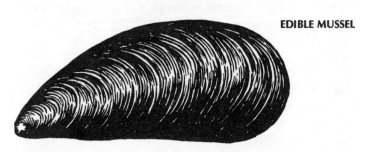

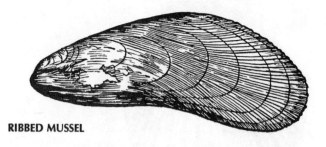

**RIBBED MUSSEL**

Another common mussel along the Atlantic Coast is the ribbed mussel (*Modiolus demissus plicatulus*), which is also known as the mudbank mussel and fan mussel. It is found in bays on tidal flats and along the banks of tidal creeks and rivers. It is easily recognized by the grooves along its dull, olive or brownish shell. They may reach 3 inches when fully grown but those usually found are much smaller.

There are many other species of mussels which are found in salt water which can be used for bait if they are large enough. Although mussels are somewhat difficult to keep on a hook, the fact that they can be obtained easily makes them a favored bait with many anglers. Mussels are usually so numerous in most places that they can be readily gathered from rocky shores, jetties, piles, and mud flats where they are found anchored. They can also be bought in many coastal fish markets.

## OYSTERS

These popular bivalves, as everyone knows, are used for food more than for bait. But they can be used for many of the smaller bottom fishes in saltwater such as flounders, blackfish or tautog, sheepshead, croakers, and spot, even though they are difficult to keep on the hook. Oysters are found on both coasts. The common edible oyster (*Ostrea virginica*) usually found in restaurants and fish markets is the most numerous along the Atlantic Coast and is also found along the Pacific Coast, where it was introduced from the Atlantic. The tree or coon oysters (*Ostrea frons*) are found growing on the roots of mangrove trees in southern waters. Oysters are gathered with dredges and tongs in deep water or by hand in shallow water.

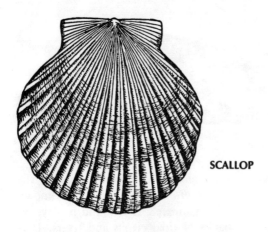

**SCALLOP**

## SCALLOPS

This is another shellfish that is considered more of a food than a bait. But in this case you can have your bait and eat it too. For only the heavy muscle which holds the two shells together is eaten in this country and the rest is usually discarded. This remainder, although somewhat soft, can be used as bait for many of the same fishes that are caught on clams and mussels. Two kinds of scallops are usually found on the market. One is the sea scallop (*Pecten grandis*), which is one of the largest and is found in the ocean from New Jersey north to Labrador. The other is the bay scallop (*Pecten irradians*), which is found in inshore waters from New England to Florida. But there are many other species of scallops found along the Altantic and Pacific Coasts. Scallops are rarely gathered by anglers solely for bait, but if you can find a place where scallop fishermen shuck or open the scallops to remove the muscle meat, you can usually get the discarded shells with the remaining meat for the asking.

## KEEPING AND HOOKING

After you have your clams, mussels, or oysters, you have the problem of keeping or preserving them for future use. They will stay alive in a cool spot away from the sun for quite a while. For long periods they can be kept in a bushel basket or wire cage or bait box submerged in salt water. Make sure that the water covers

136

them most of the time and that they are not exposed to warm air, sunlight, or rain for too long a periods. Clams, mussels, and oysters can also be kept on ice for several days.

To prepare clams, mussels, or similar shellfish for bait, you must shuck them or remove them from their shells. This can be done by inserting a knife blade between the two shells and cutting the muscles which hold them together. But most anglers —to save time, work, and a possible injury to the hands—just strike the clams or mussels with a hammer or rock or hit them against a hard object to crack the shells. This is usually done on the fishing grounds, although some anglers prefer to remove the meat from the shells beforehand and pack it in jars or other containers. When this is done the bait takes less space, weighs less, allows more time for actual fishing. If you pack this meat in an airtight container and add plenty of salt you can keep the bait for some time, especially if you place it in a refrigerator when it is not in use. The salt will also toughen the bait a bit. You can also freeze the shellfish meats for future use.

When it comes to hooking clams, mussels, and similar bivalves you will find that not too much can be done to prevent fish from stealing the bait. Some anglers steam or scald their clams or mussels and let them lie in the air or sun for a while so that they will dry out and thus stay on the hook a little better. Wrapping the soft meat around the hook with fine thread will also help to hold it in place.

**HOOKING CLAMS**

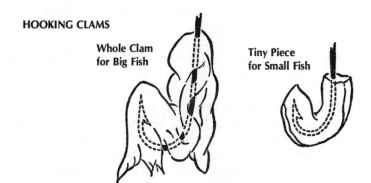

Whole Clam
for Big Fish

Tiny Piece
for Small Fish

When hooking clams for big fish such as striped bass or cod, the meat from one or more large clams should be used. Surf clams or hard-shell clams can be hooked first through the tough, muscular foot, then twisted and hooked once again; after this the softer portions should be hooked and draped around the bend and shank of the hook. The stringy mantle lying along the edge of the shell can also be used if it is pierced and wrapped around the hook several times. For smaller fish the muscular foot can be cut into sections and then hooked once or twice. The long siphons, such as those on the soft-shell clam, are tough and make a good bait if the dark outer skin is peeled off. Mussels, oysters, and scallops are even softer than clams and about the only way to keep them on a hook for any length of time is to wrap the soft meat around the hook with fine nylon or cotton thread. For some fish, such as tautog or blackfish and sheepshead, the small clams and mussels can be cracked and placed on the hook without removing the shell parts.

It is the very softness of shellfish which is attractive to saltwater fishes, and you can't go wrong by taking along these baits on your fishing trip.

## USING CLAMS, MUSSELS AND OYSTERS

When using clams for bait it isn't necessary to cover the point and barb of the hook. Leave them exposed to hook the fish more quickly and to help prevent the bait from being stolen. Small pieces of clam are good for flounders, porgies, blackfish, sea bass, croakers, spot, and other fish along the Atlantic Coast. Similar small pieces of clam can be used along the Pacific Coast for croakers, corbina, surf perch, rockfish, and flounders.

The whole insides of a big skimmer clam can be used for striped bass and channel bass when surf fishing. You can also use the whole insides of a big clam for big cod. If the cod are running small you can cut the tongue or foot of the clam into two or three portions. Smaller portions are also better for pollock, haddock, cusk and hake. One trick when using clams for these fish is to soak them in cod liver oil before putting them on the hook.

Along the West Coast you can use razor jackknife clams for surf perch. Here the best fishing usually takes place along beaches where these clams are being dug regularly. A good time to fish here is during the incoming tide when the surf perch moves in to feed on the broken clams and other marine foods exposed by the diggers.

Some anglers like to dye clams, using red and yellow liquid food coloring. You merely place the clams in a container and add a tablespoon or two of the food coloring. Then stir the contents and let it stand for a while. The length of time you let the mixture stand depends on how dark you want the clams to be. The same thing can be done with mussels, scallops, and oysters. The added color is supposed to make them more visible and attractive to the fish.

In recent years anglers have discovered that the skimmer clam makes a highly effective "chum" for striped bass and other fish. They started using the trimmings from the big clams which were being discarded by the clam-packing companies. When they couldn't get the trimmings, they would merely buy a bushel or two of the skimmers and grind up the insides for chum. You can place the chum in a chum pot or similar container and lower it under the boat. Or you can mix the ground clams with sea water and ladle the "soup" over the side or stern of the boat. The hook can be baited with the soft bellies of the clams and drifted out naturally in the current.

Chumming for stripers with clams can be done from shore or jetties or boats along the beaches, but it works best around bridges, piling, rips and tidal creeks, and other spots where bass are congregated or feeding. In the Chesapeake Bay area they also use ground soft-shell clams for chum to attract stripers to the boat.

Skimmer clams, hard clams, and soft clams can also be ground up and mixed with boiled rice and used as chum to attract winter flounders. And the stringy mantles found along the edges of the clamshell of a big skimmer clam make good baits for the big "snowshoe" and sea flounders.

Actually, all kinds of clams can be ground up, chopped up, or just cracked and used as chum for many other saltwater fishes, such as cod, porgies, sea bass, blackfish or tautog, croakers, and similar bottom species.

Mussels can also be used as chum to bring fish around a fishing spot. Both the sea mussel and the ribbed mussel can be used as chum for flounders, blackfish, sea bass, or porgies. Crush the mussels and scatter them around the boat or put them into a chum pot or mesh bag and lower it to the bottom. Every so often lift or shake the chum pot or bag to release some chum and juices in the tide.

Any other shellfish such as the oysters, razor clams, or scallops can also be used as chum if you obtain the trimmings or discarded meat and shells for this purpose. But they are usually too difficult to obtain, so most anglers depend on the more plentiful clams and mussels for chum or bait.

# CHAPTER 11

# SNAILS, WHELKS
# and CONCHS

*This chapter will deal with the snails, whelks, conchs, and other* univalve or single-shell mollusks used for bait. They are so numerous in numbers and species that only those commonly used for bait can be included.

## MOON SNAILS

These are the large sea snails which are found buried in the sand or mud from shallow coastal waters to depths of more than 200 fathoms. There are several species found along both the Atlantic and Pacific Coasts, and they are easily recognized by the typical snail-like appearance of the shells and the large meaty part or foot which spreads beyond the shell. Along the Atlantic Coast one of the largest is *Polinices heros*, also called the moon shell or sand-collar snail. It is 4 inches in diameter when fully grown. It can be found wholly or partly buried in sand or mud between tide marks and in shallow and deep water. It ranges from the Gulf of St. Lawrence to North Carolina. Another closely related moon shell or sand-collar snail is *Polinices duplicata*, which is found from Massachusetts to the Gulf of Mexico. It doesn't grow as large as the one mentioned above. On the Pacific Coast one of the largest is the Western moon snail *(Polinices lewisii)*, also known as the Lewis moon snail. It may reach 5 inches in diameter and is found from British Columbia to San Diego, California.

141

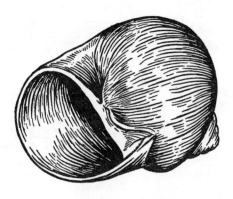

**MOON SNAIL**

The meaty part of the moon snails makes a tough bait which can be cut up and used for many bottom-feeding fish. It is used for cod and can be placed on the same hook with a piece of clam, since it is not stolen so easily by smaller fish such as bergalls or cunners.

## PERIWINKLES

These are the common small sea snails which are seen by the thousands clinging to rocks, piles, and seaweed in shallow water and high and dry between tide marks. The edible periwinkle (*Littorina litorea*), also called the common periwinkle, shore periwinkle, and winkle, is the most numerous in New England along the seashore. It prefers rocky areas from Labrador to Delaware Bay. Its shell varies in color, being black, olive-green, brownish-yellow, or gray often banded with brown. This periwinkle is commonly eaten and used for bait in Europe, from where it was introduced to Canada and then spread southward along the Atlantic Coast. It is also eaten and used as bait to a certain extent in this country. Although it is somewhat small, it can be cracked and the meat removed and placed on a hook. Several periwinkles can be strung on the same hook to make a larger bait. Periwinkles can be used for many of the smaller bottom-feeding fishes such as tautog, porgies, flounders, and croakers.

There are many other kinds of periwinkles found along both the Atlantic and Pacific Coasts which can be used for bait. Many

**EDIBLE PERIWINKLE**

of them are too small to make practical baits but others are large enough to be used. The good thing about periwinkles is that they make a fine emergency bait. They are almost always available in sufficient numbers and are so easy to gather that if you run out of other bait or have forgotten to bring it you can try these small snails.

## *WHELKS*

The whelks are the largest univalve shells found north of Cape Hatteras along the Atlantic Coast. The waved whelk *(Buccinum undatum)*, also called the common whelk and English whelk, has long been used for food in Europe and as bait in the cod fisheries. It reaches from 2 to 4 inches in length and is brownish in color. Along the Atlantic Coast it is found from Labrador to New Jersey. Along its northern range it is found close to shore, but farther south it is more common in deeper water.

Another group of whelks are the neptune shells, and one of the commonest is the channeled whelk *(Busycon canaliculatum)*, also called the conch or winkle. This is found from Cape Cod to northern Florida. It reaches from 6 to 9 inches in length and prefers a sandy bottom in shallow water. Another whelk is the knobbed whelk *(Busycon caricum)*, also called the giant whelk, pear conch, conch, or winkle. It is the largest of the Atlantic Coast whelks, sometimes reaching 10 inches in length. It is easily distinguished from the channeled whelk since it has a row of knobs on the shoulder near the top of the shell. This whelk is found from Cape Cod to Florida.

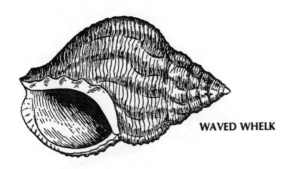

WAVED WHELK

CHANNELED WHELK

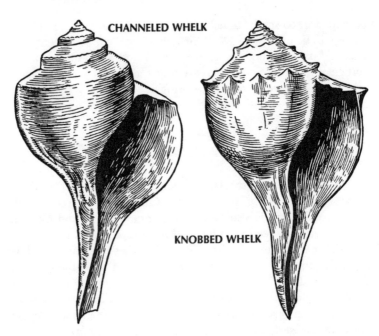

KNOBBED WHELK

South of North Carolina to Texas, the left-handed whelk *(Busycon perversum)*, also called the lightning shell, is the species usually found. There are many other kinds of whelks found along the Atlantic and Pacific Coasts and most of the larger ones can be used for bait.

Sometimes whelks can be bought in fish markets or from bait dealers, but usually you'll have to obtain your own. Those that are found in deep water are taken by commercial fishermen. In waters of moderate depth some whelks can be caught by leav-

144

ing dead fish or crushed shellfish in wire traps overnight. The whelks will crawl into the trap and can be hauled out in the morning. In shallow water you can often gather some whelks by wading or diving for them. A few may be washed high and dry on the beach or stranded in tidal pools and can be picked up.

Whelks make a tough bait and are often used for cod, either alone or together with softer baits such as clams. The pests like bergalls or cunners will quickly steal the clam bait but have a hard time with the tougher whelks. Thus the angler can be fairly sure that his hook always has some bait on it, and he doesn't have to haul in and look at it too often. In fact, the whelks are so tough that many anglers pound them with a wooden mallet or other instrument to soften them a bit, and also to allow the fluid to ooze out. Whelks can also be cut up into tiny pieces and used for fish such as tautog or blackfish, porgy or scup, sea bass, and many other bottom fishes.

## CONCHS

The conchs are another group of very large sea snails which are used for bait in tropical waters. One of the largest is the giant conch *(Strombus gigas)*, also called the queen conch, white conch, and fountain shell. It is a very large shell which may reach a foot in length and weigh 5 pounds. The beautiful pink and white shells are often seen in curio shops and in homes on mantels. This

GIANT CONCH

conch is found in southern Florida, especially in the Keys, as well as in the Bahamas and West Indies. It crawls around on the ocean bottom and on the coral reefs. Many other species of conchs are found in tropical waters. One of these, the Florida conch (*Strombus pugilis alatus*), is found from Cape Hatteras to the Gulf of Mexico and is quite common in the shallow waters of Florida.

Conchs are usually caught by diving for them in shallow water. But at times you can capture a good supply by lowering a basket or trap filled with dead fish or meat and leaving it there to attract the conchs. In some areas they are popular as food, but anglers consider them more important as bait for fish such as bonefish, permit, groupers, grunts, and snappers. The conch meat is also cut up or ground up and thrown overboard as chum to attract various saltwater fishes.

## LIMPETS

The limpets, which are small univalve shells shaped like cones and are found attached to rocks in between tide marks or in shallow water, are sometimes used for bait. There are many kinds found along the Atlantic and Pacific Coasts. One species used on the West Coast is the white-cap limpet (*Acmaea mitra*). This has a high, white conical shell which may be an inch in height. Limpets are well camouflaged to resemble their surroundings and they are hard to see. They cling to the rocks tightly but can be removed by slipping a thin knife blade quickly under the shell.

Most of the snails, whelks, and conchs can be kept for several days, like clams, in a cool spot or on ice. Or they can be

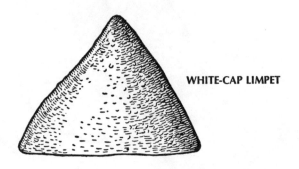

**WHITE-CAP LIMPET**

suspended in wire cages or similar containers in salt water. They can be opened with a hammer or hatchet, but if these tools are lacking the shells can be hit one against another or on some hard object. A knife is useful for extracting the meat from the shell and for cutting it up into pieces of the right size. A club or wooden mallet is also handy for pounding the tough meat to make it softer and better bait. Conchs can be baited like clams except that you only have to hook them once or twice to keep them on the hook.

Of course, this list of snail-like baits is far from complete and there are many others which can be used for bait. Almost any shellfish which is large enough and can be gathered in sufficient quantities can be cracked open and tried for bait. You will generally find that they will take some kind of saltwater fish.

Snails, whelks and conchs can be kept and preserved in many of the same ways as the clams covered in the previous chapter. They can also be hooked and used for many of the same fish as clams.

# CHAPTER 12

# SQUID and OCTOPUS

*A*lthough scientists consider squid and octopuses to be mollusks like clams, mussels, oysters, and other shellfish, they are so unique in structure and habits and so important as bait that they rate a special section. Millions of pounds of squid are used each year by commercial fishermen and anglers, especially in the North Atlantic. They are also popular as food in many countries and to a certain extent in this country among people of Oriental and Mediterranean descent.

The common Atlantic squid *(Loligo pealii)*, also called the blunt-tailed squid and inkfish, is so strange in appearance that it is easily recognized. The long, round body which tapers to the tail end and has two fins, has an opening on the opposite end into which the head fits. The head has two large, staring eyes and then tentacles or arms which surround a black, parrotlike beak which is the mouth. Squid swim backward very rapidly by squirting out a stream of water from a siphon found under the neck. Live squid vary in color, changing rapidly into different blends and tints of red, brown, yellow, green, or blue depending on its reactions and surroundings. When dead the squid turns white.

The common Atlantic squid usually averages 5 to 8 inches in body length. It is found from Massachusetts Bay to South Carolina from the shoreline to depths of 50 fathoms. It is rare north of Cape Cod where the short-tailed squid *(Ommastrephes illecebrosus)*, also called the sea arrow or flying squid, is more commonly found. This squid has shorter fins than the common

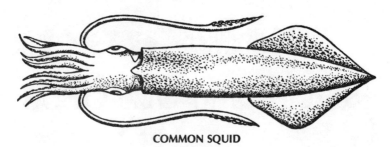

**COMMON SQUID**

squid and is usually found in deeper water from the Bay of Fundy to New Jersey. There are several other species of squid found along the Atlantic Coast, from tiny 2 or 3 inchers to the giant squid, which may reach more than 50 feet in overall length.

Along the Pacific Coast the common squid is *(Loligo opalescens)*, which ranges from Puget Sound to San Diego and reaches an overall length of about a foot. Other species of squid found in the Pacific run from tiny 2-inch specimens to giants measuring several feet.

## OBTAINING, KEEPING, AND HOOKING

During certain years squid are scarce, whereas in others they are abundant, but commercial fish houses, fish markets, and bait dealers usually have some for sale either fresh or frozen. Squid are usually taken by commercial fishermen in traps, pound nets, otter trawls, or haul seines. But during certain seasons and in some areas squid come close to shore, especially at night, and these can often be caught from boats, piers, or land with seines or dip nets. A light on a boat or pier or shore will attract small bait fish and the squid will often gather to feed on them.

Squid are also sometimes stranded on shore in large numbers and can be picked up, especially late at night or early in the morning. They can also be snagged with one or more treble hooks on the end of a line if the hooks are baited with one or two shiny bait fish. The hooks and bait should be moved up and down to attract the attention of the squid, and when it tries to envelop the bait a quick jerk on the line will often hook it.

Squid are difficult to keep alive in captivity since they require a lot of room and plenty of salt water. They are rarely used

150

in the live state unless they are caught and placed on the hook within a short time. Most of the squid are frozen or are kept on ice or in a refrigerator until used. They can also be cleaned, washed, cut up, and packed in containers or jars with plenty of salt and kept in a cool place for future use.

The whole squid is a favorite bait for swordfish and is also used for some of the marlins, tunas, and striped bass. For these fish the squid is usually used with one or two large hooks. The simplest way is to hook the squid once through the tail with a single hook. Another method is to run the single hook through the center of the squid with the bend and point coming out at the head or mouth. When using two hooks, one hook is run through the body and comes out at the head or side, while the other hook is run through the tail section. A flexible wire leader can be used to connect both hooks. To prevent the tail of the squid from

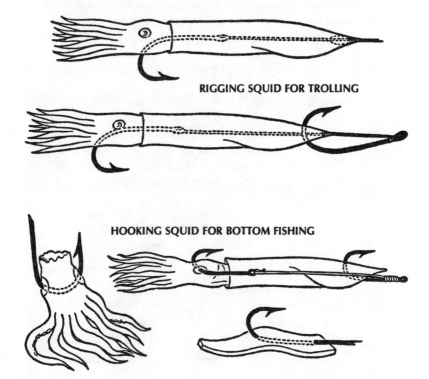

**RIGGING SQUID FOR TROLLING**

**HOOKING SQUID FOR BOTTOM FISHING**

sliding down the leader, a ball of string is often wrapped around the leader just inside the tail section to help hold it in position.

In Canadian and New England waters anglers often use whole squid rigged in "daisy chain" fashion and troll these slowly for giant tuna. Here several squid are rigged one behind the other without any hooks—only the last one contains a hook. This chain is trolled slowly about 30 or 40 feet behind the boat. The tuna often hit the rig and grab and steal the hookless squid. Eventually, the same fish or another tuna grabs the squid with the hook. The daisy chain should be trolled just fast enough to stay on top of the water, but not so fast that the squid wash off or fall apart.

An emergency rig for striped bass is often made by bending back the barbs on two big 7/0 hooks and slipping the eye of the second hook over the first and the eye of the third hook over the second, so that you have a series of three hooks lined up. The squid is then hooked so that the first hook, with the eye to which the leader is tied, runs through the tail section of the squid, the center hook runs through the body, and the last hook pierces the head. In all these methods the tail section is always nearest the leader so that the squid rides backward when trolled or retrieved during a cast.

Some anglers also use a half-round lead weight which is hammered or soldered onto the shank of a hook just below the eye. Then the tail end of the squid is cut off slightly and the fins are removed so that the squid can be threaded on the shank of the hook. The tail end is then tied flush against the lead weight, producing a squid bait which can be cast more easily or trolled below the surface.

**THREE-HOOK SQUID CASTING RIG USED FOR STRIPED BASS**

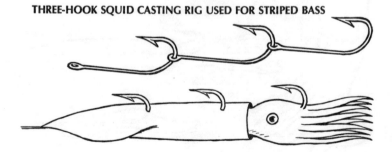

Small live squid 6 to 8 inches long are also used for white sea bass along the Pacific Coast. They can be hooked through the tail and lowered into the water and allowed to settle to the bottom. Then reel in some line so that the squid is just off the bottom. Hold it there a few minutes and if you get no bite, reel in your squid about halfway up to the surface and then let it sink to the bottom again. Then reel it back up again and let it drop down once more. Keep repeating this process until a fish takes it.

When bottom fishing for striped bass, cod, tilefish, pollock, channel bass, large weakfish, and bluefish, a small whole squid or large portions are used. The head with tentacles left on (the two longest ones can be cut off) makes a good bait for striped bass. So does the body section. Pieces of squid are often used together with clams or other soft baits on the same hook. The soft baits are often stolen by the fish, but the tough squid usually remains. The snow-white color of the squid also makes it one of the more attractive baits.

For smaller fish, such as the porgy or scup, sea bass, pollock, fluke, or summer flounder in Atlantic waters, and for rockfish, cabezon, lingcod, and sand bass in Pacific waters you can use strips of squid. These can be cut in triangular or rectangular shapes anywhere from 1 to 4 inches long.

Long, narrow strips of squid are also used like pork rind in conjunction with artificial lures such as plugs, spoons, metal squids, feather lures, spinners, and jigs, and these can be cast or trolled. The squid makes a tough bait; all you have to do is pierce it once or twice with a hook and it will stay on for a long time.

## OCTOPUS

This close relative of the squid can also be used for bait in many areas where it is found. Along the Atlantic Coast the octopus is not commonly found in northern waters. In the warmer waters of Florida, Bermuda, and points further south they are more numerous. In the Pacific Ocean various species of octopus are more common, being found from Alaska to tropical waters. Although most of them prefer deep water, especially the larger

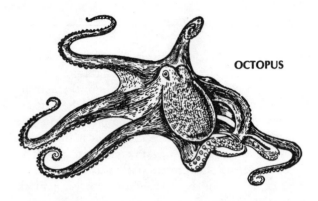

**OCTOPUS**

specimens, some are also found in shallow water. These can often be caught by turning over rocks in shallow water or tidal pools or probing with a gaff hook or spear into crevices or holes around reefs and rocks. The entrances to octopus dens are often littered with the remains of crabs and shellfish on which they feed. It is also claimed that a handful of salt poured into the hole of an octopus's den will make it come out. They can also be caught in traps with small funnel openings baited with dead fish or crabs.

The octopus makes a tough bait. The whole ones have been used for swordfish, and the tentacles which are split open and cut up into small sections are used for many saltwater fishes. If the skin is peeled off and the meat is pounded to soften it, the result is a more attractive bait.

The octopus is very popular in Hawaii both as food and bait. There they are caught by diving or by a special lure made of a cowrie shell, a stone, wood, and a hook. This lure is lowered near an octopus lair or is dragged along the bottom until an octopus grabs it. Then the line is jerked hard to hook the octopus. The Hawaiians cut up the octopus and use it for such fish as the uku or snapper and the ulua or jack.

The octopus also makes an excellent bait for morays and other eels found in salt water. It can also be used along the Pacific Coast for rockfish, cabezon, sculpin, lingcod, and sand bass.

# CHAPTER 13

# CRABS

*T*he crabs are very numerous both in species and numbers in the salt waters of the world. The Atlantic and Pacific shores of the United States have their share of these crustaceans which are eaten by many saltwater fishes. This despite the fact that most crabs have tough shells and pincers for protection. However, crabs do have periods when they are soft and helpless and this is when they usually make the best bait.

Before we take up the different kinds of crabs individually, perhaps it would be helpful to explain the various stages in which crabs are found. Crabs shed their hard covering at intervals as they grow, to make room for the increase in size. Just before they shed this covering they are known as "shedder" or "peeler" crabs. To tell if you have a shedder, try breaking off one of the moving pincers on the large claws or one of the points found on each end of the top shell. If it breaks with difficulty and leaves no meat exposed, it's a hard crab. If the shell breaks easily and leaves the soft, newly formed meat of the new shell exposed, the crab is a shedder. After they shed their shells they are "soft-shell" crabs, and when their new shell starts to harden, but still caves in when pressed, they are called buckrams, leather-backs or paper-backs. Finally the shell hardens and they are hard-shell crabs again. Crabs are used for bait in all their stages, but those in the soft-shell or shedder stage are usually preferred.

155

## BLUE CRAB

Of all the crabs found along the Atlantic Coast, the blue crab (*Callinectes sapidus*), also called the common edible crab, blue-claw crab, and sea crab, is the most popular for food and bait. This is the crab that is usually sold in the fish markets and served in restaurants in the hard or soft-shell stages. It is found from Cap Cod to Florida and around the Gulf of Mexico to the Mississippi. The blue crab is easily recognized by its large size, the dark green back, white belly, and long claws which are bright blue, blending into red at the tips. It reaches 6 inches or more in breadth along the top shell. It is a swimming crab and the hind legs are shaped like paddles to propel it through the water.

Blue crabs are found in the salt and brackish waters of bays, sounds, and rivers, where they prefer muddy bottoms covered with eelgrass or sea lettuce. They are most active and numerous in northern waters from May to October, when they frequent the shallower waters. During the winter they move off into deeper water.

Although blue crabs can be bought in the hard- and soft-shell stages in many fish markets and from commercial fishermen and bait dealers, many anglers prefer to catch their own. Shedder crabs are also sold by some bait dealers but they are usually high in price.

Hard blue crabs can be captured in fairly large quantities by means of traps. The standard crab trap is the wire-box type in

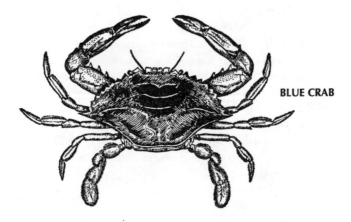

**BLUE CRAB**

which the four sides fall open when the trap is on the bottom. When the trap is raised the four sides close, capturing any crabs that have entered to feed on the dead fish or meat which is tied in the center of the trap. This type of trap can be bought in many fishing tackle and hardware stores along the seacoast. Another kind of trap used for crabs can be made from wire mesh in the shape of a bag. The open end is fairly wide, while the closed end is flattened. A line is tied to the open end or entrance and this trap can be baited with crushed clams or mussels or fish to attract the crabs. These two traps can be used from bridges, piers, jetties, or the shore where the water is fairly deep. If you use more than one trap you can usually obtain enough crabs for your needs in a short time. However, most of these will be hard crabs because few shedder or soft crabs enter such traps.

One of the best ways to obtain shedder or soft shell crabs is to wade in shallow water on the tidal flats and scoop up the crabs with a long-handled crab net. At first you may have difficulty in spotting the crab amid the eelgrass and sea lettuce, but if you stand still you will soon see them either moving around or partly hidden under the weeds. And it will take a while to catch on to their tricky maneuverings before you are able to capture them in the net consistently. Many of these crabs will also be hard ones, but you will often find a shedder crab or soft-shell crab hidden among the weeds and you can scoop it up. If you see one crab carrying another you will usually find that the one underneath is either a shedder or soft-shell crab.

A variation of the method above is to use a rowboat with one man slowly rowing or poling and another one in the bow of the boat with a crab net ready to scoop up the crabs. This method has the advantage or covering more territory and it can be used in deeper water around piers, railroad trestles, bridges, and pilings. The crabs are usually more plentiful at night, when they come out of hiding, and can be easily seen in the water with the help of a flashlight or spotlight. Usually the best time to go crabbing with a dip net is during low tide, when the water is shallower and the crabs are more concentrated in smaller areas.

Another way you can capture hard blue crabs in small numbers is to tie a piece of fish or a fishhead to a string and lower it

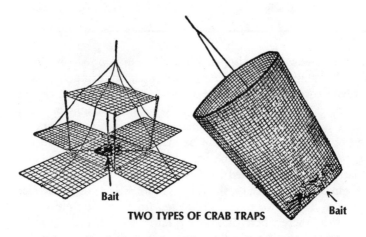

**Bait**

**TWO TYPES OF CRAB TRAPS** **Bait**

into the water. When a crab starts eating the bait he can usually be drawn slowly toward shore or the surface of the water and eased over a net, then scooped up.

When you are crabbing, only the larger blue crabs are usually kept for bait. In fact, some states have laws which prohibit the taking and keeping of blue crabs under a certain size. The female crabs carrying eggs are also protected in most states. The best policy is to check local and state laws before you go after blue crabs.

Hard blue crabs will live for quite a while out of the water if they are kept in large containers in a cool spot away from the sun. For longer periods they can be kept in large floating boxes or bait cars in the water. Shedder crabs and soft-shell crabs can be packed in one layer of seaweed, moss, straw, or grass in a tray and kept on ice for several days. But hard crabs, shedder crabs, and soft-shell crabs should always be kept in three separate containers.

To hook large, whole blue crabs for big fish such as tarpon for bottom fishing, the best method is to keep the crab alive. The large claws or pincers can be broken off and the hook should be run through the edge of the top shell from the bottom up. This should be done carefully in order not to crack the shell or make too big a hole. Another method is to remove one of the walking legs and insert the point of the hook into the hole left there and then curve the hook around and let the point and barb emerge between the other legs. The hard crabs can also be secured to the hook by tying them with thread.

158

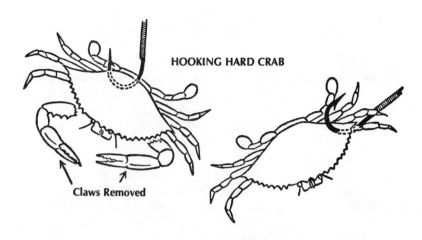

**HOOKING HARD CRAB**

Claws Removed

When preparing shedder crabs, remove the big claws; these can be cracked open and the meat inside can be used for bait. Then remove the top shell by inserting your thumbnail under it in the back part of the crab. Now the crab can be turned over. Using a hard instrument like a knife handle, hit the remaining shell on the belly in several places to crack it into small sections. These pieces of shell should be peeled off, leaving the soft body of the crab. The remaining legs should be cut or twisted off.

If you are fishing for big fish, the whole body of the crab can be used. For smaller fish or if you are short of bait, you can cut the crab in half or into quarters. The same thing can be done with a soft-shell crab which has already cast off its hard covering. The shedder and soft-shell crabs are rather delicate baits and are hard to keep on a hook. The hook should be inserted two or three times into the portion used and twisted each time to help it stay on. Many saltwater anglers use fine thread to tie the crabs around a hook.

Soft-shell blue crabs are very effective for striped bass and are widely used in the Chesapeake Bay. Here you use a whole, big, live soft-shell and an 8/0 long-shank hook which is attached to the crab with rubber bands to keep from killing the crab. In other words, do not run the hook through the crab, but merely lay it on top of the crab and lash it to the body with two or three thin rubber bands. The crab is then lowered into the water gently from a boat and allowed to drift out with the tide right below the surface or the water, just as a crab naturally floats out in the current. This fishing is done mostly at night and you have to go by feel to know when a fish picks up your crab. Usually this is indicated by the line's speeding up as it moves off the reel spool.

Fishing in Chesapeake Bay you can also catch channel bass, cobia, and black drum with soft-shell crabs. And striped bass can also be caught on the bottom with soft-shell blue crabs when fishing in the surf.

Small hard-shell blue crabs also make an excellent bait for big tarpon, especially along the West Coast of Florida at Boca Grande. Here you use a bottom rig with an egg sinker which is attached with weak cord or soft wire so it flies off when a tarpon is hooked. The best hooks for this fishing are Sobeys in sizes No. 5/0 or 6/0.

You can also use the small live blue crabs for permit. Here a smaller No. 2/0 or 3/0 hook is inserted through the crab from the underside and out through the back near one of the points of the top shell. For best results remove the two big pincer claws also. Presentation of the crab is very important when fishing for the wary permit. You should cast it about 4 or 5 feet ahead of the permit and a few feet beyond the fish, then reel it back so that the fish swims into it. Casting too close to a permit will startle it. When a permit approaches the crab, lower your rod and let the bait settle toward the bottom. Then when the fish picks up the crab, let it move off a few feet so that it can swallow it or get it deeper into its mouth. Then set the hook.

While fishing for permit you may also be able to cast the small blue crab toward any bonefish you see. If you are going after bonefish only, you can use a somewhat smaller hook with the crab bait. Here about a No. 1 or 1/0 hook is best.

You can also try the larger hard-shell blue crabs for such fish as grouper and jewfish. Fish the crab at slack tide in holes around wrecks, rock jetties, and under bridges and pier pilings. For these fish use a big No. 10/0 or 12/0 hook.

## LADY CRAB

The lady crab (*Ovalipes ocellatus*) is another swimming crab which is often used for bait, especially in surf fishing. It is found

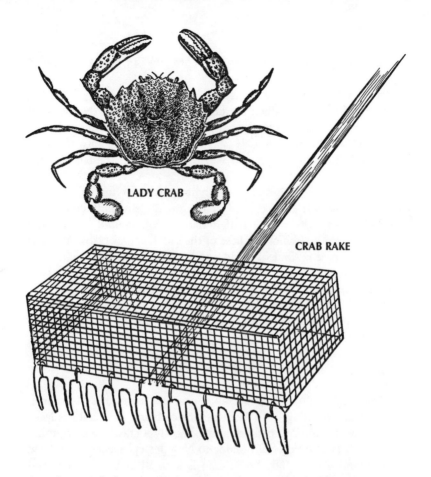

**LADY CRAB**

**CRAB RAKE**

along the sandy beaches from Cape Cod to the Gulf of Mexico. It is easily recognized by its overall yellow or tan color and the purplish or reddish circular spots on its back. The shell, which is somewhat round, reaches 3 inches in diameter. This crab is also called the calico crab, sand crab, and speckled crab.

The lady crab can swim efficiently with its two paddles, but it is usually found crawling along the sandy bottom. When approached, it buries itself in the sand leaving only the eye-stalks protruding. If you see these crabs crawling around you can usually catch some at low tide with a regular crab net, scooping, them up before they disappear in the sand.

When the crabs cannot be seen, they can often be caught by raking the area to dig them out. An ordinary garden rake can be used for this purpose if you attach a wire basket into which the crabs will fall. This basket is attached with the opening facing the teeth of the rake. When the rake is pulled through the soft sand you can usually feel the crab strike the teeth, then you twist the handle of the rake quickly and the crab will fall into the wire basket. Sometimes the crab will be impaled on the teeth of the rake.

Like the blue crabs, the best lady crabs for bait are the shedder or soft-shell ones. But the small, hard lady crabs with shells about the size of half dollars are often used, since their shells are not as thick as those of the older, larger crabs. You can impale three or four of these small crabs on one big hook.

Lady crabs can be kept, prepared, and hooked like the blue crabs described earlier. They are especially popular as bait for striped bass, but can also be used for channel bass, black drum, cod, kingfish or northern whiting, and many other species.

## GREEN CRAB

Although the green crab (*Carcinides maenas*) is also considered a swimming crab like the blue crab and lady crab, it lacks the two swimming paddles and is mostly a crawling or running crab. It is common from Maine to New Jersey, especially in New England waters. The green crab is a small crab with the shell reaching about 3 inches in width and 2 inches in length. It is a dark, drab green color spotted with yellow or yellow-green.

The green crab is most numerous in rocky areas, where it is found between the tide marks or in shallow water or pools, hiding in crevices or seaweed or under rocks. These crabs can often be seen in tidal pools at low water. To obtain them, you can turn over the loose stones between tide marks or in shallow water. In tidal pools they will often emerge from their hiding places if you throw some crushed mussels, clams, or other shellfish into the water and then sit quietly. Or you can tie a dead fish to a string, and when the crabs come out to eat it you can catch them by hand or with a small dip net. To obtain green crabs in large quantities, construct a wire trap with one or two funnel entrances similar to the minnow traps, but with larger openings. These, of course,

**GREEN CRAB**

must be baited with dead fish, crushed mussels, clams, or other bait and left overnight.

Green crabs are hardy and will live for days out of the water if kept in a cool spot. Or they can be kept in live boxes submerged in salt water. Only crabs of the same size should be kept in the same container.

Although green crabs are also found in the soft and shedder stages, they are usually used for bait in the hard stage, and mostly for tautog or blackfish. The larger crabs can be cut in half or quarters, whereas the smaller ones are used whole. The larger pincer claws are usually removed before baiting the hook. The crabs stay on best if the hook is run between the legs or through the body and then into one of the leg holes after you twist off one of the legs.

## FIDDLER CRABS

These small crabs are easily recognized because the males have one large claw and also because they live in sand or mud burrows along salt marshes or brackish bays. Three species are commonly found along the Atlantic Coast from Cape Cod to Florida. One of the most numerous is the mud fiddler (*Uca pugnax*), also called the marsh fiddler. It is olive or dark green, with yellowish claws. It prefers the mud flats of bays, where it digs burrows in the sedge banks.

Another fiddler crab often used for bait is the sand fiddler (*Uca pugilator*), also called the china-back fiddler. It grows some-

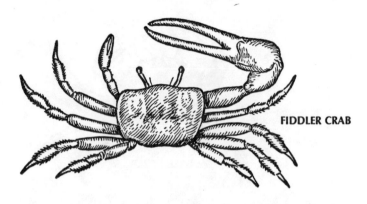

**FIDDLER CRAB**

what larger than the mud fiddler and is much lighter in color, having a shiny, gray back with markings of brown, dark gray, or violet. The claws are whitish or pale yellow. Although it is often found living in bays together with the mud fiddler, it usually digs its burrows in sandier soil. It is preferred over the other fiddlers by most fisherman for bait.

The largest of the three fiddlers found from Cape Cod to Florida is the red-jointed fiddler (*Uca minax*), also called the soldier crab, a name often applied to the other species of fiddlers and hermit crabs. It is easily recognized by the red marks at the joints of the large claw, and the gray or brown color of its shell. It prefers marshes in brackish or almost fresh waters, where it digs holes above high-water mark.

On the Pacific Coast the two species of fiddler crabs usually found are (*Uca crenulata*), which ranges from San Diego south, and (*Uca musica*), which is found from Mexico to Canada. They burrow in the salt marshes just as do the Atlantic Coast fiddlers.

Fiddler crabs are often sold by bait dealers, but the supply is somewhat undependable and many anglers obtain their own. Those that live in shallow burrows can be dug up with a clam hoe or fork. Where they are numerous they can often be herded into a trap which can be set up quickly and easily with some boards. Two long boards can be hammered together to form a corner and this is dropped between the fiddlers and their burrows. They will crowd into the corner and can be scooped up quickly. After fiddler crabs disappear into their burrows they will emerge again in 10 or 15 minutes if you stay still and avoid making quick movements.

164

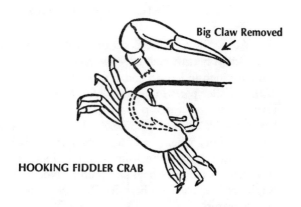

**HOOKING FIDDLER CRAB**

Big Claw Removed

Fiddler crabs will usually live for several days in a box or other large container if it is kept in a cool spot. If you want to keep them for any length of time, they should never be packed so tightly that they are on top of one another. However, if they are going to be used soon, then there is no harm in packing them close in a small container.

To hook fiddler crabs, remove the large claw. Then you can run the point and barb of the hook into the hole where the big claw was attached and thread the crab up on the bend of the hook as far as it will go. Another way is to force the point and barb of the hook up to the bend between the crab's legs. Still another way is to run the hook from the underside of the crab, through the body, and out through the shell.

Fiddler crabs are a favorite bait for tautog or blackfish in northern waters and for sheepshead in southern waters. They can also be used for redfish or channel bass, sea trout, pompano, and black drum in southern waters.

## HERMIT CRABS

These crabs, which live in empty snail shells, are familiar to anyone who has gone to the seashore, where the small kinds are often numerous in shallow water. There are many species of hermit crabs found in Atlantic and Pacific waters. Some live in deep water, others prefer shallow water, and a few in the tropics live on land.

165

Along the Atlantic Coast one of the commonest hermit crabs is the small hermit crab (*Pagurus longicarpus*), which reaches only about an inch in length and is usually found occupying the shells of the smaller periwinkles or snails. It is abundant in quiet shallow waters and tidal pools from Massachusetts to Florida. A larger species (*Pagurus policaris*), which is light red or brown and lives in empty whelk and moon snail shells, is known as the big hermit crab. It is found from Maine to Florida and prefers rocky and shelly bottoms of bays and sounds. North of Cap Cod a large, bright red species of hermit (*Pagurus bernhardus*) is found in deeper waters.

In tropical waters one of the largest hermits is the sea soldier (*Petrochirus bahamensis*), which when fully grown is often found occupying large conch shells. Another large hermit crab is the soldier crab (*Cenobita diogenes*), which is found in Florida and the West Indies. These crabs live on land most of the time, but return to the water during the breeding season. They are sometimes found far inland dragging around their shell homes, which are magpie shells.

Along the Pacific coast one of the commonest hermit crabs found in tide pools is *Pagurus samuelis*. Another species is *Pagurus granosimanus*, which is most numerous north of Puget Sound. And the hairy hermit (*Pagurus hirsutiusculus*) is another crab often found along the West Coast. All three of these hermits have an extreme range from Alaska to Lower California, but each species has a certain region where it is most abundant.

Of course, there are many other species of hermit crabs found along the Pacific and Atlantic Coasts which make just as

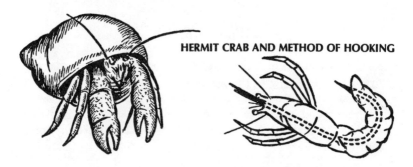

HERMIT CRAB AND METHOD OF HOOKING

good bait as those mentioned above. Those that are numerous and can be gathered with ease are the ones that usually find their way into the saltwater angler's bait box.

Hermit crabs can be picked up easily in shallow water or on land when they are needed for bait. Sometimes they can be attracted in fairly large numbers by baiting the area with dead fish, crushed clams, or similar food. At other times large numbers of hermit crabs are washed ashore by storms.

The sea-dwelling hermit crabs will stay alive for quite a while in their shell homes if they are kept in a cool spot out of the sun. They can be kept for longer periods in bait cars or in other containers submerged in water. Of course, the land-dwelling hermits will live out of the water for a long time.

When hermit crabs are used for bait they must be removed from their shell homes. This can be done by cracking the shell with a rock or other hard instrument. A lighted match or other heat applied to the shell will also bring the crab out of its home. The large claws of the hermit are removed before the crab is placed on the hook. When the whole hermit crab is used, the hook can be run through the entire body starting from the hard head and into the soft tail portion. Or you can pierce the hard body and then run the hook through the tail. For small fish the soft abdomen or tail alone can be used. Hermit crabs can be used for bonefish, pompano, permit, sheepshead, blackfish or tautog, snappers, and many other saltwater fish that eat crabs.

## OTHER CRABS

Some of the other crabs that can be used for bait at times include the many species belonging to the genus *Cancer*. These are found along both the Atlantic and Pacific Coasts. They are often called rock crabs, edible crabs, or market crabs. Along the Atlantic Coast the two species usually found are the rock crab (*Cancer irroratus*) and the Jonah crab or northern crab (*Cancer borealis*). Along the Pacific Coast, *Cancer magister* and *Cancer antennarus* are the ones commonly found. These crabs, as their name implies, live among rocks, although they may also bury themselves partly in the sand. Most of them are some shade of yellowish or reddish-brown and most of them are edible. In shallow water they can be picked up by hand or with a crab dip net. But in deeper water special crab traps baited with dead fish are usually used.

Then there is the ghost crab (*Ocypoda albicans*), also called the sand crab, which is found from New Jersey south along the Atlantic Coast. It lives in burrows along sandy beaches near and above high-water mark. These crabs are fast runners and very difficult to catch, especially during the daytime. But at night when they are more numerous they can often be blinded by a flashlight or trapped some distance from their burrows.

The large stone crab (*Menippe mercenaria*) can be used for bait in Florida and other southern waters where it is found. But this crab is so popular for food that it is now rather scarce and high priced, so you cannot depend on obtaining it in sufficient numbers to use for bait.

Of course, there are many other crabs both large and small found along the Atlantic and Pacific Coast which can be used for bait. Just because a crab is not listed here does not mean that it cannot be used for bait. Try any crab that can be obtained in the area you are fishing and you will generally find that some kind of fish will take it.

# CHAPTER  14

# SHRIMP and OTHER CRUSTACEANS

*A*lthough the shrimp and other crustaceans dealt with in this chapter have shells similar to those found in crabs, they differ in many other ways. Shrimp have become very important with saltwater anglers, as more and more are beginning to use them for many saltwater species.

## SHRIMP AND PRAWNS

Shrimp and prawns of one kind or another are widely used for saltwater fishing. In the south the smaller ones are called shrimp while the larger ones are known as prawns. Most shrimp are easily recognized since they look somewhat like small lobsters, but without the two large claws. Instead, they have many tiny claws, a pair of long antennae, and bodies which are often colorless, translucent, or pale gray, green, blue or pink.

## EDIBLE SHRIMP

The edible shrimp (*Panaeus setiferus*) is the one usually caught by commercial fishermen and found in fish markets and restaurants. It is also called the common shrimp, southern shrimp, white shrimp, jumbo shrimp, and prawn. This shrimp may reach up to 10 inches in length, but most of those found do

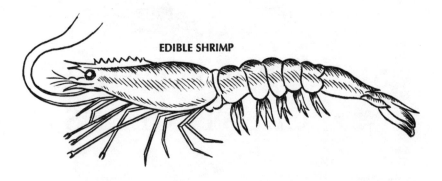

**EDIBLE SHRIMP**

not exceed 6 or 7 inches. The edible shrimp is found from Virginia to the Gulf of Mexico. The adult specimens are usually found in deeper offshore waters, but the younger ones live in bays, sounds, rivers, and other sheltered waters.

Two other shrimp related to the common shrimp above are also caught by commercial fishermen. One is the Brazilian shrimp (*Penaeus brasiliensis*), which is found from Cape Cod to Florida. Another is the brown-spotted grooved shrimp (*Penaeus duorarum*), also called the "pink" shrimp, which is caught in large numbers in the Gulf of Mexico. Of course, there are other species also caught by commercial fishermen, and in recent years quite a fishery has developed off Maine for a smaller species which is now served in many restaurants and sold in fish markets.

Most of the large edible shrimp are caught by commercial fishermen either offshore in large boats or inshore and in coastal waters in smaller craft. They use mostly otter trawls, but cast nets and seines are sometimes used by the smaller operators.

The smaller shrimp venture close to shore or into shallow water at night in southern waters, and the angler can often capture them then. A large dip net and light can be used to scoop up the shrimp from shore, docks, piers, and bridges.

Shrimp are sold live by some bait dealers, especially in Florida and other southern fishing spots. But most of the shrimp are dead when bought. To keep them alive you need large tanks with running salt water. You can also keep them in bait cars suspended in salt water. Smaller quantities can be kept alive in styrofoam plastic pails, bait buckets, and other containers. Dead shrimp should be kept on ice or frozen. Also, the tails can be shucked and the meat can be kept in heavy brine in jars in a refrigerator for quite a while.

Shrimp are hooked in several ways, depending on the size of the bait, the fish sought, and the method of fishing used. The live shrimp can be hooked through the hard shell just behind the head. Care should be taken so that the vital parts are not pierced. These can be seen as a dark spot inside the body. They can also be hooked through the tail at about the third or fourth segment. Here you run the hook from the underside into the tail and out through the top. The smaller dead shrimp can be threaded on the hook, running the point in at the head, then through the body and finally into the tail. With the larger shrimp the tail section can be used alone, removing the shell and using only the meat on the hook. For small fish this tail portion can be cut into chunks of the desired size.

## USING SHRIMP

One of the best ways to use a big, live shrimp is to hook it through the head or tail with a small No. 1 or 1/0 hook and then let it out in the current from a boat, pier, or bridge. Usually no weight is needed, but at times you can add a clincher or clamp-on sinker on the leader to get the bait down faster and keep it there.

Another way to fish a live shrimp is to cast it out and let it sink toward the bottom. Most of the time a fish will grab it before it gets down to the bottom. If it does reach bottom without being taken, let it lie there a short time; then lift it off the

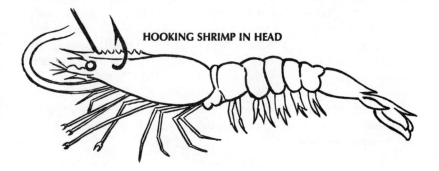

HOOKING SHRIMP IN HEAD

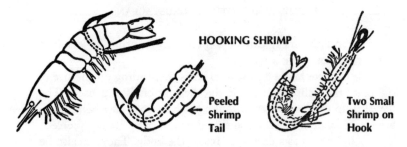

**HOOKING SHRIMP**

Peeled Shrimp Tail

Two Small Shrimp on Hook

bottom and let it settle back again, and keep doing this to prevent the shrimp from hiding in the weeds or among the rocks.

Live shrimp are widely used in southern waters for sea trout or southern weakfish. Here a "popper" float rig is utilized. This consists of a 3-foot leader attached to the fishing line. The popper float is added to the line and leader about 3 feet above the hook. A light clincher or clamp-on sinker is then put on the leader between the hook and the float. Then you hook a live shrimp through the head and the entire rig is cast out from a drifting boat moving over the flats where sea trout are found. As the boat moves along over the grassy flats, the cork float is popped or jerked every so often so it creates a splash which attracts the sea trout to the scene.

You can also fish the popping rig and shrimp from an anchored boat. Here you let the current take the float and bait out to sea trout holes or along drop-offs. The same thing can be done when fishing for snook or tarpon. Or you can cast the shrimp without a float toward the edge of the mangroves or under bridges where these fish lie, letting it drift with the current or swim around in the right spot.

The easiest way to catch a bonefish is also with a live shrimp. Here you use a No. 1/0 or 2/0 hook and cast the bait ahead of any bonefish you see cruising by. Let it sink, and if the shrimp is alive and kicking the bonefish will usually spot it. If the shrimp is not moving give it a slight jerk as the bonefish approaches it.

Live shrimp also make an excellent bait for many bottom species in southern waters. You can use them for snappers, grunts, sheepshead, grouper, and similar fish either with or without a sinker.

Shrimp also make good chum to attract various fish to the scene. Here you can grind or chop up the whole shrimp. Or you can save the tails for bait and just grind or chop up the head and body. If you locate some shrimp boats early in the morning, when they are cleaning out their nets, you can often obtain shrimp from them. You can also try fishing close to such boats, since they are actually chumming when they dump out their nets and discard dead shrimp, crushed shrimp, crabs, and small fish.

Shrimp can also be used for flounders, pompano, permit, channel bass or redfish, croakers, and northern and southern whiting.

## COMMON SAND SHRIMP

The sand shrimp, which belong to the genus *Crago*, include many species along both the Atlantic and Pacific Coasts. Although they rarely grow longer than 3 inches, with the average closer to 2 inches, these shrimp are also used for food to a certain extent. They are commonly found in the shallow waters of bays, sounds, and inlets but also frequent deeper water offshore. They prefer sand bottoms, where they bury themselves, but are also found hiding in the seaweed and among rocks. Sand shrimp are usually translucent, pale gray in color, and flecked with spots or various tints matching the bottom where they are found. They are sometimes called glass shrimp because of their clear, glassy appearance. But this name is also applied to other small shrimp.

One of the most numerous sand shrimp along the Atlantic Coast is *Crago septemspinosus* or *Crangon vulgaris,* which is found from Labrador to North Carolina. It is also found along the

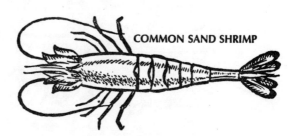

COMMON SAND SHRIMP

Pacific Coast, but here the California shrimp (*Crago franciscorum*) is the one usually found. It ranges from Alaska to San Diego and is caught by commercial fishermen with trawls for the market. Another species, the black-tailed shrimp (*Crago nigricauda*), is caught in smaller numbers along the Pacific Coast. But there are many other closely related forms found in Atlantic and Pacific waters.

The sand shrimp can sometimes be caught near shore in seines or dip nets or in tidal pools along rocky coasts. They form an important food supply for fishes such as striped bass, weakfish, bluefish, flounders, croakers, and many others, and can be used as bait for these fish.

## COMMON PRAWN

The common prawn (*Palaemonetes vulgaris*), also called the grass shrimp, glass prawn, mud shrimp, harbor shrimp, and pin shrimp, is a small variety reaching about an inch and a half in length. It makes a good bait for many saltwater fishes. It is found from Massachusetts to the Gulf of Mexico in bays, ditches, and estuaries, over mud bottoms, and in the eelgrass. It can be distinguished from the sand shrimp by its longer antennae and the sharp spine it has between the eyes. It has a translucent, almost colorless body with brownish spots.

Although the common prawn can be bought from some bait dealers and tackle stores, many anglers prefer to catch their own. Where they are fairly abundant this is often a simple job if you just need enough for one or two anglers. They have been scarce for many years although they have come back to some waters.

These small shrimp can be netted with a small dip net made

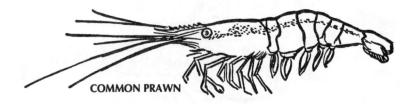

COMMON PRAWN

of fine cloth or wire mesh. Look for them along the edge of the shore in coves, tidal creeks, and mud flats. They are often found hiding in the eelgrass.

For larger quantities a fine-meshed minnow seine can be used to obtain them. Of course, this is a two-man operation if a long net is used. One man can handle a small seine up to about 6 feet long with the ends tied to poles, but longer nets require two men.

Some bait dealers and anglers also catch these shrimp by towing or pulling a funnel-shaped net along or close to the bottom. This is done from a boat so you can cover more territory and obtain more shrimp in a shorter period of time.

If you want to use the grass shrimp alive, you can transfer them into a pail filled with seawater or put them in a bait car as you catch them. Although the small shrimp will live in a small container filled with salt water if the water is changed frequently and kept cool, a large wire-meshed, box-type container which can be placed in the water is better, especially if you want to keep the shrimp for more than a day or two.

But if you want to keep shrimp alive just for the day's fishing you can pack them without water in almost any wooden or plastic box. One or more holes should be bored in the bottom of this box and covered with wire screening. Then pack a layer of sawdust or wood shavings on the bottom of the box. On top of this add a layer of cracked ice. Now place a burlap bag over the ice. Next, cover this with another layer of sawdust or wood shavings, then you can scatter some shrimp over this material. After this add another layer of shavings or sawdust and on top place some more shrimp. This can be done with several alternate layers of shrimp and sawdust or shavings until all your shrimp have been packed. Finally, on top of all the layers put another burlap bag soaked in salt water. Then place a cover on the box and keep the container out of the hot sun or rain.

If the above sounds like a lot of trouble, you can keep shrimp healthy and alive for a day's fishing in one of those big styrofoam coolers or a styrofoam bait container. Don't add any water to this container, but you can put in some rockweed, sea lettuce, or other seaweed which has been soaked in salt water.

These small shrimp are very popular with anglers who fish for weakfish, since they make an excellent chum to attract the fish to the boat. Just dribble one or two shrimp at a time into the water, but do this steadily without any break. This same chum will attract striped bass, bluefish, tautog or blackfish, porgies, croakers, and northern whiting or kingfish. You can also use the shrimp as bait for these fish.

To bait shrimp, you can thread them on the hook head first and push them up the shank until two or three cover the entire hook. A light wire hook is best for this. Shrimp hooked in this manner are not easily stolen from the hook, but will soon die; they'll live longer if you just hook them through the tail. One, two, or three shrimp can be used on a single hook, depending on the size of the hook and the preferences of the fish.

The common prawn or grass shrimp can be used for herring, white perch, mackerel, flounder and many other fishes found in brackish and salt waters.

## GHOST SHRIMP

These shrimp, also known as burrowing shrimp, live in underground burrows in mud flats or beaches. Three species are found along the Pacific Coast, of which *Callianassa gigas* is the largest, reaching a length of 5 inches. These are found from British Columbia to Lower California. Another common ghost shrimp is *Callianassa californiensis,* which is found from Alaska to Lower California. These two species prefer the bays, where there are mud flats. The third species, *Callianassa affinis*, prefers open beaches along rocky shores in southern California. There is another ghost shrimp found along the Atlantic Coast, but it is not well-known or widely used as bait there.

The ghost shrimp are pink or cream colored and have one large claw which either extends out ahead of the creature or is folded back over the front half of the body. These shrimp can be dug with a shovel or fork on the mud flats at low tide. Although they may burrow anywhere up to 3 feet, most of them do not go much deeper than 20 inches or so. After turning over the mud or

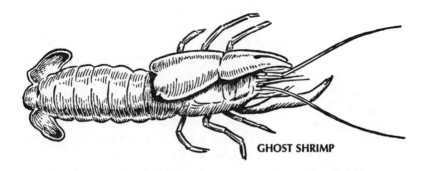

**GHOST SHRIMP**

sand with the fork, search through it quickly but thoroughly to locate the shrimp. Ghost shrimp can be used for halibut, croakers, white sea bass, sculpins, and many other fishes found along the Pacific Coast.

Of course, this list of shrimp and prawns is far from complete. There are many other varieties found along our coasts which can be used when they can be obtained in sufficient quantities.

## SAND BUGS

The sand bug (*Emerita talpoida*) is also called the beach bug, sand crab, mole crab, and mole shrimp. It is also known as the sand flea, but this confuses it with the true sand fleas or beach fleas, which are much smaller.

The sand bug is easily recognized by the oval or egg-shaped body, smooth back, and several stout, hairy legs on the underside. They may reach up to an inch and a half in length but usually average somewhat smaller. The shell is tan or sand-colored tinged with pink or light purple. The Atlantic species is found from Cape Cod to Florida while a related form (*Emerita analoga*) is found along the Pacific Coast from Oregon to Panama.

**SAND BUG AND METHOD OF HOOKING**

The sand bugs are found along the open sand beaches, where they burrow into the sand directly under the breaking surf. An incoming wave causes them to leave the sand and swim about, but as soon as the wave starts to recede they burrow into the sand again. They move up the beach on an incoming tide and back again to low-water mark on the outgoing tide. However, sometimes they get stranded near high-water mark when the tide drops and can be found buried in the wet sand.

Sand bugs live in colonies numbering in the hundreds or thousands, and they usually give themselves away by telltale streaks caused by the slightly protruding head parts as they burrow into the sand backward. Sometimes they can be found swimming around in tidal pools, but usually they have to be dug from the wet sand under the breaking waves. This can be done by waiting until a wave sweeps up the beach and then, as the water recedes, digging your hands and fingers as deep as possible and feeling for the sand bugs as you pull against the rushing water.

However, the quickest way to obtain the sand bugs in large numbers is to make a scoop trap with a long handle. This can be made in a variety of forms, but usually resembles a giant dustpan with the long handle facing toward the opening instead of away from it as in the conventional scoop. The frame can be made from strips of wood or heavy wire and covered with quarter-inch or half-inch wire mesh. The larger mesh is better, since it permits most of the sand and broken shells to escape.

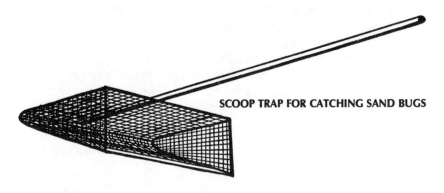

**SCOOP TRAP FOR CATCHING SAND BUGS**

To catch the sand bugs with this trap, all you have to do is wait until a wave sweeps up the beach, then drop your scoop into the receding wave and drag it toward you with the bottom of the trap scraping lightly against the sand. If you pick a spot where sand bugs are numerous, a few scoops will give you all the bait you need.

The sand bugs can be kept in damp sand in a container for quite a while. One of those big styrofoam coolers for drinks or sandwiches is ideal for this. Keep the sand bugs in a cool spot and they'll live for days. But since they are usually available during the fishing season, a fresh supply can be obtained as needed. Most of the sand bugs you catch will be hard-shelled ones, but a few may be soft-shelled, especially during the summer and early fall. These make excellent bait, but they do not stay on the hook too well and may have to be tied down with thread. A single hard-shelled sand bug can be hooked for smaller fish by running the point through the underside and out through the top shell. This should be done carefully so as not to make too large a hole or crack the shell.

Sand bugs make an excellent bait for pompano in southern waters and are widely used along the beaches of Florida. There, you use a rig with anywhere from two to five small No. 1 hooks on dropper loops above the sinker, baiting each hook with a whole sand bug. Then you cast the rig out into likely spots from the beach or a pier. Usually the best fishing takes place when the surf is fairly rough but the water is clean.

Sand bugs are also used along the Pacific Coast when surf fishing for corbina, yellowfin croakers, spot-fin croakers, and surf perch. Here you cast the sand bug out, let it lie in one spot, then reel it in about 2 or 3 feet, allowing it to rest in one spot about a minute or two before reeling it in again for 2 or 3 feet; keep repeating this until the rig is near shore or up on the beach.

For larger fish such as striped bass, channel bass, and black drum you can thread several sand bugs on the hook and shank, and even up on the leader. You can also do this if you get small sand bugs. Sand bugs can also be used for bonefish, sheepshead, tautog or blackfish, and northern or southern whiting.

## *SPINY LOBSTERS*

The spiny lobsters which are found in warm waters are easily recognized since they resemble the common lobster and freshwater crayfish except that they lack the two large pincer claws. In fact, they are often called saltwater crayfish. They are also called rock lobsters, but this name is usually applied to those imported from South Africa for food. Spiny lobsters are blue, yellow, and brown and are covered with many spines. The Atlantic spiny lobster (*Panulirus argus*) is found in Florida, the Bahamas, and West Indies. A closely related species, *Panulirus interruptus*, is. found in Pacific waters as far north as Southern California.

Spiny lobsters live in coral reefs, rock bottoms, and under kelp, hiding during the day and coming out at night to search for food. They are usually caught commercially in traps with funnel entrances which are baited with dead fish and lowered to the bottom. You can also spear them by wading in shallow water or diving in deeper water and searching for them in their hiding places. They usually give themselves away be revealing the two long antennae. Spiny lobsters should be handled carefully to avoid the sharp spines on the back and antennae. Gloves are recommended when grabbing them, since they kick or flap their tails violently and can cut your hand.

Spiny lobsters are often sold in fish markets for food, but at prices which make them an expensive bait. If you plan to catch your own spiny lobsters check the local laws to find out the seasons, size limits, bag limits, and other regulations governing their capture.

The spiny lobsters can be kept alive in large crates suspended in salt water. The tail is the part usually used for bait, and the hard shell covering is removed leaving the light meat. The head, body section, and legs can be crushed and thrown into the water to attract fish. Spiny lobsters are favored for bonefish, permit, snappers, groupers, grunts, sheepshead, and many other fishes in tropical waters. You can use a whole lobster on a big hook for big grouper or jewfish.

## COMMON LOBSTER

The common or American lobster (*Homarus americanus*) is known to almost everyone as a popular seafood. It also makes a good bait for many saltwater fishes, but because of its popularity as food and its high price, it is rarely used now. At one time, back in the 1800's when lobsters sold for a penny apiece, lobster tails were used for striped bass. They can still be used for striped bass, cod, blackfish or tautog, and many other saltwater fishes. But unless they can be caught or obtained cheaply, they are rarely used for this purpose today.

Catching lobsters in large numbers requires considerable equipment in the way of a boat, lobster pots, buoys and ropes, and bait. A few lobsters can sometimes be taken in shallow water by diving. Lobsters are found from Labrador to North Carolina along the Atlantic Coast, but they are most numerous in New England, especially Maine, and in Canadian waters.

Fewer lobsters are caught now in a given area than in the past, but the demand for them increases, so they bring fancy prices on the market and in restaurants. To maintain the lobster fishery, the spawning females are protected, size limits have been established, and artificial propogation is carried on at a few hatcheries. Also, special licenses or permits are needed to fish for them in some areas. Thus it is doubtful whether lobsters will ever become so numerous again that they will be widely used for bait.

# CHAPTER  15

# SALTWATER BAIT FISHES

*T he bait fishes found in salt water are numerous both in numbers* and species and are favorite foods with most game fishes. They range in size from 2 or 3 inches to 2 feet or more and a weight of several pounds. They are found in the open ocean, often many miles offshore, as well as in the surf, bays, inlets, rivers, and even fresh water. They are generally found in schools ranging from a few individuals to hundreds of thousands. These minnows of the sea seem to spend their entire lives battling the waves, tides, currents, and storms and fleeing or hiding from birds and larger fishes.

## CATCHING, KEEPING, AND PRESERVING

Before we take up the individual bait fish themselves, perhaps it would be best to discuss general methods of obtaining and keeping these fish. The most efficient and quickest method of obtaining bait fish in large numbers is usually by means of a seine. Small seines of 4 to 6 feet in length can be handled by one person, but longer ones require two or more men. In shallow water, seines can be hauled by wading, but in deeper water one or two boats are needed. The general procedure is to start some distance away from shore and to draw the seine toward land, forming a half-circle so that the two ends of the seine touch land and cut off the escape of the bait fish. Another way is to anchor one end on shore and swing the other end around until it touches land, then pulling the seine toward shore.

Of course, in order to make a good haul, you should look for schools of bait fish swimming along or milling about. Low tide is a good time to do your seining because the bait fish are more concentrated in a smaller area then. Another good time is at night, when the bait fish hug the shoreline in compact schools to escape the larger game fish. Bait fish also gather under lights at night, so seining around piers, bridges, and shore lights can be productive. But before you do any seining, check your state laws to find out if there are any regulations on the subject. Some states require a permit or specify the length, mesh and width of the seine used.

Another way to obtain bait fish is by means of a "drop" or "umbrella" type of net which is usually square in shape and has lines attached to each corner for lifting. There are many inexpensive types and designs on the market. Or you can make one using wire, cord, and either cheesecloth, mosquito netting, or wire screening. They can be any size from 3 to 10 feet square. The smaller ones are best because they can be worked by hand. The larger ones require supports or pulleys for hauling. There are portable nets on the market which are small and have a collapsible frame.

These drop nets can be lowered to the bottom in shallow water or to a depth of 2 or 3 feet in deeper water where certain kind of bait fish gather. Then soaked bread, crushed clams, mussels, crabs, or ground fish can be dropped above the net and allowed to sink into it. When the bait fish gather and are thick over the net, lift it quickly to catch them. After a while the bait fish will become suspicious and you'll have to wait a while or try a new spot.

Still another way to catch bait fish is by means of traps. These can be bought in tackle stores and come in a variety of shapes, sizes, and materials. They are usually designed for freshwater minnows, but can also be used in salt water for many kinds of bait fishes. They are usually round or rectangular and are made of wire, cloth mesh, or plastic. They have one or more funnel entrances through which the bait fish can enter but find it hard to escape once inside. You can also make your own traps using wire screening or wire mesh formed around a wood or wire frame.

These bait fish traps are baited with bread, crushed clams, mussels or crabs, shredded or ground meat or fish, and similar foods. They are then lowered to the bottom where bait fish are plentiful. In deep water it is a good idea to tie a buoy to the trap so that it can be located. In a swift tidal current or river it may be necessary to weigh down the trap with stones or similar weights so that it isn't carried away or rolled around. The same thing can be done when there is a strong wind or storm, but then the safest policy is to remove the traps from the water.

If you want to catch a large number of bait fish in funnel traps you will generally need more than one or two. For best results these traps should be examined every few hours during the day and removed from the water before dark unless you also want to catch eels. Otherwise the eels will enter your traps during the night and eat up your bait fish.

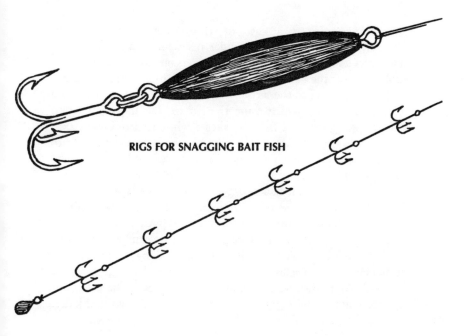

RIGS FOR SNAGGING BAIT FISH

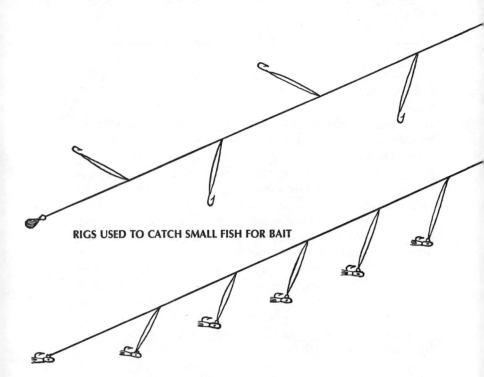

RIGS USED TO CATCH SMALL FISH FOR BAIT

You can also use a "cast" or "throw" net to catch bait fish, especially mullet. This is a circular net which comes in various diameters and is thrown so that it spreads out like a parachute or umbrella over the bait fish. There is a cord attached to the center which can be tied to the wrist. The outer edge of the net is lined with lead weights which cause the net to sink like an inverted cup, trapping the bait fish. It takes a while to acquire the skill needed to use a cast net, but it pays to own such a net and learn how to use it for those days when bait fish cannot be obtained by other means.

Some of the bait fishes, especially the larger specimens, can be caught on hook and line using tiny hooks baited with bits of sea worm, clam, shrimp, or crab. You can quickly make a rig for this by tying a series of short loops on your line and adding a tiny hook on each loop. You can also snag bait fish by casting lures or treble hooks into a school. Here again, a special snagging rig can be made by tying several treble hooks one above the other and adding a sinker or weight on the end. This is cast out and jerked to snag bait fish.

Bait fish in thick schools near shore in shallow water sometimes can be captured with dip nets or by kicking them out of the
water. Bait fish are also washed ashore when chased by fish or
during storms.

Of course, bait fish of various kinds are sold by tackle stores,
boat liveries, commercial fishermen, and bait dealers. But there
are not always bait fish on hand, especially fresh or live ones.
They are sold mostly iced or frozen. So most anglers who want
fresh or live bait fish catch their own.

After the bait fish are caught, transfer them immediately to
a large container of salt water. Small numbers of bait fish can be
kept in minnow buckets or styrofoam coolers. For longer periods
of time the bait fish should be kept in bait cars or a live box,
which can be a big wooden frame box with wire mesh and a
hinged door through which the bait fish can be removed. However, only certain kinds of bait fish can stand prolonged confinement in a bait car. Many are too delicate to tolerate the handling
or confinement and soon die. There are aerators and circulators on
the market which can be used with tanks or containers to provide
fresh water and oxygen for bait fish. If you do not have such a
gadget you can keep bait fish for fairly long periods in big plastic
garbage cans or trash cans. However, the water has to be changed
or fresh water has to be added at regular intervals, and it must be
kept cool to keep the bait fish alive and kicking.

However, for most saltwater fishing bait fish are used dead,
and these can be kept on ice, frozen, or in brine or special solutions. The brine solution should be strong and in an airtight jar
for best results. Bait fish can also be preserved in a solution of 1
percent formalin and 99 percent water. The bait fish should then
be packed in an airtight jar and the solution poured into it. If the
solution starts discoloring it should be spilled out and fresh solution should be added to the jar. This can be done two or three
times or until the solution remains clear. If the bait fish are stiff
you can use less formalin; if they are too soft add a bit more
formalin. From 5 to 10 percent glycerin added to the solution
will help to keep the bait fish flexible. Bait fish preserved in such
solutions are best when used in casting or trolling, where they are
used almost like artificial lures with some action. For bottom
fishing or still-fishing you can't beat fresh bait fish.

**METHODS OF HOOKING BAIT FISH**

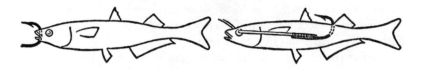

## METHODS OF HOOKING

The basic methods of hooking bait fish are as follows: When still-fishing with live bait fish, run the hook through the back just in front or behind the dorsal fin, being careful not to strike the backbone. Another way is to run the hook through both lips or just the upper lip. The bait fish can also be hooked through the side or belly. When using a dead bait fish you can thread it on a long-shank hook by forcing the point into the mouth and out through the belly. Or you can run the hook through the eyes and then into the body near the tail. A variation of this is to run the hook into the mouth and out of one of the gill openings and then into the body.

Bait fish can also be "sewn" on the hook so that they will have a permanent bend, which will cause them to spin or wobble when pulled through the water. One of the simplest methods is to run your hook into the bait fish's mouth and out the gill opening. Then tie a half hitch around the bait fish's body just back of the head and insert the hook about midway between the dorsal fin and tail. Finally you tighten up on the leader, putting a bend into the minnow, and secure the half hitch. See Chapter 2 on minnows describing and illustrating methods of sewing bait fish on a hook.

But since bait fish vary in structure and there are many kinds of fishing methods in salt water, other ways of hooking are often used. Many of these will be described in the following sections dealing with the individual bait fishes.

188

## MULLET

There are many species of mullets found throughout the world and they are especially numerous in tropical waters. And wherever found, they are a favorite food of the larger saltwater fishes and make good bait. Two species are commonly found in the United States and these are the ones usually used for bait. The striped mullet (*Mugil cephalus*), also called the common mullet and jumping mullet, is one of the most abundant, being found from Cape Cod to Brazil along the Atlantic Coast and from Southern California to Chile along the Pacific Coast. It has a dark blue back, silvery sides, and noticeable dark stripes along the upper part of the body. The white mullet (*Mugil curema*) is also known as the silver mullet and is likewise found from Cape Cod to Brazil, but it is more plentiful along its southern range than the striped mullet. The white mullet looks much like the striped mullet except that its back is more olive-green and it lacks the dark stripes, thus having a more silvery appearance. The striped mullet may reach 2 feet in length and the white mullet 3 feet, but most of those found usually are between 3 inches and a foot long.

Mullet are usually found in bays, sounds, inlets, and rivers, where they feed on the bottom mud and sand, obtaining organic matter from these materials. They usually spend the summer months up north in these protected waters; then in late summer and fall they leave the bays and migrate southward along the coast in large, compact schools. They hug the shoreline closely, swimming through the heaviest surf at times, and can easily be seen by the dark patches and ripples they create on top of the water. They also leap out of the water when frightened or when chased by larger fish.

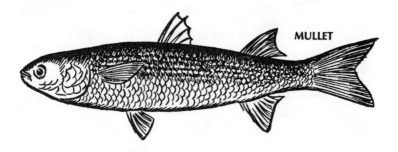

MULLET

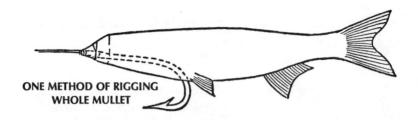

ONE METHOD OF RIGGING
WHOLE MULLET

When migrating in these compact schools they can be caught with seines or cast nets. During these migrations they seem to stop only on dark nights to rest or to escape the larger fish. That is usually the best time to seine them, when they are trapped in a corner of a jetty or when hugging the shoreline.

You can also snag a few mullet by casting a lure or snagging rig with treble hooks into the compact school and reeling or jerking fast and hard. Mullet have also been known to take a tiny hook baited with doughballs or bread or worms in some areas. Mullet can also be bought live or dead from some bait dealers, tackle shops, commercial fishermen, and fish markets.

Mullet usually die quickly unless they can be kept in large tanks or pools with plenty of cool, well-aerated water. Most of them are used live as soon as they are caught or are frozen or kept on ice for future use.

For still-fishing with live mullet, hook them through one or both lips or through the back. Another method, used for tarpon, is to run a flexible wire leader with the hook through the mullet's mouth, with the aid of a needle, and then out near the tail. The bend of the hook ends up at the mullet's mouth. A variation of this is to run the needle with leader into the mullet just back of

SPLIT MULLET BAIT AND METHOD OF HOOKING

190

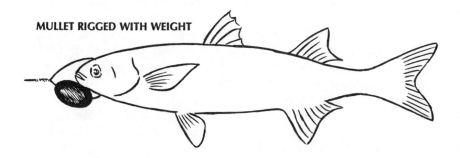

**MULLET RIGGED WITH WEIGHT**

the gill opening to the other side of the backbone. Then the needle is run along the backbone and out near the tail on the opposite side of the mullet from where it entered. Finally the leader is drawn through the bait until the hook shank is buried in the body at the head end of the mullet. Of course, in these methods the mullet soon dies and is used dead.

The mullet can be still-fished on the bottom for tarpon with plenty of slack line coiled on shore or on the bottom of the boat, so that a tarpon can pick up the bait and swallow it without feeling the pull of the line.

Mullet are also rigged whole in trolling for sailfish, tuna, marlin, dolphin, tarpon, and other large game fish. Here the backbone and intestines are usually removed and the hook is sewn in place so that it protrudes from the underside of the mullet and the leader emerges from the mouth. The mouth is sewn tight and lashed around the leader with thread. Other methods call for removing the head and dorsal fins and cutting the front part of the mullet at various angles, depending on the preferences of the captain, guide, or angler. Then the hook is sewn in place so that it protrudes through the underside of the mullet.

To make a mullet stay or swim below the surface of the water when trolling, you can rig it with a sliding or egg-shaped sinker which rests just below its nose. This is especially effective when the water is rough and the weight keeps it just below the surface most of the time. It should swim naturally through the water without spinning. Check the bait in the water near the boat at the trolling speed to see if it is swimming properly.

To rig this weighted mullet you first insert a hook into the belly of the mullet so that the hook eye rests in its mouth. Then

191

slip the sinker on the end of the wire leader and push this end through the head of the bait and through the eye of the hook. Then bend the end of the wire into a small loop and twist it around the wire leader in a haywire twist.

One of the best baits you can use for tarpon and snook is a live mullet. Many anglers and fishing guides spend many hours catching live mullet for these fish. Rather heavy tackle is used because most of the fish run big and the fishing is done near bridges, piers, and piles. A medium weight rod and a 3/0 or 4/0 reel filled with 30- to 50-pound test line is best. A 6- to 10-foot wire leader is attached to the end of the line along with a 5/0 or 6/0 Sobey hook. This hook should be needle-sharp, and when a tarpon takes the bait you should strike hard two or three times to set the hook.

The best-sized mullet to use for tarpon is from 8 to 12 inches in length. They can be somewhat smaller for snook. You can hook the mullet either through both lips or just the upper lip. The mullet can then be allowed to swim out naturally from an anchored or drifting boat where tarpon are seen rolling or known to be present.

If you want to fish the mullet at a certain level or keep it away from the bottom, add a cork, plastic, or styrofoam float a few feet above the bait. This is a good technique for bridge or pier anglers because the tide or wind will take the mullet out to different spots. Live mullet can also be cast toward a school of tarpon seen rolling or feeding on the surface.

Live mullet can also be used to catch roosterfish in the Pacific. Dead mullet can also be used for these fish if allowed to sink and then reeled in slowly with some rod action.

You can also scale the mullet, remove the head and then split the mullet lengthwise along the backbone up to the very end of the tail. The backbone is taken out and the part near the head is rounded off. This provides two split-mullet baits similar to strip baits, and they are used on a safety-pin attachment with a single hook.

These silvery bait fish can also be cut into strips or chunks of varying sizes and used for bottom fishing in the surf or from a boat or pier. Most anglers scale the mullet before cutting it, since the tough scales many lodge against the point of the hook and prevent penetration. Of course, if you get small whole mullet you can use these for bottom fishing without cutting them up.

Besides the fish mentioned above, mullet will also catch striped bass, bluefish, channel bass, weakfish, summer flounder, grouper, snappers, and many other saltwater fishes.

## MENHADEN

The menhaden is a member of the herring family and is a popular bait fish for many saltwater fishes. It is known by many names in various areas, some of which are mossbunker, bunker, razor-belly, fatback, pogy or pogie, bug fish, hardhead, bony fish, greentail, and chebog. It is also called the shad, shiner, herring, and yellowtail, but these confuse it with other fishes with the same names. There are several species of menhaden found in the Atlantic and the Gulf of Mexico, but the most common is *Brevoortia tyrannus,* which is the one usually caught commercially and used for bait. It ranges from Nova Scotia to Brazil, and commercial fishermen catch huge numbers with purse seines to be processed into oil and animal and poultry feeds.

The menhaden is a flat, deep-bodied fish with a fairly broad back and a thin belly. It is a bluish color above, with silvery sides which often have a brassy tinge. The adults have one large dark spot on the shoulder just back of the gill opening and smaller spots scattered along the upper sides. It may reach 18 inches in length, but most of those found run from about 4 to 12 inches in length.

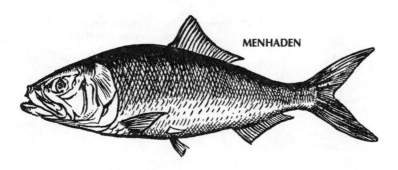

MENHADEN

Menhaden are usually found swimming in compact schools along the Atlantic Coast in bays, sounds, inlets, rivers, and the ocean near shore. North of the Carolinas they are found migrating north in the spring of the year and south in the fall, whereas in more southerly waters they are usually present the year round. The schools of menhaden are usually easy to spot since they mill around in compact groups and create a characteristic ripple on the surface of the water. Or their bodies give the water a brassy tinge. You can often see them jumping out of the water, especially when chased by larger fish.

Since menhaden are found in such compact schools and swim slowly or mill around in circles, they can easily be caught by means of a purse or haul seine. The average angler buys his menhaden from a commercial fisherman or bait dealer, but when they are found close to shore they can be caught in seines or other gear used in catching bait fish or small fish. The menhaden usually die quickly and are preserved by freezing or icing. It is a very oily fish and will soften and spoil quickly. Freshly caught menhaden will stay on a hook fairly well, but when it softens it may have to be tied on with thread.

In recent years more and more anglers seeking striped bass and big bluefish have been catching live menhaden or bunkers, keeping them in well-aerated containers or tanks and using them for these fish. If you see schools of bunker moving on top, you can often snag a few by casting lures into them and then jerking hard to foul-hook one of the bunkers. You can also make up special rigs for this snagging by using a trolling weight weighing an ounce or two and adding a treble hook behind it. Or you can

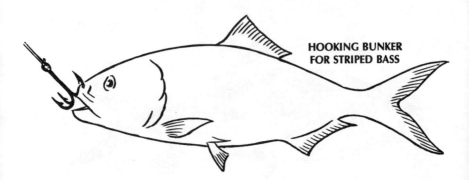

HOOKING BUNKER
FOR STRIPED BASS

**HOOKING BUNKER FOR BLUEFISH**

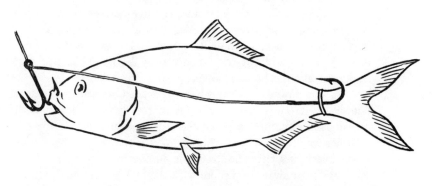

make up a special snagging rig with a sinker or weight on the end and four or five treble hooks spaced a few inches apart on the leader.

Bunkers are difficult to keep alive for any length of time so the minute you hook one, run a hook through the back or lip and let it out right where you snagged it. This means, of course, that you have to locate some stripers or blues not far from the source of your bait. Usually when bunkers are thick or traveling in schools, there are some big stripers or blues under them. Often you can see the big fish break when chasing and feeding on the bunkers.

If you use a single hook of about 6/0 or 7/0, hook the bunker through the back. Or you can use a treble hook in sizes No. 3/0 or 4/0 and hook the bunker in the back just behind the head or through the upper lip. If big bluefish are around, a tandem hook rig with one treble hooking the upper lip of the bunker and another one in the belly is better to hook these fish.

Although spinning outfits can be used to drift the live bunkers, a conventional outfit with revolving spool reel gives you better control of the bait, and also of a big fish after it is hooked. You have to let the bunker out by letting out some line. Usually about 100 feet behind a drifting boat is good. When a striper or blue picks up the bait, the line will move off the reel faster. You have to let out more line to give the fish time to swallow the big bait. This means you have to thumb the spool lightly or leave the click on so that the line comes off smoothly when the fish is moving off with the bunker.

Usually in weak or slack tides the live bunker can be fished with no weight and allowed to swim around near the surface. But in strong currents or when drifting fast, and when the stripers are deep, you can add a 1- or 2-ounce drail between the line and leader to take the bunker down.

A whole bunker can also be used dead. One way is to cast it out or let it out with the tide, then reel it back slowly with occasional rod action to make the bait look alive and crippled. Another way to use a dead whole bunker is to run your boat close to the beach or a jetty and lower the bunker into the water. Then move the boat away from shore with the reel in free spool, allowing line to run off the reel. When you have most of the line off your reel, stop the boat and reel back the bunker slowly along the bottom.

You can also use a dead whole bunker with a 2- to 4-ounce trolling weight ahead of the leader and let this out from a drifting boat so that the bait moves slowly along the bottom. If there is no wind or tide you can troll the dead bunker very slowly with such a rig.

You can also use small whole bunkers bottom fishing or surf fishing for such fish as striped bass, bluefish, channel bass, and weakfish. And you can use a large, dead menhaden for the big game fish such as tuna and sharks. Here you drift the whole bunker out in the tide without any weight or you can add a float several feet above the bait to keep it at a certain depth.

Menhaden can also be scaled and filleted and the meat can be cut into strips or chunks. Or the bunker can be cut crosswise into steaks of any thickness required. The heart of a menhaden can be used for mackerel, and a hairnet filled with ground menhaden and tied around a hook can be used for giant tuna.

Bunkers are also used in chumming for bluefish, mackerel, tuna, sharks, and other saltwater fish. A meat grinder is used to grind the oil bunker and this is dribbled into the water to create a "slick" or chum stream which attracts the fish to the scene. This is a messy job and some bait dealers and commercial fish houses sell menhaden already ground up or frozen in blocks. Menhaden can also be cut up into chunks and the smaller ones can be used whole as chum for the larger game fish.

## ATLANTIC HERRING

The Atlantic or common herring (*Clupea harengus*) is also called the sea herring and Labrador herring. Young herring are canned as "sardines" and are also called whitebait. The herring is one of the most numerous fish found in the North Atlantic, with many millions of pounds taken annually and processed for food. But they have been scarce in some areas in recent years and catches have fallen off. The Atlantic herring is found from Labrador to Cape Hatteras, but is most plentiful north of Cape Cod.

Although the Atlantic herring is a thin fish like most of the members of the herring family, it doesn't have as deep a body as the menhaden, shad, or alewife. Its back is greenish or bluish and the sides are silvery. It grows up to 18 inches in length but most of those caught are not over a foot long.

The herring are found swimming in large schools with the smaller ones hugging the shoreline and the bigger ones venturing

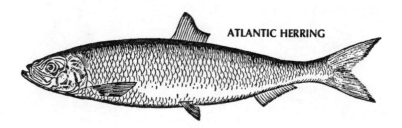

ATLANTIC HERRING

out into deeper water. They are caught commercially in weirs, seines, traps, and dip nets. The larger herring can be taken at times on hook and line with tiny fish baits, cut-fish, or small lures such as flies, spoons, spinners, and jigs. They can also be snagged with various kinds of snagging rigs.

Herring are difficult to keep alive for any length of time unless you have large tanks with fresh salt water circulating through them. They have a soft flesh and must be frozen or kept on ice at all times to prevent them from spoiling.

Likewise, herring are difficult to keep alive on a hook and soon expire, especially if they are caught and kept in a small container. The best way to use them alive is to catch them and then impale them on the hook immediately when they are still lively. Although they can be hooked through the lips or back like other bait fishes, many anglers like to use tiny hooks and run them into the belly.

A whole live herring can be used for striped bass or bluefish by hooking it through the back with a single 6/0 or a 3/0 treble hook and letting it out in a tide or current from shore, a pier, bridge, or a boat. Usually you don't need a weight or sinker, but if the current or tide is strong or you want to get down deep, you can add a light weight ahead of the leader, while drifting in a boat.

A whole dead herring makes a first-rate bait for a giant tuna. A good spot to fish them is near commercial fishermen who are pulling their herring nets. Tuna usually gather here to feed on the herring which fall out of the net. Use a whole big herring on a 10/0 or 12/0 hook. The hook should be buried in the back of the

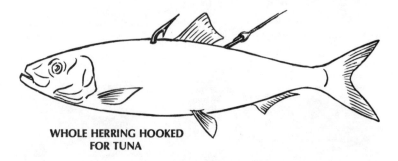

**WHOLE HERRING HOOKED FOR TUNA**

bait, allowing only the point and barb and eye to show. A cork or plastic float can be added anywhere from 15 to 25 feet above the herring. Then let it out near the nets or spots where tuna are showing or feeding.

When trolling for giant tuna you can sew the big hook in the body cavity of the herring, and the hook can be buried entirely or allowed to protrude from the belly. Herring are also used in New England and Canadian waters as teasers for tuna. These "daisy chains" consist of a dozen or so herring tied about a foot apart and trolled behind the boat to attract the big fish. The herring do not have any hooks in them, except the last one, which can be rigged with a big hook.

Herring can also be used as chum for giant tuna, sharks, and other fish. Throw the smaller whole herring out or cut up the big ones into chunks and toss these out. The herring can also be ground up and used like menhaden for chum.

Herring can also be cut into strips and chunks and used for various fish on the bottom. Try them for striped bass, bluefish, weakfish, cod, pollock, haddock, whiting, and other species.

## PACIFIC HERRING

The Pacific herring (*Clupea pallasii*), also called the California herring, is the West Coast relative of the Atlantic herring. It is similar to its relative in general appearance and reaches about the same length of 18 inches. The Pacific herring is found from San Diego north to Alaska in dense schools and is caught in large quantities commercially in nets and seines for food.

Like the Atlantic herring, the Pacific herring is fragile and difficult to keep alive. Most of them are dead when used for bait. But some of them find their way into live bait tanks on party boats and are used as chum when alive.

Most anglers on the Pacific coast use the herring for salmon, and these can be fresh or frozen. The smaller herring from about 3 to 5 inches are rigged whole and are often used behind a big metal spoon or "dodger" which acts as an attractor. Here the needle is .used to draw a leader through the vent of the herring and out the

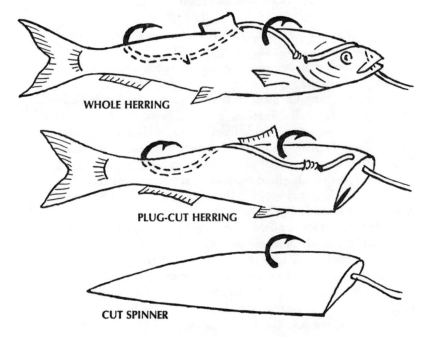

WHOLE HERRING

PLUG-CUT HERRING

CUT SPINNER

mouth. A treble hook is attached to the end of the leader at the vent and the shank is then drawn up into the bait's body. One of the hooks is buried in the bait, leaving two of them exposed. Some anglers also thrust a sliver of wood or a toothpick into the herring's eye, then bend the herring into an arc and force the pick in so that the bend stays in position. The mouth of the herring is also sewn or clipped so that it stays closed. There are also other ways in which the whole herring can be sewn to the hook or hooks giving it a bend which causes it to wobble or revolve in an attractive manner.

The herring can also be "plug-cut" for salmon. Here the head is cut off at an angle slanting from the back to the belly and toward the tail. Then one or two hooks are used to hook the bait, with the leader coming out at the front of the bait where the head was.

You can also cut fillets or strips from the sides of a big herring in the shape of a pennant. The edges of these strips or "spinners," as they are called, are then beveled on the inside meaty part and hooked with a single hook.

Herring can be used for Pacific salmon either by slow trolling or by "mooching" from a drifting boat. Here there is usually a trolling weight or drail added a few feet ahead of the bait. You can use either a spinning rod or conventional rod and try various depths by letting out line and varying the trolling speed of the boat. Usually the silver or coho salmon are just below the surface or only a few feet down. But chinook or king salmon lie and feed deep, often near the bottom, and this is there you have to troll your herring.

Too many anglers using herring bait for Pacific salmon strike these fish too soon or too fast and fail to hook them. When you feel a fish taking the bait, the best procedure is to feed some slack line before trying to set the hook, so that the salmon can swallow the bait.

Besides salmon, Pacific herring can be used for striped bass, white sea bass, black sea bass, halibut, Pacific yellowtail, albacore, tuna, and many other fishes found in those waters.

## PACIFIC SARDINE

The Pacific sardine (*Sardinops caerulea*), also known as the California sardine, Monterey sardine, and pilchard, is an important commercial fish on the West Coast; millions of pounds have been taken each year for canning for food or processing into meal and oil. Large numbers are also used by commercial fishermen and sportsmen for bait. However, they fluctuate between abundance and scarcity, and catches have fallen off during many years.

The Pacific sardine is found from Alaska south to the Gulf of California. Since it belongs to the herring family, it resembles the Pacific herring somewhat except that the sardine has low, raised

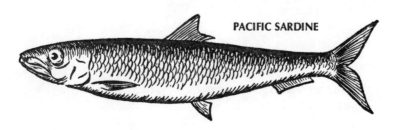

PACIFIC SARDINE

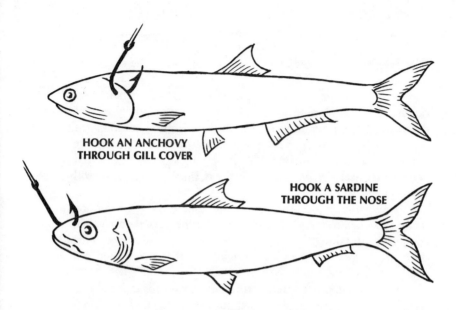

HOOK AN ANCHOVY
THROUGH GILL COVER

HOOK A SARDINE
THROUGH THE NOSE

ridges on the gill cover which the herring lacks. And it doesn't quite reach the length of the Pacific herring, running only to about 14 inches. There are several other species of sardines found in U.S. waters.

Most of the sardines are caught by commercial or sport fishing boats in nets and seines. They are kept alive in large tanks filled with well-aerated water on the live-bait boats and are used for chumming. They are thrown out alive in small quantities, or even only one or two at a time, to bring yellowtail, albacore, or tuna up to the boat. Then a live sardine is hooked through the nose or tail and is cast toward the feeding fish. Live sardines can also be used for barracuda, halibut, bonito, and white sea bass. Dead sardines make good bait for striped bass and the larger ones can be scaled or filleted or cut into chunks for this fish. You can also use strips or chunks of the sardine for bottom fishing for rockfish, lingcod, halibut, and greenling.

### ALEWIFE

The true alewife (*Pomolobus pseudo-harengus*) is also known by many other names, such as branch herring, river herring, wall-

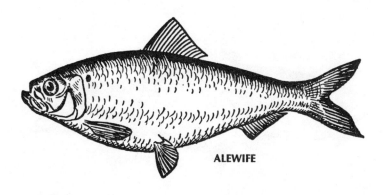

**ALEWIFE**

eyed herring, big-eyed herring, goggle-eye, spring herring, blear-eyed herring, buckie, and Gaspereau. It is found from Canada to the Carolinas, where it ascends rivers and streams to spawn. It reaches about a foot in length and resembles the shad in general appearance and structure. It is caught in large numbers by commercial fishermen for food and can be used as bait for many of the fishes which feed on the other herrings.

Alewives start making their spawning runs up brooks during April and in May in New England waters. They can be caught with dip nets in narrow brooks. In larger rivers and lakes they can be snagged with lures or treble hook snagging rigs. After you have a live alewife, hook it with a single No. 5/0 hook or a 3/0 treble hook through the back just ahead of the dorsal fin. Then cast it out and allow it to swim around. In a canal or river you can follow the bait downstream by walking along the shore as the current sweeps it along. When a striped bass or other fish grabs it, give some slack line so that it can swallow the bait.

## GLUT HERRING

The glut herring (*Pomolobus aestivalis*), also known as the blueback, summer herring, May herring, school herring, black-belly, sawbelly, and kyach, is related to the alewife, which it resembles closely. It is found from Nova Scotia to Florida but is most common from Chesapeake Bay south. It also ascends streams to spawn but does not venture into fresh water as the

203

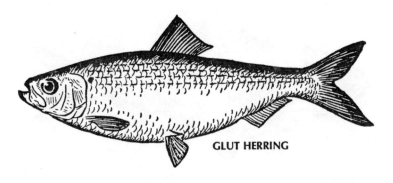

**GLUT HERRING**

alewife does. It reaches about a foot in length and can be caught
and used in much the same way as the other herrings for many of
the same fishes.

## HICKORY SHAD

The hickory shad (*Pomolobus mediocris*), also known as the
shad herring, fall herring, and tailor herring, is another species
which resembles the alewife, glut herring, shad, and other herrings. However, it reaches a larger size than the alewife or glut
herring, but not as large as the true shad. Some hickory shad
reach 2 feet and almost 3 pounds. It also has a lower jaw which
protrudes more than in the other herrings. It is a more active fish
than the other herrings and feeds on larger foods, often chasing
small bait fish. Therefore it can often be caught on hook and line
with artificial lures. The smaller ones can be used whole, and the
larger ones are cut up into sections or strips for many saltwater
fishes.

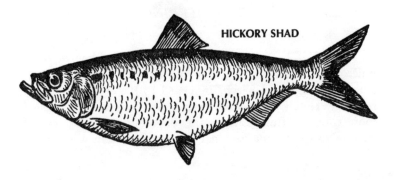

**HICKORY SHAD**

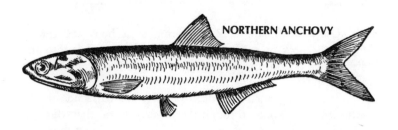

NORTHERN ANCHOVY

## ANCHOVIES

The anchovies are another large group of bait fishes which resemble the herring somewhat in the compressed body shape and delicate flesh. Along the Pacific Coast two species are usually caught and used for bait. One is the northern anchovy (*Engraulis mordax*), also known as the California anchovy. It is found from British Columbia to Lower California and reaches about 7 inches in length. There are also two subspecies of this anchovy found in California waters. Another anchovy found in the Pacific is the deep-bodied anchovy (*Anchoa compressa*), also known as the sprat, which reaches about 6 inches and is found from Point Conception south to Lower California. As its name implies, it has a much deeper body than the northern anchovy.

The anchovies are widely used as bait in the Pacific waters and several million pounds a year may be caught for this purpose. They are used for chumming and bait on commercial and sport fishing boats. Many of the methods used in hooking sardines and herring can be used with anchovies.

Live bait or party boats and private boats use the anchovies as chum to attract albacore, yellowtail, and tuna up to the boat. In the beginning you should throw quite a few of these live bait fish out into the water. The game fish will spot them and will start "boiling" some distance from the boat. Then gradually decrease the number of live anchovies you toss out as the fish work their way closer to the boat. Finally, throw just one anchovy at a time, but steadily without a break. This will tease and hold the fish close to the boat, where you can cast a live anchovy on a hook toward the waiting fish.

Choose the livelier "greenback" rather than the dying "blackback" anchovy from the bait tank. It will last longer on the hook. Use a small No. 4, 2, or 1 tuna-style hook and run in through the neck or nose of the anchovy. Then cast it into any boils you see or into the spot where albacore, yellowtail, or tuna are feeding.

When using anchovies dead or alive for barracuda in the Pacific, run a 2/0 hook through the lower jaw and then through the head of the bait. A light sinker is added about 3 feet above the hook and then this rig is cast out and allowed to settle to the bottom, after which it is a slowly retrieved toward the surface.

Whole dead anchovies can also be trolled for Pacific salmon. The bait is rigged with a sharp bend in its body so that when it moves through the water it wobbles and darts from side to side. There are also clear plastic bait heads with a diving lip which can be used. You push the anchovy into this plastic head, where it is held in place with a straight pin.

Small whole anchovies or bigger ones can be cut up and put on a hook and used for such fish as halibut, lingcod, sculpin, greenling, and rockfish.

## PILCHARD

The pilchards are the "herrings" and "sardines" of southern waters, since they closely resemble these fish in appearance, shape, and habits. The one usually found in Florida, Bermuda, and the West Indies is the *Harengula sardina*, which is the most abundant and used most often for bait. The hard-scaled pilchard is another somewhat smaller species which is not as plentiful.

Like most herrings or sardines, pilchards are bright, silvery fishes with large scales which are easily removed or lost. The back is a greenish blue-gray and the body is deep. The eye is big for a fish which only average from 3 to 6 inches in length. It may reach 8 inches, but the smaller sizes are more common.

Pilchards can be found swimming in small, compact schools offshore and inshore. They are especially plentiful around such structures as jetties and breakwaters, piers, bridges, and docks. In deeper offshore waters they are often chased by various game fish and form a compact "ball," especially when surrounded by sailfish. Then they are easily caught in a net or seined in large quantities. Or you can cast a lure or treble hooks with a weight and snag or foul-hook a few for bait.

Pier and bridge anglers use so-called "pilchard rings" to catch these bait fish below these structures. You can buy these rings on many piers or in tackle shops, or you can make your own from fine stainless steel leader wire. The rings are strung in chain fashion so they interlock and then a sinker or weight is added to the end. This ring is lowered into the water where pilchards are thick, or you can chum a spot with soaked bread to attract them. They dart around after the bread and get caught in the rings like in a gill net.

You can also catch pilchards with dip nets or umbrella type nets lowered into the water under them. Here too, it helps to drop some bread or other food over the net to draw the small fish into it. And pilchards will also bite on plain, tiny gold- or silver-plated hooks, or the same hooks can be baited with bits of shrimp or tiny slivers of fish.

Like most of the herring family, pilchards are very delicate and require immediate using if you want them alive. They can be kept alive in bait cars, live wells, or big tanks with well-aerated water. Many fishing piers and boats have such live wells where the pilchards can be kept and used on a hook alive.

Used alive and hooked through the back or nose, they make good bait for Spanish mackerel, cero mackerel, king mackerel, snook, sea trout, barracuda, and even sailfish if the pilchards are fairly large in size. You can also use pilchards plain or on a jig or other lure from a drifting boat at various depths. Or you can use a bottom rig with a whole pilchard or a piece of one for many different kinds of saltwater fish found in southern waters.

## KILLIFISHES

The killifishes, of which there are many species, are a favorite bait with saltwater anglers. The one usually used along the Atlantic Coast is the common killifish (*Fundulus heteroclitus*), also called the hardhead, mummichog, mummy, mud minnow, and

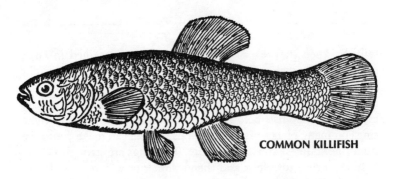

**COMMON KILLIFISH**

mud dabber. It is found from Labrador to northern Florida. Another closely related form (*Fundulus grandis*) is found from Florida to Texas. Both are easily recognized by the rugged body with single dorsal fin on the back near the rounded tail. They are a drab, olive-green color with yellowish or whitish bellies. Some specimens have light, narrow vertical bars or small spots along the sides. They reach up to 5 or 6 inches in length. The killifishes are plentiful in most saltwater bays, tidal creeks, and rivers right up to fresh water, especially over mud bottoms where there are plenty of weeds. They are very gregarious and are usually found in schools and can be caught in large numbers with seines, umbrella type nets, or in minnow traps baited with crushed clams, mussels, crabs, or bread.

The killifishes are very hardy bait fish which will live out of the water and on the hook for a long time. They can be kept in damp seaweed for hours on a cool day. On hot days the container should be kept on ice or the killies should be kept in a minnow bucket or other container filled with salt or fresh water. Unlike other saltwater bait fishes, which cannot stand the change from salt to fresh water, killies can be kept in fresh water almost indefi-

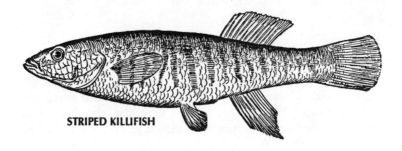

**STRIPED KILLIFISH**

nitely. But for best results, if you want to keep them a long time put them in a large bait box or car floated or submerged in salt water.

The killifishes can be used for many saltwater fishes such as striped bass, weakfish, bluefish, and sea bass. They are especially popular for the summer flounder or fluke, and when these fish are running, most of the bait dealers and boat liveries in New England, New York, and New Jersey carry the killies for bait.

Another killifish sometimes used for bait is the striped killifish (*Fundulus majalis*), also known as the Mayfish, bull minnow, and bass killy. It is often found in the same waters as the common killifish, but it differs quite a bit in appearance and can easily be recognized. It is lighter in color, has a longer, more pointed snout, slimmer body, and dark vertical or longitudinal stripes along the sides. It also reaches a larger size, with a maximum length of 8 inches. The dark stripes along its sides sometimes cause this bait fish to be mistaken for a young striped bass by anglers who catch them in their seines or traps. It is considered inferior as a bait fish to the common killifish.

Still another killifish used for bait is the broad killifish (*Cyprinodon variegatus*), also called the sheepshead minnow. It is found from Cape Cod to Florida and has a much broader body than the common killifish. It rarely grows more than 3 inches long.

## SILVERSIDES

The silversides are often called saltwater minnows since they are very numerous in numbers and form an important food supply for many marine game fishes. There are many species found along the Atlantic Coast and the Gulf Coast but one of the most abundant is the common silverside (*Menidia menidia*), which is found from Maine to the Carolinas. It is also called the spearing, sperling, friar, sand smelt, white bait, and shiner, but the last two names are also applied to other bait fishes. Along the Pacific Coast the grunion (*Leuresthes tenuis*), the jack smelt (*Atherinopsis californiensis*), and the top smelt are also members of the silverside family.

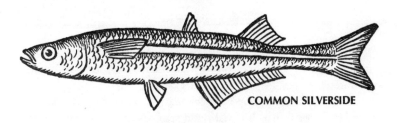

COMMON SILVERSIDE

The silversides are easily recognized by their pale green color and the silvery bands running along both sides of their bodies. The common silversides may reach 5 or 6 inches in length but most of those found run from about 2 to 4 inches. They are present most of the year in some waters such as bays, tidal rivers and creeks, and the surf, but are most numerous during the late summer, fall, and early winter. They can easily be caught in seines, drop nets, or minnow traps, especially at night. The larger specimens sometimes appear in the fish markets, since they make good eating. Silversides make good bait for many saltwater fishes, but they are rather delicate and die quickly in confinement or on a hook. So they are used mostly dead and can be bought fresh or frozen in small packages. They can be used for striped bass, bluefish, weakfish, mackerel, bonito, false albacore, summer flounder or fluke, sea bass, cod, and silver hake or whiting.

## SMELTS

The smelts, of which there are many species along both the Atlantic and Pacific Coasts, often make a good bait for a wide variety of saltwater fishes. The American smelt (*Osmerus mordax*), also called the ice fish and frost fish, is the most common variety along the Atlantic Coast and is found from the Gulf of St. Lawrence to Virginia. It lives mostly in tidal creeks, rivers, and bays and goes up to fresh water to spawn. It is also found landlocked in freshwater lakes. It reaches a foot in length but most of them range between 6 and 10 inches. It is a popular food fish and is sold in fish markets. When numerous it can be caught with dip nets and will often bite on a hook and line covered with bits of fish, sea worms, or grass shrimp. It is often caught through the ice in freshwater lakes. Smelt can be used for such fish as cod, summer flounder or fluke, and other saltwater species.

Another member of the smelt family includes the capelin (*Mallotus villosus*), found in Arctic waters and sometimes ranging as far south as Cape Cod; this can be used as bait for cod, haddock, pollock, and halibut in northern waters. Then there is the candlefish or Eulachon (*Thaleichthys pacificus*) and the surf smelt (*Hypomesus pretiosus*), which are found along the Pacific Coast. Also, the several members of the smelt family known as whitebait are found along the Pacific Coast. These Pacific smelts are used for many fishes such as salmon, white sea bass, barracuda, yellowtail, albacore, the bonitos, and the smaller tuna.

## SAND LAUNCE

The sand launces, known as sand eels, are an important item of food for many saltwater game fish, and they make good bait fish. They look like miniature eels and are found in huge numbers both in North Atlantic and North Pacific waters. But they usually reach less than a foot in length and they have a forked tail which the common eel lacks. Along the Atlantic Coast the common sand launce (*Ammodytes americanus*), which ranges from Labrador to Hatteras, is the species usually caught and used for bait, and to a certain extent for food if big enough. Sand eels prefer sandy bottoms where they have the habit of burying themselves 5 or 6 inches in the sand. Along the surf they are sometimes left in the damp sand above low-water mark and can be dug up with shovels, forks, or clam rakes. Other times the sand eels can be found in large, compact schools swimming slowly and milling around over shallow and deep waters. Then they can best be taken in drop nets or seines. Sand eels are very abundant during the late fall and early winter and during storms; they are often washed up high and dry on the beaches or are chased there by larger fishes.

Sand eels are fairly hardy bait fish and can usually be kept alive in damp seaweed for a few hours or so in cool weather. They are also a tough bait and stay on the hook well. A whole sand eel

**SAND LAUNCE**

can be hooked through the eyes and then the hook can be imbedded in the body near the tail. The larger ones can be cut in half for the smaller fishes. Sand eels can be used for striped bass, bluefish, weakfish, mackerel, and summer flounder or fluke. They are also very popular as bait for silver hake or whiting. And you can use them for cod, haddock, or pollock. For these you can put three or four of the sand eels on one hook. Many saltwater anglers also find them effective when trolled behind a spinner for such fish as striped bass, weakfish, and bluefish.

This chapter includes most of the smaller bait fish commonly used for bait in salt waters. But there are many others which the angler will come across, and these can be tried for bait. Any small fish a few inches long can usually be used for bait with good results in saltwater fishing.

# CHAPTER 16

# COMMON EEL

*The common eel* (Anguilla rostrata), *also called the American* eel and freshwater eel, is a favorite bait fish with many saltwater anglers for such fish as striped bass and bluefish. The common eel is found from Labrador to Brazil and is most numerous in the bays, sounds, tidal creeks, rivers, and rocky shores, and in freshwater rivers, ponds, and lakes. It is easily recognized by its snakelike shape. The eels vary greatly in body color, being gray, olive, brown, or blackish along the back, and yellow, white, or silvery along the belly. The females reach up to 4 feet in length, but the males reach only about half that size.

The common eel has an interesting life history which has been fully understood only since the early part of this century. It was discovered that they spawn in the ocean, southwest of Bermuda in the depths. After the young eels hatch it takes a year before they reach the coast and enter the bays and rivers. The female eels enter rivers and head upstream, spending most of their lives in fresh water. The males remain in salt water and brackish water of rivers and bays. The eels live there for several years until they mature, and then in the autumn the females make their way down the rivers to the sea, where they meet the males and migrate to their spawning ground to repeat the cycle.

Although both the female and male eels can be used for bait, most of those usually taken for this purpose are the smaller saltwater males. They can be caught by many methods, but the eel pot is the favorite and usually the most dependable way to get

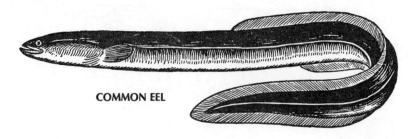

COMMON EEL

them when needed. These are similar to the minnow traps with funnel entrances, although the eel pots usually have wider openings to permit the larger, eating-size eels to enter. But for most bait purposes the regular wire-caged minnow traps or eel pots with small openings will work fine. These can be bought or constructed from wire mesh around a heavy metal or wood frame.

Eel pots can be placed on the bottom of saltwater bays, sounds, tidal creeks, or other bodies of water where eels are present. They should be set in the daytime or just before dark and examined the following morning. They can be baited with meat, dead fish, crushed crabs, clams, and mussels. Or you can place some bread in the trap; this will attract the smaller bait fishes, which in turn will attract the eels. If the eel pots are set among weeds or in deep or muddy water, they should have a small buoy attached so that they can be located. The majority of the eels caught in the eel pots can be used for bait; however the really tiny ones can be released, and the very large ones can be skinned for their skins and the meat can be eaten.

Eels can also be caught on hook and line with small long-shanked hooks baited with pieces of fish, sea worms, shedder crab, or clam. However, this is usually a slow process unless many lines are put out, and most of this fishing is done at night. Further, too many eels caught on hook and line will be too big for bait.

You can also catch eels by "bobbing." A dozen or so sandworms or bloodworms are threaded and strung on fine linen or silk thread and rolled into a ball. The whole mess is lowered to the bottom on a string, and when the eels bite into it they can be lifted out of the water and into a waiting net or bushel basket or pail.

214

When eels are numerous they can also be caught in seines. Or they can be speared at night, using a spear with several prongs and a strong flashlight to spot them on the bottom. Finally, eels can often be bought in fish markets or from fishing tackle and bait dealers.

The common eels are very hardy creatures and will live out of the water for a long time in cool weather. They can be kept in damp seaweed if you plan to use them soon. For longer periods either tanks with running fresh or salt water or wire cages or bait cars suspended in salt water will enable you to have eels on hand whenever you need them.

The live eel is one of the deadliest baits you can use for big striped bass and bluefish. Use anywhere from a 5/0 to 8/0 claw-type or O'Shaughnessy hook. And instead of attaching it directly to the line or leader, you first add a snap-swivel on the end of the line and put the hook on it. Then when the eel twists and turns, it is less apt to tangle up your line.

There are several ways to hook an eel. Some anglers run the hook through both lips. This works fine if you run the barb and point well away from the tip of the nose or snout. Otherwise the eel will twist and break its own jaws and escape. You can also run the hook through the lower jaw well back from the lips. Another way is to run the hook into the mouth and out through the side of the jaw. Some anglers also run the hook through both eyes. And still other anglers fishing in Chesapeake Bay for cobia hook the eel through the tail.

For striped bass, live eels work best at night and from a drifting or anchored boat. You can cast the eel out about 20 or 30

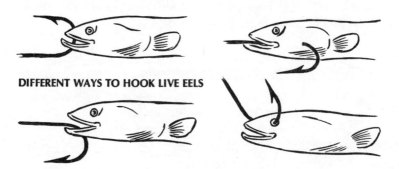

**DIFFERENT WAYS TO HOOK LIVE EELS**

feet from the side of the boat and let the bait head for the bottom with plenty of free line. But keep feeling the eel on the end all the time. The second it gets hung up or tries to hide in the weeds or rocks, raise your rod tip to make it clear the bottom.If you feel the eel quivering or moving away, or if the line starts to slip out fast, it usually indicates a striper is after the bait or already has it. Stripers usually don't fool around with eels—they grab them quickly, move off, and swallow them. But it pays to wait until the fish moves for a few seconds before setting the hook.

You can also cast a live eel from a boat toward the beach, shore, or rocks or jetties and then reel it back very slowly. The same thing can be done when surf fishing from beaches, rocky shores, or jetties. Here you don't have to reel it back immediately, but let it swim around. When fishing in a tidal river, inlet, or a strong tide or rip, you can let out line so that the eel moves a good distance out. Then you can reel it back in slowly against the current and repeat. Most of this fishing is done without any float or weight on the line. But if you are fishing very shallow waters with rocky bottoms or weeds or want to control the depth at which the eel swims, you can add a float or bobber a few feet above the eel.

Live eels can also be trolled slowly close to the bottom using weighted or wire lines. Or you can fish them on the bottom using a sinker to keep them down deep. However, they tend to tangle up the line and rig when fished this way and most anglers would rather use them without a bottom rig or sinker.

You can also try using live eels when fishing offshore in deep water. They make good baits for sharks, tuna, dolphin, marlin, and other fishes. Here you merely let them out from a drifting boat and let them swim at various depths.

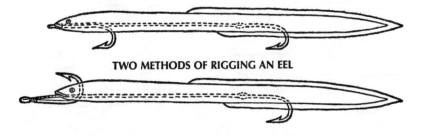

TWO METHODS OF RIGGING AN EEL

**Wire Runs Through Jaws and Eye of the Hook**

### RIGGING EEL FOR OFFSHORE TROLLING

One of the most popular ways to use the eel is to rig it with one or two hooks and cast it out, then retrieve it or troll it through the water to give it some action. Each angler has his own pet method of rigging a whole eel. Long needles are used to pull the line, wire, or light chain to which the hooks are attached through the body of the eel. When two hooks are used the front hook usually emerges at the head or neck of the eel, while the other hook comes out near the vent or a few inches from the tip of the tail. In most methods the hooks emerge on the underside of the eel, but in one method the hook comes out on top of the head. In still other methods small metal squids or metal action heads are attached to the front of the eel to provide action and weight. Or the head of the eel is removed and the skin is pulled back and a lead weight inserted to create an eel-bob. The size of the whole eels used will usually range from small "shoestring" eels measuring 7 or 8 inches, up to big 18 or 20 inchers.

Big rigged eels are also trolled offshore for such fish as white marlin, blue marlin, tuna, and swordfish. Here they are usually rigged with one big hook and trolled on top of the water fast enough so that they stay there and the tail slaps the water in a lively attractive manner.

The skin of the common eel is also used on various eelskin lures for casting or trolling. Most of these are usually a heavy metal tube, ring, or weight with a hole. The skin is tied around a groove on the head, permitting the incoming water to inflate the skin when it is cast or trolled. Eelskin can also be draped over a metal squid or attached to one by means of a ring. You can also cover a big plug with an eelskin after first removing the hooks and then replacing them.

Whole eels or eelskins that have been rigged can be kept for future use in large jars with heavy salt brine. The eelskins will keep for a long time in such salt preparations; however, the whole

217

eels tend to get hard, and then when they are removed and used they tend to become soft and soon fall apart. Although such preserved eels will usually catch as many fish as a fresh eel, many anglers like to rig eels that have been recently killed because they are tougher and last longer.

# CHAPTER 17

# OTHER SALTWATER BAIT FISHES

*T his chapter will include many of the larger bait fishes and small* fishes used for bait, as well as those which were not covered in the previous chapters. Many of these bait fishes are used for such offshore fish as swordfish, the marlins, tuna, sailfish, and shark, so they often run to a good size. Catching and preparing these baits take up a great deal of time, but it is a chore that cannot be avoided if you want to have a successful fishing trip.

## PREPARING WHOLE, STRIP, AND CUT BAITS

Most offshore anglers do not prepare their own baits since that is the job of the captain or mate on the boat that is chartered for this fishing. And since the art of rigging and preparing these baits requires considerable practice, most anglers are content to depend on the fishing guides for their rigged baits. Also, each fishing area has different methods for preparing and rigging baits, depending on the prevailing conditions, and it is always best to follow the advice of the local fishing guides.

However, for the angler who must prepare his own baits, a description of the methods commonly used may be helpful. A whole bait must be prepared so that it swims naturally and doesn't revolve when trolled through the water. In order to give the baits more action, the backbone in the bait fish is often broken in several places or is removed entirely. The instrument

219

THREE METHODS OF RIGGING WHOLE BAIT FISH

for removing the backbone consists of a copper, brass, or stainless steel tube with one end sharpened. This is pushed over the backbone, cutting it free from the rib bones. Then a wooden plunger is driven into the tubing to clean out the backbone left inside: Such "deboners" can be bought in most coastal fishing tackle shops.

The simplest and quickest way to prepare a whole bait fish is to run the hook through the nose with the point facing either up or down. But this method has its drawbacks, since it fails to hold the bait securely and is easily knocked off the hook by a fish or the resistance of the water rushing against the bait. However, it can be reinforced by tying the hook in with line.

One of the commonest methods of rigging is to insert the hook through the gills and then force it out through the belly. The hook is then sewn in place and in most cases the mouth and gill openings are also sewn up. In some baits a bridle is tied from the bait's mouth to the leader wire to keep it riding naturally. The hook can also be placed so that it emerges from the side or back of the bait.

A whole bait fish can also be slit open, the intestines and often the backbone removed, and the hook placed inside. The leader attached to the hook runs out through the mouth, and then belly and gills and mouth are sewn up. Here the hook can protrude from the belly or be buried entirely inside the stomach cavity.

Still another method of rigging a whole fish is to tie the hook ahead of the bait with a length of wire chain or line as a connection between the mouth of the bait fish and the bend of the hook. Here the bait fish trails a couple of inches or so behind the hook.

220

**TWO-HOOK RIG USED WITH WHOLE FISH FOR SHARKS**

There are many other methods used to rig whole fish, and some of these will be described in the sections dealing with the individual bait fishes.

Strip baits cut from the sides and bellies of various fishes such as bonito, albacore, dolphin, and mackerels are widely used in offshore trolling. They have various lengths, shapes, and thicknesses, depending on the bait fish used, the fish sought, the area fished, or just the preference of the fishing guide, captain, or angler. Most of these fish strips run from about 8 to 14 inches in length and from an inch to 2 or 3 inches at the widest part. Both ends taper to somewhat of a point, with the front or middle of the strip usually being the widest part. The strips range from 1/8 to 1/2 inch in thickness at the center and are thinned or beveled along the edges. Then the strip is impaled on a hook which is attached to a wire leader with a safty pin catch holding the front part of the strip. This front part of the strip can also be tied on to the leader with twine to hold it more securely.

**STRIP BAIT ON SAFETY PIN CATCH RIG**

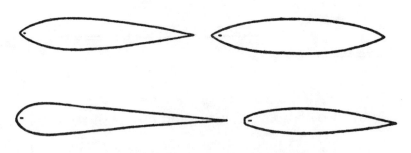

**SOME SHAPES USED IN CUTTING STRIP BAITS**

Other strip baits are made by cutting a wider portion from the belly of a fish, folding the strip, and placing a hook between the folds. Then the strip is sewn along its entire length. A variation of this method is to cut two identical strips, place the hook between them, and sew around the edges, making a single bait. In both of these methods the fleshy part of the strips is hidden on the inside and the skin is on the outside.

Some of the larger bait fishes can also be filleted or cut into steaks or chunks and used for many fish. Still others are used whole dead, while others are used alive. These will be covered in more detail in the sections dealing with specific bait fishes.

Although frozen or iced bait fish can be used in an emergency to provide baits and strips, they are not nearly as good as freshly caught bait fish prepared on the spot and used immediately for fishing. However, since fresh bait is not always available, many anglers prepare their baits or strips in advance and keep them frozen or on ice until used. But freshly caught bait fish last the longest and usually make the most effective baits.

## USING STRIP BAITS

Strip baits can be trolled on flat lines or on outriggers, and they should be moved fast enough so that they stay on the surface of the water most of the time. They are very good for dolphin and should be trolled about 5 or 6 knots behind the boat. Troll along weedlines, near weed patches, driftwood, boxes, and any other floating objects. Strip baits are also good for white marlin and sailfish.

You can also troll the strip baits underwater for many fish. Here you can use a two-hook rig to hold the strip and add a feather lure or plastic skirt ahead of the strip to keep it swimming below the surface. Such strips are especilly effective for Allison or yellowtail tuna and wahoo.

## ATLANTIC MACKEREL

The Atlantic mackerel (*Scomber scombrus*), also called the common mackerel, is known to almost everyone as popular food fish and to saltwater anglers as a fine game fish and bait fish. It is easily recognized by its streamlined shape, blue or greenish back, and irregular dark bars. It averages about a foot in length and a pound in weight, but may reach almost 2 feet and a weight of several pounds.

Another species of mackerel, the chub mackerel (*Pneumatophorus colias*), is found in many of the same waters as the Atlantic mackerel and resembles it very closely, but it is not numerous and rarely reaches more than 14 inches in length.

The Atlantic mackerel ranges from Labrador to the Carolinas with seasonal migrations of vast schools of fish. They spend the winter in deeper, more southerly waters and the spring and summer in shallower, colder, more northerly waters along their range. They are most plentiful in New England, especially Maine, and in Canada during the summer months. Generally the smaller mackerel are found closer to shore than the larger specimens.

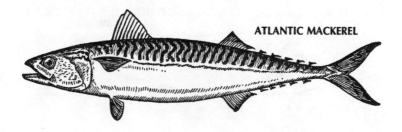

ATLANTIC MACKEREL

The Atlantic mackerel are taken in huge numbers by commercial fishermen using purse seines, gill nets, and traps. Sports fishermen also catch many on rod and reel, for food and bait. They can be chummed to a boat with ground menhaden or bunker and will strike pieces of fish or artificial lures such as spoons, flies, diamond jigs, and metal squids. A rig with a diamond jig on the end and three or four plastic tube lures above it will take them two and three at a time when they are thick. You can also buy mackerel from commercial fishermen, fish markets, or bait dealers.

Mackerel can be kept alive for quite a while in large tanks or bait cars where there is plenty of fresh seawater circulating. They are used dead most of the time, however, and can be kept on ice or be frozen until used. They turn soft quickly, and they stay on the hook best if used soon after they are caught.

Live mackerel make a very good bait for big striped bass or bluefish. Those up to a foot or slightly more in length are best for this. The mackerel are usually hooked through the back with a single No. 5/0 to 7/0 hook. Or you can use a small treble hook in sizes No. 3/0 or 4/0 instead of the single hook. Some anglers like to use a double hook, with one hook going through the mackerel's back and the other hook swinging free. For bluefish the two hooks can be separated by a few inches of wire leader, and one hook can go into the mackerel's back near the head and the other one near the tail.

Light lines are best when fishing with live mackerel since the bait swims more naturally and isn't hampered in any way; many anglers use spinning rods and reels filled with 15- or 20-pound test lines. But here again—handling the live bait, controlling big fish, and working around obstructions, other

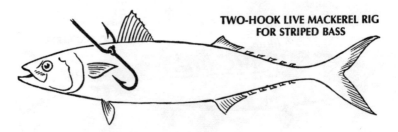

**TWO-HOOK LIVE MACKEREL RIG FOR STRIPED BASS**

boats, and similar hazards make many anglers turn to conventional revolving spool reels. These can be used with the shorter conventional surf rods and 30-pound test lines.

Mackerel are fished from drifting or anchored boats and are usually fished on a free line without any float or weight. However, you can add a float or bobber a few feet above the bait, if you want. And when fishing in channels or strong tides or when you want to get the bait deep, you can add a light egg or oval sinker a few feet above the bait. When a striped bass grabs the mackerel, let it run with the bait for at least 20 seconds. Then reel in the slack line and set the hook.

Live mackerel or dead ones can also be used for tuna, billfish, sharks, and other fish offshore. Here chumming with ground bunker is usually done to bring the fish up to the boat. Then you drift a live or dead mackerel out in the slick. To get the mackerel deep you can use a free line, but if you want to control the depth you can add a cork or plastic float above the bait.

Small, live "tinker" mackerel have also been used successfully to catch school tuna in recent years. These mackerel run from 6 to 10 inches in length and are kept alive in bait wells until used. Then they are hooked on small "albacore" or "tuna" style hooks through the back. Here, too, chumming with ground bunker is first done to bring the school tuna near the boat. Then the mackerel is lowered into this slick and allowed to swim around freely. To keep mackerel below the surface in a strong tide or current, you can add a light clamp-on or clincher sinker or a couple of split-shot sinkers on the leader a few feet above the hook.

Big, whole, dead mackerel are also rigged with one or two hooks and are trolled or presented to giant tuna, white and blue marlin, swordfish, and sharks. Several mackerel are also trolled slowly in "daisy chain" fashion with only one of them, usually the last one, containing a hook.

And finally you can use a small, dead whole mackerel or cut a big one up into chunks or strips and use it for various fish such as striped bass, bluefish, weakfish, pollock, cod, whiting, fluke, and sea bass.

## PACIFIC MACKEREL

The Pacific mackerel (*Pneumatophorus diego*), which resembles the Atlantic mackerel somewhat but is a closer relative to the chub mackerel, is an important food fish which is also used for bait. It ranges from Alaska to Lower California but is not common north of San Francisco. It reaches up to 2 feet in length and a weight of several pounds, but most are under 18 inches long.

Pacific mackerel are caught in purse seines, dip or scoop nets, gill nets, haul nets, and on hook and line. They are caught by anglers on sea worms, clams, fish bait, and lures such as flies, spoons, and metal squids.

A whole live mackerel makes an excellent bait for such fish as black sea bass, white sea bass, yellowtail, striped marlin, and sharks. Those from 10 to 14 inches are best for these fish. You can also troll a dead mackerel for the striped marlin, or fish with a dead one for the fish mentioned above. And a whole mackerel can be rigged with one or two hooks and presented to swordfish.

Mackerel can also be cut up into chunks or strips and used for many fish. Strips up to 6 or 7 inches long and an inch wide are used with a sinker and are lowereed from a live-bait or party boat and then reeled back in to catch yellowtail and kelp bass.

You can also sugar-cure mackerel for bait and use the strips or chunks in the Pacific surf for surf perch, spot-fin and yellowfin croakers, and rockfish. You can cure your own mackerel by filleting them, brushing the fillets with a few drops of anise oil, then covering them with a mixture of salt and sugar and keeping them in a jar or jug until ready for use.

## COMMON BONITO

The common bonito (*Sarda sarda*) is also called the Atlantic bonito and northern bonito, and is found from Maine to South America, mostly in the deeper offshore waters, but occasionally it

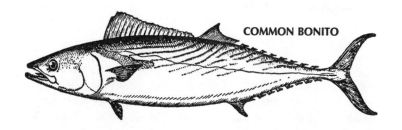

**COMMON BONITO**

comes inshore to feed on smaller fishes. It is a streamlined fish with gray-blue back, silvery sides, and dark stripes running obliquely along its back. It runs from about 3 to 10 pounds in weight with a maximum of about 15 pounds. It is fished for by anglers for sport or bait with lures such as feathers, spoons, metal squids, plugs, jigs, or natural baits such as strips or chunks cut from smaller fish. There are also other species of bonitos related to the common bonito found in Atlantic and Pacific waters.

Live bonito can be used for the bigger marlin such as the blue and black marlin. Here the fish can be rigged with a line running through the eye sockets and then tied around a big hook on the outside or on top of the head of the bait. Then the bonito is dropped overboard and is trolled at about 3 or 4 knots behind the boat. A bonito rigged in this manner will stay alive for a long time.

You can also use the bonito dead, rigging it in several ways with the hook in front of the fish just ahead of the mouth. Or the hook can be buried entirely inside the fish or one or two hooks can protrude from the belly. Then the bait can be trolled on an outrigger so that it skips on top of the water. Or it can be presented to a swordfish seen on or just below the surface of the water.

A whole bonito also makes an excellent bait for sharks and can be used live or dead. A live bonito can be allowed to swim around either on a free line or under a cork or plastic float. This can be done from a drifting or anchored boat and at the same time you can chum with ground bunker. You can also drift a dead bonito out into this chum slick. If you see a shark approaching the dead bonito you can pull it with your rod tip a couple of times to make it dart, flash, and look alive.

227

## OCEANIC BONITO

The oceanic bonito (*Katsuwonus pelamis*), also called the oceanic skipjack, striped tuna, and striped bonito, is found in the warmer seas but may range as far north as Cape Cod in the Atlantic and British Columbia in the Pacific. It is a heavier fish than the common bonito, with some specimens reaching up to 40 pounds, but it is more commonly under 20 pounds in weight. The oceanic bonito has a blue-green back and a silvery belly and is distinguished by the lateral line which curves sharply downward below the second dorsal fin and by the four longitudinal stripes on the lower part of the sides.

The oceanic bonitos usually travel in large schools offshore near the surface, chasing and feeding on smaller fishes. They can be caught on live bait fish such as sardines and anchovies and on artificial lures such as metal squids, spoons, and feathers. The oceanic bonito provides strip baits for many offshore fishes.

You can also rig a whole oceanic bonito for swordfish. Large bonitos of 4 or 5 pounds are used in swordfishing and two methods are usually used to rig the bait fish. One calls for removing the insides and backbone of the bait and sewing the hook either entirely inside the fish or protruding from the belly. The hook points face toward the head of the fish as in most rigged baits.

The other method, developed by W. E. S. Tuker, who has taken many large swordfish off Chile, calls for cutting open the belly of the bonito and removing the insides, but leaving the backbone in the bait. The main difference, however, is that the two hooks are placed in the bait so that the points face toward the

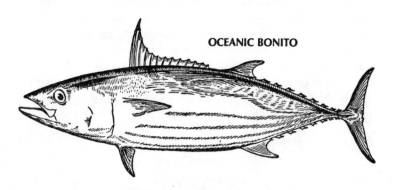

**OCEANIC BONITO**

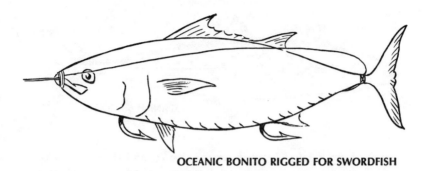

**OCEANIC BONITO RIGGED FOR SWORDFISH**

tail, where it is tied securely. Then the leader is brought back over the fish's back toward the head and is tied to the line that sewed up the bait's mouth. The bait is trolled head first, but when a swordfish strikes it, he cuts the weak line tying the fish's mouth to the leader and the bait turns around, tail facing the angler, while the swordfish is mouthing and swallowing it.

Oceanic bonito can also be used whole for blue and black marlin and sharks, or it can be cut up for many smaller saltwater species.

## SPANISH MACKEREL

The Spanish mackerel (*Scomberomorus maculatus*) is found along both the Atlantic and Pacific Coasts, being most numerous in the warmer waters. It is also called Sierra mackerel and spotted mackerel. It is a streamlined, slim fish with deep blue back, silvery sides and belly, and it is covered along the back with bronze spots. The second dorsal fin, which is yellowish and edged with black, begins in front of the anal fin. The Spanish mackerel is usually found at the surface, where it travels with others of its kind in large schools. It may be several miles offshore or may move in close to shore where it can be caught from piers and even jetties.

Spanish mackerel run from 2 to 5 pounds in weight but may reach 25 pounds. It is a popular food fish taken commercially in gill nets and purse seines. Sportsmen catch them on small metal squids, spoons, feather lures, and jigs.

Two other mackerels closely related to the Spanish mackerel

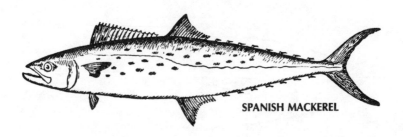

SPANISH MACKEREL

are the king mackerel (*Scomberomorus cavalla*) and the cero mackerel (*Scomberomorus regalis*), which both reach a larger size than the Spanish mackerel, but the smaller ones can be used for bait for many of the same fishes that take Spanish mackerel. The whole mackerels can be rigged with anywhere from one to three big hooks and used for big marlin, giant tuna, swordfish, and sharks. Strips can be cut from the belly and used for sailfish, white marlin, and dolphin.

## *DOLPHIN*

The dolphin (*Coryphaena hippurus*), also called the dorado, is easily recognized by its shape, with the blunt head and long dorsal fin and gaudy coloring of blues, greens, purples, and yellows. It is a fish of the open ocean, found both in the Atlantic and Pacific but being most numerous in warmer tropical waters. Along the Atlantic Coast it frequents the Gulf Stream and may follow it up as far north as New England during the summer months. Dolphin are a popular sport and food fish with anglers and are caught trolling or casting with strip baits, spoons, feathers, plugs, and

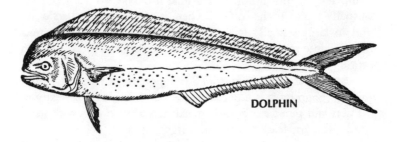

DOLPHIN

jigs. Look for them around floating boxes, logs, patches of weeds, and other debris. Dolphin reach 60 or 70 pounds in weight but most of those caught fall under 25 pounds. The smaller dolphin can be rigged whole and used for such fish as blue marlin, black marlin, and sharks. You can also cut strips from the sides and belly of the dolphin and use these while trolling for sailfish, white marlin, other dolphin, barracuda, and other offshore fish.

## FLYING FISH

There are many species of flying fishes found in the warm waters of the world and most of them make good baits for the larger game fishes. One that is often used for bait is the California flying fish (*Cypselurus californicus*), which is found along the Pacific Coast from Point Conception to Baja California. It reaches a length of 18 inches but most of those seen or caught will be smaller.

Flying fish are easily recognized by the long winglike pectoral fins, large pelvic fins, and the extension of the lower half of the caudal fin or tail. They are usually found in the deeper offshore water, where they travel in small schools under the surface and leave the water to glide through the air for distances up to several hundred feet when disturbed by a boat or larger fish. They make good eating but are caught mostly for bait in gill nets. They can often be netted at night, and at times they also fly on the deck of a boat and can be picked up. They have also been known to bite on a tiny hook and line baited with a tiny bait fish or piece of fish. But before you try to catch them, you first have to chum with the tiny minnows or ground fish to bring them up to the boat.

Flying fish die soon after caught and mostly are used dead. They are commonly used for striped marlin, tuna, and swordfish in the Pacific and can be used for sailfish and white marlin in the Atlantic. You can also cut them up or use whole ones dead while drifting or fishing on the bottom.

Whole flying fish are rigged for trolling by hooking them through both lips or rigging a hook 2 or 3 inches ahead of the

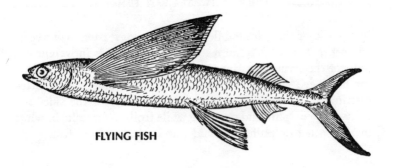

**FLYING FISH**

mouth, which is sewed up. Or you can rig them with the hook protruding from the belly or side. The wings are usually tied so that they lie flat against the body.

## NEEDLEFISH

The long, slim needlefishes, which belong to the family *Belonidae*, are numerous in species and numbers in the warmer waters of the Atlantic and Pacific. They resemble the freshwater garfish, being elongated and having long, thin jaws armed with numerous pointed teeth. They run from several inches to 4 feet in length and are known by various names such as garfish, needlegar, billfish, houndfish, agujon, sea pike, longjaws, and timucu, depending on the species and the locality found.

Needlefish can be caught at night in cast nets or dip nets or by spearing. They leap out of the water or skim along the surface with great speed and can pierce a man's body with their sharp beaks. They have also been known to hit small lures such as plugs, spoons, and jigs and take pieces of fish bait on a hook. When fishing for them it's a good idea to first chum with ground or cut-up fish, then cast out your bait.

**NEEDLEFISH**

Needlefish can be used alive for many big fish and can be rigged whole and trolled for sailfish and marlin. You can also put one on a big jig and drift with it for king mackerel, amberjack, barracuda, and other fish. Or you can troll a small needlefish on a jig for snook.

## BALAO

The balaos or half-beaks are more popularly called the "ballyhoo" among offshore anglers. They resemble the needlefishes except that instead of having two long jaws they have only a long lower jaw.

There are many species found in the warmer waters of the world; but the common half-beak or balao (*Hemiramphus brasiliensis*), which sometimes ranges as far north as Cape Cod as a straggler, is usually used as bait. However, it is most plentiful off Florida and in the Caribbean.

The balaos or half-beaks are very slim fish with greenish backs, silvery sides, and, of course, that long lower beak which protrudes far beyond the upper jaw. Most of them average several inches in length but some species may reach a couple of feet. The best size to use for bait is from 6 inches to a foot or so. Your choice will, of course, depend on the size of the fish you are after. But most of the time you don't have much choice if you buy your ballyhoo from a tackle shop or a bait dealer. They are sold fresh, iced, or frozen in these places, but you have to take the sizes they have available.

You can, however, go out and try to catch your own ballyhoo. This is easier said than done, since these fish swim in small compact schools in the open ocean and first have to be located. They are most plentiful over reefs, or you might look for schools being chased by game fish. To catch them in large numbers you need a seine or cast net which will encircle the school and trap them. Or you can go out at night in a boat with lights which attract them and then try to net them.

A live ballyhoo can be hooked through the lower jaw and trolled slowly for sailfish. Once caught, however, ballyhoo are

**BALAO**

difficult to keep alive and are usually used dead for most fishing. They are a favorite bait with offshore trollers, especially for sailfish, white marlin, dolphin, king mackerel, wahoo, barracuda, albacore, and the smaller tunas. If you can get big ballyhoo you can also try them for blue marlin.

For most of the above fish they are usually trolled from outriggers or on flat lines so that they skip on top in an attractive manner. They are rigged on bead-chain and wire rigs usually with one hook, but for such fish as king mackerel, wahoo, and barracuda a two-hook rig is better since these fish tend to chop off the tail of the bait without getting hooked. But before you rig a ballyhoo, break off most of the beak, leaving only about an inch for wrapping the soft wire around.

Another good way to use ballyhoo for many fish, and especially for king mackerel, is to drift with the bait fish so that it sinks and moves well below the surface. You can lift and lower your rod every so often so that the ballyhoo looks alive, flashing and glittering in the depths. You can also rig the ballyhoo on a jig and drift or troll it for many fish.

You can also use a whole ballyhoo or a piece on a hook for bottom fishing with a sinker to catch grouper, snappers, grunt, and many other southern species.

**THREE WAYS TO RIG BALLYHOO**

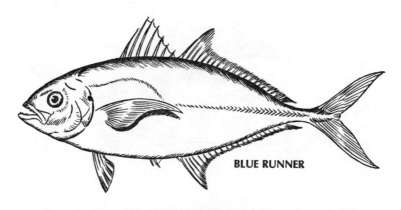

**BLUE RUNNER**

## BLUE RUNNER

The blue runner (*Caranx crysos*) is also called the yellow jack, yellow mackerel, hard-tailed jack, and just plain runner. It is related to the jacks, scads, and pompanos. And like these fish, it has a flat, streamlined body and deeply forked tail. In color it is bluish or greenish above and golden or silvery below. There is usually a small dark spot on the gill cover. It may reach a length of 22 inches and a weight of 4 pounds, but most of those caught will run much smaller, usually between a half-pound and a pound or two in weight.

Although the blue runner has been known to range along the Atlantic Coast from Cape Cod to Brazil, it is not too plentiful in northern waters and is more commonly caught and used for bait in southern waters. It is especially plentiful off Florida and is also found in the West Indies and the warmer waters along the Pacific coast.

Sports fishermen often catch blue runners when fishing from shore, piers, bridges, and boats while seeking other species or when casting or trolling with small lures or using various natural baits. The angler seeking these fish for bait can also use light spinning tackle and cast tiny spoons or jigs. Adding a small piece of shrimp to these lures will bring more strikes. You can also troll from a boat with a rig made up of anywhere from three to five tiny yellow or white jigs spaced a few inches apart. Look for blue runners around buoys, markers, piers, jetties, mouths of inlets, and over reefs, rocky bottoms, and wrecks.

**TWO WAYS TO HOOK LIVE BLUE RUNNERS FOR SLOW TROLLING**

**Line Through Back Holds Hook**

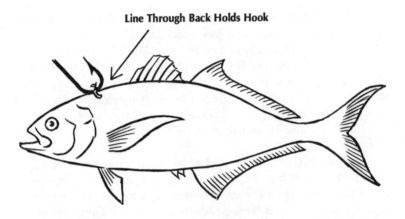

You can keep the blue runners alive in a large tank or container with well-aerated water. They'll keep fairly well in such tanks or bait wells until used for bait.

Live blue runners can be used for sailfish, amberjack, barracuda, sharks, and other fish found offshore, by hooking one through the back and letting it swim out while the boat drifts with the tide or wind. This can be done with or without a cork or styrofoam float above the hook. For best results do not let the bait swim too close to the boat. Blue runners have the habit of trying to hide in the shadow of the boat. If this happens, start the motor and let the bait drop back some distance behind the boat.

You can also troll a blue runner very slowly behind a boat.

This can be done with or without an outrigger or from a kite. Here you should hook the runner through the back just behind the head. Or you can run a line with a needle through the back or through both eye sockets and then tie the line around the bend of a hook on the outside. This way the bait swims more naturally and lives longer.

When using blue runners for king mackerel or barracuda you may want to add a second hook on a short wire leader behind the first and run this through the tail of the bait.

Blue runners can also be used live or dead just off the bottom when fishing for grouper of jewfish. You can also cut the runner into chunks or strips and use it for bait with a bottom rig.

## PINFISH

The pinfish (*Lagodon rhomboides*) is also called the sailor's choice and is a very popular bait fish in southern waters. It is found from the Carolinas south to Florida, in the Caribbean and along the Gulf of Mexico. It is also a fine panfish and is caught for food, but it is small, rarely going over 8 or 10 inches in length and a

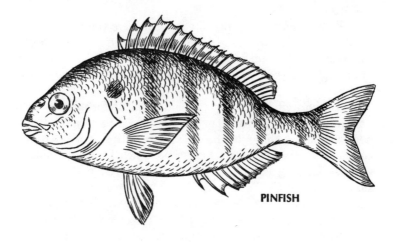

PINFISH

few ounces in weight, so many anglers do not bother with cleaning and eating them.

However, other anglers try to catch pinfish for bait, and this is best done from piers, docks, bridges, jetties, or boats in tidal rivers, inlets, or passes and close to shore in the ocean. They are most plentiful over shallow, grassy flats.

You can catch pinfish in wire mesh traps by baiting them with fish, crabs, clams, or shrimp scraps. Then set the trap on the bottom in places where pinfish are found and leave it for a day or two.

Most anglers, however, catch pinfish on tiny hooks baited with small pieces of fish or shrimp. It's a good idea to first chum with ground-up bits of fish or shrimp or with canned cat or dog food to bring the pinfish around under a boat, pier, or dock.

Pinfish are pretty hardy and can be kept alive in a tank, bait well, or plastic can for a good length of time. They also stay alive on a hook for long periods and make excellent bait for many saltwater species.

You can use a live pinfish by hooking it through the eye sockets or through the back and letting it out on a plain line from a drifting or anchored boat or from a pier or jetty. This is a good way to catch tarpon, amberjack, cobia, channel bass or redfish, and big sea trout.

Pinfish can also be used for sailfish. Here you use a plastic or styrofoam float anywhere from 10 to 15 feet above the hook. The pinfish is let out from a drifting boat offshore, and when a sailfish takes the bait you let it run with it before trying to set the hook.

A highly effective way to use a live pinfish for snook is with a sliding sinker rig and a 5/0 or 6/0 hook on a 3-foot leader. If you hook the pinfish throught the eye sockets or lips, it will face the current and stay alive for a long time. Then let it out in such spots as inlets, passes, tidal rivers, deep holes, channels, and along drop-offs.

Live pinfish can also be fished on a regular bottom rig for grouper, red snappers, and other large fish. Or you can cut the pinfish in half or chunks or strips and use it for many bottom fishes.

## BUTTERFISH

The butterfish (*Poronotus triacanthus*) is also called the harvestfish, dollarfish, skipjack, and shiner, depending on where you live along the Atlantic Coast from Canada to the Carolinas where this fish is usually caught. It is very popular as a food fish, being fat, oily, and delicious in flavor—hence its name "butterfish," indicating that it is highly prized on the table.

The butterfish is easily recognized by its flat, deep body, the single elongated dorsal fin on its back, and a similar anal fin along its belly. It has a short head, blunt snout, and a forked tail. The butterfish is bluish gray above and blending along the sides to a silvery belly. It is a small fish, rarely reaching more than a foot in length.

Butterfish usually show up in Maine, Massachusetts, Rhode Island, and New York waters in the spring, summer, and fall. They may come into fairly shallow water near shore at times and can be seen swimming near the surface.

Millions of pounds of butterfish have been caught annually along the Atlantic Coast by commercial fishermen using pound nets, traps, gill nets, and otter trawls. They have been caught at

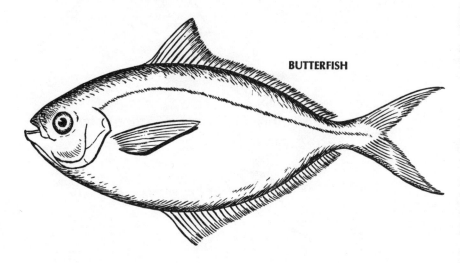

BUTTERFISH

times on a tiny hook baited with a bit of clam or sea worm, but you can't depend on locating them or catching them this way too often. Therefore most anglers buy their butterfish either fresh or frozen from fish markets, bait dealers, boat liveries, or commercial fishermen.

Butterfish are rather delicate and even if caught alive are difficult to keep in a tank or on a hook for any length of time. So most of them are used dead, and being oily they must be kept on ice or be frozen until used. Once they thaw out and have been exposed to warm air or the water, they quickly soften and are harder to keep on the hook.

You can use a whole butterfish in the larger sizes for such fish as giant tuna and sharks. Here you can hook the butterfish

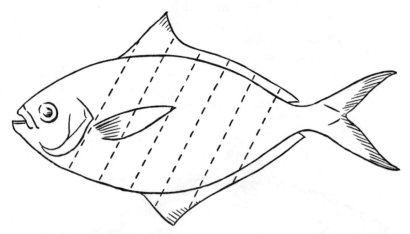

**CUTTING BUTTERFISH INTO CHUNKS AND METHOD OF HOOKING**

through the back with a big hook and let it out from a drifting or anchored boat while chumming with ground bunker and chunks of butterfish.

Tons of butterfish are also used for bluefish, especially on the party boats and private boats fishing off New York and New Jersey. Here chumming is also done with a ground bunker to bring the bluefish up to the boat. Then a butterfish is cut into narrow steaks and one of these is impaled twice on a hook. Then you let the bait out in the chum slick. Besides bluefish you may also hook bonito, false albacore, and school tuna on this cut butterfish bait.

Butterfish can also be cut up into various sizes and shapes and used when surf fishing for striped bass, bluefish, and weakfish. You can also cut up butterfish and use it with a bottom rig for cod, pollock, whiting or silver hake, sea bass, and other bottom fish. Or cut the butterfish into long narrow strips and use it for fluke.


## SPOT

The spot (*Leiostomus xanthurus*) is also called the Lafayette. This name was given to the fish by New Yorkers when these fish suddenly appeared in great numbers in 1824 when Lafayette visited this country. These fish still make occasional sporadic visits to northern waters, but they are more commonly found farther south from Virginia to the Gulf of Mexico.

The spot is a member of the croaker family and the male can make a drumming sound. It is readily recognized by the small black spot just behind the gill cover, from which it derives its name. Another distinguishing feature is the 12 to 15 oblique bars running from the back downward along the sides.

The spot is a small fish, rarely going over a foot or so in length or a weight of more than a pound and a half. Most of those that are caught range from a few inches to 8 or 10 inches in length. However, they often make up in numbers what they lack in size, and millions of pounds have been caught by commercial fishermen.

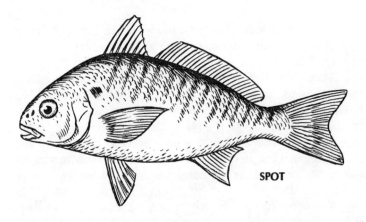

**SPOT**

The spot is also a popular fish with many saltwater anglers, and thousands are caught for food from piers, docks, shore, boats, and bridges along the Atlantic Coast, especially in our southern states. They run from spring to fall, with the summer months best. They are found over sand and mud buttoms and often ascend rivers up to brackish and even fresh water.

To catch spot on hook and line you need tiny No. 8 or 10 hooks, which can be baited with bits of sea worms, clam, mussel, shedder crab, or shrimp. To bring them around a boat or pier or other spot you can try chumming with cracked shellfish, ground fish, or canned cat or dog food. Then if you use a multiple-hook rig with several hooks you can often catch them two or three at a time.

Spots are pretty hardy fish and can be kept in a plastic garbage container, bait well, or tank for fairly long periods. Of course, the water should be kept cool and changed often or aerated.

You can use a live spot for bait by hooking it through the back and then letting it out with or without a float from a pier, bridge, or boat to catch such fish as tarpon, king mackerel, cobia, snook, and sharks.

You can also use a whole dead spot on a bottom rig, hooking it through the head or tail and fishing it deep for tarpon. In this case it's a good idea to cut off the tail so that the bait doesn't spin in a tide or current.

And anglers fishing for channel bass in the surf often use spot for bait, especially the head part. Here you run a 7/0 or 8/0 hook up through the lower jaw and out through the nose.

You can also cut up a spot into steaks, chunks, or strips and use it for bluefish, weakfish, sea trout, snappers, and many other fishes.

## GRUNTS

The grunts comprise a large family of fish in warm and tropical waters. They include the French grunt, gray grunt, white grunt, blue-striped grunt, and the margates, pigfish, and porkfish. There are many other grunts, and they are so numerous that it is no problem to find or catch a few when you want them for food or bait.

Grunts are really "panfish of the sea," and millions are caught commercially and by anglers for food and sport. The Florida crackers have been eating "Grits and Grunts" from way back, and they are still a popular dish on the table. They can also be a pest to those anglers seeking other fish, as the smaller bait-stealing grunts clean a hook time after time.

And most of the grunts you'll catch will be on the small side, running from a few inches to a foot or so in length. However, certain species reach 2 or 3 pounds and a few reach even bigger sizes.

The grunts resemble the porgies, have deep, compressed bodies, sloping heads, and sharp dorsal spines. Many of them have stripes or bars running across the head and the body. The inside of the mouth of many grunts will be a bright orange red.

The grunts are numerous in Florida waters, especially in the Keys. They are also found in Bermuda, the Bahamas, and throughout the Caribbean. Look for them around bridges, piers, docks, and over reefs and rocky bottoms. In clear water you'll see them swarming by the hundreds in all sizes and with mixed species. They are especially active at night and this is the time to catch the bigger specimens.

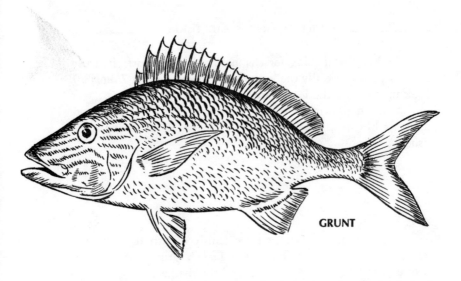

**GRUNT**

To catch the smaller grunt for bait, use tiny hooks baited with pieces of shrimp, crab, or almost any cut fish. These baits should also be small unless you want a bigger grunt. Grunts are essentially bottom fish, so lower the baits as close to the bottom as you can. You can also catch grunts in wire traps with fairly large funnel-type openings baited with crushed shrimp or crabs and left overnight.

Grunts are very hardy and can be kept alive in tanks, bait wells, or bait buckets filled with water. Of course, to keep them for long periods of time the water should be cool and well aerated.

A live grunt can be used for sailfish, either with or without a float, let out from a drifting boat offshore where these fish are found. You can hook the bait through the back.

You can also use live grunts for amberjack, tarpon, and snook by hooking them through the back and letting them out from piers, bridges, or boats. Here it's a good idea to first clip off the sharp dorsal spines with cutting pliers or shears.

One grunt, the "pigfish," has been used to attract sea trout. A big live one is tied to a line under the boat, and the noises it makes draw big sea trout to the spot. Then a smaller pigfish can be used as bait in the same spot.

And because grunts can withstand the pressure in deep water, they make excellent bait for red snappers, grouper, and other fish found in depths. Here you often need heavy sinkers or weights to get the grunt down to the bottom.

There are many other bait fish which can be used in saltwater fishing. One of these is the bonefish, which is a popular game fish in tropical waters. It makes a good bait when rigged with one or two big hooks and then trolled for blue marlin and giant tuna.

The smaller albacores can also be whole for such fish as swordfish, marlin, and sharks. They can be cut up into strips and used for sailfish, white marlin, and dolphin. Strips can also be cut from the different kinds of tunas and also used for offshore trolling.

The smaller barracudas can be rigged with two or three hooks and used whole for sailfish, tuna, and marlin. A whole barracuda also makes an excellent bait for big grouper when lowered and trolled slowly near the bottom. Strips cut from the barracuda are also used.

The various snappers such as the mangrove snapper and others found in warm waters can be used for bait in the same way as the grunts. Porgies can also be used alive or cut up for bait.

Small bluefish have been used successfully to catch tarpon, king mackerel, cobia, and sharks.

The silver hake or whiting makes a good bait for big tuna, marlin, and sharks. It can be fished alive or dead from a boat offshore where these fish are found. Ling, hake, small cod, and pollock can also be used for tuna and sharks.

Small saltwater catfish hooked through both lips make a good bait for tarpon and for grouper and jewfish. Here it's a good idea to clip off the sharp spines before using them for bait.

Strips cut from the whip ray have been used when trolling for sailfish and white marlin and other fish offshore. Chunks cut from rays make a top bait for sharks. Long, narrow strips cut from rays and skates can be used when fishing for summer flounder or fluke. The same thing can be done with dogfish or small sharks.

Finally, in an emergency or after you catch your first fish, you can cut pieces from almost any fish and try it for the same kind or a different fish. Most fish are cannibalistic, and strips cut from silver hake or whiting can be used to catch others of the same kind. Strips cut from summer flounders of fluke will catch other flounders. A piece of channel bass will often catch other channel bass, and so on.

# CHAPTER 18

# THE SALTWATER BAIT BUSINESS

$M$*any of the natural baits used in freshwater fishing can be* propagated and the bait dealers can often raise unlimited quantities to meet the demand for these baits. But it is more difficult or impractical to propagate most saltwater baits because they require natural conditions which are hard or expensive to create artificially. So up till now most natural saltwater baits have been obtained from the ocean or tidal waters as needed. The baits have been kept alive or preserved in some manner until they were sold and used by anglers.

Since saltwater fishing is seasonal in most areas, very few people devote all their time to obtaining or selling natural baits. The demand for saltwater baits in most areas runs from April to October, the peak months being June, July, and August. Of course, the further south you go the longer the season; Florida, for example, is fished by many thousands of anglers during the winter months. But at best, the saltwater bait business is rarely an all-year-round affair.

Most of the saltwater baits are obtained, handled, and sold by commercial fishermen, fish markets, boat liveries, bait dealers, and fishing tackle stores. The handling of natural baits is usually a side line with many of these places, their major incomes coming from other products or services. The commercial fishermen, for example, obtain menhaden, herring, mullet, mackerel, squid, crabs, clams, and other baits mostly for food or for processing into various products; but they often sell lesser quantities to

247

sport fishing boats, bait dealers, and tackle stores to be used for bait. If the demand for bait is large and the baits wanted are plentiful, some of the commercial fishermen may spend quite a bit of time trying to obtain them, but usually they stick to their main business of fishing for the food markets.

When it comes to sea worms, there is a fairly large business built around these baits along the Atlantic Coast from Long Island, New York, to New England and Canada. The great majority of the bloodworms and clam worms come from Maine. The industry supports hundreds of diggers, shippers, and wholesalers who supply the retail outlets.

To be a digger doesn't require much of an investment—a fork or hoe, a pair of boots, a bucket for the worms, and a man is in business. A digger can spend anywhere from two to four hours a day on the flats when the tide is low. During favorable seasons he can dig anywhere from 300 to 1,000 or more worms a day, but as more and more worms are removed each year, the pickings become slimmer and fewer worms are taken. And the weather can affect the digging, since too much rain drives the worms deeper into the ground and hot weather kills the worms quickly. Digging worms is also hard work and seasonal. In addition Maine requires that a digger be a resident of the state for at least five years and take out a license. Small quantities of sea worms are also dug in Massachusetts, Rhode Island, Connecticut, and Long Island, New York.

Sea worm diggers can make anywhere from $500 to $10,000 in one season. The worm industry is considered an important one in Maine, because it employs quite a few people and in one year as much as $2,767,190 was paid to the diggers. And the diggers are the low men on the totem pole because the shippers, wholesalers, and retail bait outlets make an even bigger profit on the sale of worms.

The digger takes his worms to the shipper, who buys them from him and sorts, packs, and ships the worms to the wholesalers. The shipper must have storage space such as a cool basement, where the worms are kept until shipped. He also needs large wooden trays and plenty of rockweed to keep the worms in.

The wholesalers, are usually found in the larger cities. They supply the retail outlets such as the fishing tackle stores and boat liveries. The wholesaler usually handles other kinds of baits besides worms.

The number of sea worm diggers in Maine has increased from 400 in 1953 to around 1,500 in 1975. So more worms were dug to meet the demands of fishermen and the price of the worms, like everything else, skyrocketed. But as more and more worm diggers turned over the flats in search of worms, the size of the worms taken decreased and many flats failed to produce sufficient numbers to make it worthwhile to dig them. As a result, more and more worm diggers migrated to other counties in Maine to do their digging, abandoning the flats around Wiscasset, which was the major source until recently. Now many of the worms are coming from Washington County. Still others are being imported from New Brunswick and Nova Scotia in Canada.

Nowadays bloodworms and sandworms are being shipped to all parts of the country for saltwater fishing—even as far as Florida and California—and most of this shipping is done by air so that the worms arrive alive and healthy.

Naturally, the opportunities in the well-established sea worm industry are somewhat limited, and those who want to get into the saltwater bait business will find less competition and more openings in handling other bait. The bait fishes such as mullet, spearing, herring, sand eels, and killies can often be seined in large numbers and sold to bait dealers or to the anglers themselves. Some bait dealers such as tackle stores and boat liveries seine the bait fish themselves, but others are too busy and will often buy from anyone who can supply them with such baits. The equipment for seining bait fish is not too expensive. It requires seines, a small boat or two for deep-water work, and two or three men to handle the operations. Of course, some bait fish such as killifish must be kept alive, and tanks or bait cars are needed to hold them. Others which die quickly can be kept on ice or frozen until sold.

In Pacific waters there is a big demand for sardines, anchovies, and herring for the sport fisheries, especially on the live-bait boats which carry big tanks filled with these bait fish which are used alive. These bait fish can also be iced or frozen and sold through tackle shops, bait dealers, and boat liveries.

The fleet that catches these bait fish usually works at night in sheltered harbor areas or early in the morning along the coast. They use lights on the boats and skiffs to attract the bait fish, then set a net around them. Or if they see schools of the bait fish swimming on the surface, they surround them with seines and nets.

Catching these bait fish is a big investment in the big boat you need and the lighter skiffs. You also need tanks to keep the bait fish alive until they can be sold to the sport fishing fleet. And since sardines, anchovies, and herring run in cycles—from being scarce to being overfished—there are some years when you can't catch enough to make a decent profit or even expenses.

There is also a very good demand for shedder crabs such as the blue crab and calico or lady crab. But these crabs are never obtained in very great quantities and it often takes a great deal of time and hard work to get them. The green crabs and fiddler crabs are often numerous in some areas, and since they are hardy and live a long time out of the water, it is often profitable to handle them if they can be caught in large numbers.

The edible or jumbo shrimps can be obtained from commercial shrimpers or dealers and then sold as bait to tackle shops or the anglers themselves. These have to be iced or frozen and, of course, they are used dead.

The live shrimp industry is a big one in Florida, where millions of shrimp are caught and sold all over the state. They are usually caught by individuals who operate from small skiffs and either seine or dip the shrimp out of the shallow water along the flats. This is usually done at night with a light on the boat. The winter months are best for the larger shrimp, whereas during the summer months you can catch smaller shrimp by pushing a net through the grass on the flats.

The live shrimp are delivered to wholesale houses, which keep them in big tanks that are well aerated with pumps to provide oxygen for the shrimp. Special tank trucks are used to transport the live shrimp to tackle stores, bait dealers, boat liveries, and fishing piers. All of these outlets also have tanks of varying sizes in which the shrimp are kept alive until sold to the fishermen.

It is a risky business because many shrimp are lost due to warm water, lack of oxygen, polluted water, hot or cold weather, and disease. And the supply is undependable because shrimp come and go with the seasons and the weather and may fail to show up in any numbers in their usual haunts. And, of course, with the big demand for live shrimp there has been a tendency to overfish them and deplete the natural supply.

During the height of the fishing season there is often a great demand for certain kinds of bait, and if you can supply the retail outlets with the baits they need you can often do a good business. Many of these outlets run short of bait or have difficulty in obtaining them through regular channels, and they will welcome a supplier they can depend on. Usually it pays to specialize in one or two kinds of baits since it takes a great deal of time and work to get and handle several kinds of baits. Of course, if you act only as a distributor or wholesaler, you can handle a large variety of baits, but you must be situated in a spot where there are many retail outlets.

Many fishing tackle stores and boat liveries sell natural baits to their angler customers and, although handling such baits is often a nuisance and a risk and often not profitable, these businesses realize that it attracts more customers. Many anglers like to buy their baits on or near the fishing spots and they will go to the tackle store or boat livery or marina which handles these baits rather than to a place that doesn't have them.

The fact that there are fewer saltwater fishermen than freshwater fishermen also helps to keep the business smaller. But saltwater anglers have been increasing in numbers each year, and in many areas and during certain seasons the demand for saltwater baits often exceeds the supply. If the bait dealers can meet this demand the resulting turnover makes it a profitable venture during the fishing season.

The dream of many bait dealers and saltwater anglers has

been to raise natural baits artificially in unlimited numbers. Up until now this has been difficult, but in recent years more and more experiments have shown that such saltwater bait raising may be profitable in the future. Most of these experiments and projects have been done to increase the supply of shellfish or fish for food. But their methods can often be adapted to bait raising too.

For example, researchers at the University of West Florida have been experimenting with lugworms and have found that they can breed, raise, and keep and ship the worms readily. They have found that they can rear the lugwoms to marketable size (3 inches or larger) in 120 days. Lugworms can be used as bait for many saltwater species.

It has also been proven that oysters, mussels, and clams can be cultivated and grown artificially with a high yield. Mussels have been cultivated in France since the 13th century. There they anchor poles in shallow water and attach seed mussels to these poles. They also use the "raft" method to produce mussels for the market. Here a wooden raft is anchored in deeper water, and ropes up to 1/2 inch thick and 30 feet long are suspended from the raft. The small mussels attach themselves to the ropes and thrive and grow until they reach adult size.

In Florida and Texas they have been trying to raise shrimp in tanks or ponds for food and bait. They have succeeded in raising millions of shrimp at the University of Miami's mariculture facility. But they have found that in order to succeed, such an operation must be hundreds of acres in size. And to be profitable you need at least four harvests each year, which limits the size of the shrimp to the smaller, faster-growing species.

Other experiments have shown that certain saltwater fish such as mullet, eel, and killifish can be raised in tanks or ponds and sold for bait. In fact, such fish culture has been going on for centuries in many foreign countries. They have been raising saltwater fish mainly for food, but it can also be done to raise some of these fish for bait.

But a lot more research and work must be done to make such mariculture economical and profitable. Many problems must be solved and a lot of money will have to be spent before such bait raising in salt water on a large scale becomes practical. The high price of most land, ponds, marshes, and wetlands or the construction of tanks or artificial ponds makes such operations a big investment.

But in time most of these problems can be solved and saltwater bait raising will become as common and as profitable as raising worms or minnows for freshwater fishing. It has to be done, because the natural supply of these saltwater baits is limited and is being depleted. If we want saltwater baits in the future, we will have to raise many of them artificially.

# Index